AF560584

CULTURE AND CONSCIOUSNESS

CULTURE AND CONSCIOUSNESS

Literature Regained

WILLIAM S. HANEY II

MOTILAL BANARSIDASS PUBLISHERS
PRIVATE LIMITED • DELHI

Indian Edition: Delhi, ***2006***
(First Published by Associated University Presses, London, 2002)

ISBN: 81-208-2755-4

MOTILAL BANARSIDASS
41 U.A. Bungalow Road, Jawahar Nagar, Delhi 110 007
8 Mahalaxmi Chamber, 22 Bhulabhai Desai Road, Mumbai 400 026
236, 9th Main III Block, Jayanagar, Bangalore 560 011
203 Royapettah High Road, Mylapore, Chennai 600 004
Sanas Plaza, 1302 Baji Rao Road, Pune 411 002
8 Camac Street, Kolkata 700 017
Ashok Rajpath, Patna 800 004
Chowk, Varanasi 221 001

Printed in India
BY JAINENDRA PRAKASH JAIN AT SHRI JAINENDRA PRESS,
A-45 NARAINA, PHASE-I, NEW DELHI 110 028
AND PUBLISHED BY NARENDRA PRAKASH JAIN FOR
MOTILAL BANARSIDASS PUBLISHERS PRIVATE LIMITED,
BUNGALOW ROAD, DELHI 110 007

Contents

Preface

C*ULTURE AND CONSCIOUSNESS* ARGUES THAT THE VAST INTERDISCIPLINARY boom in consciousness research has enormous implications for literary and cultural studies, and that the potential benefits of this research in the twenty-first century are momentous and "will be ignored at our great peril"—to repeat Howard Mancing's words regarding cognitive science (1999, 167). My objective in this book is to show how consciousness studies can help us reassess our approach to key issues and the fundamental assumptions of contemporary theory and criticism. I indicate how major points of contention in the humanities can be elucidated through a perspective that accommodates the full range of mind and consciousness. Debates in recent theory surrounding the two basic questions about identity and truth—whether they are given or made, individual or social—cannot be resolved solely on the basis of the mind or reason, which is a fragmentary and partial content of consciousness.

My argument unfolds in eight chapters; the first three theoretical and the others largely applied. In the first three chapters I lay the foundations for a definition of intersubjectivity that includes yet goes beyond Habermas's idea of an interaction mediated by language and resulting in mutual understanding and agreement (1987, 294–326). In chapters 4 to 8 I apply the notion of intersubjectivity to the reading of specific works of literature. Chapter 1 traces the history of modern research into consciousness and indicates how the theory and praxis of consciousness in the East can provide a model for the cooperation scientists propose between phenomenology and cognitive science. It explains that the Western mind/body dualism is really a monism, that the mind and body comprise the material building blocks of experience as distinct from consciousness (*purusha* or Atman). Chapter 2 compares the views of the self formulated by modern literary theory and Shankara's Advaita (nondual) Vedanta, and suggests that the deconditioning of the mind and disburdening of the personality in postmodern culture can induce something akin to the emptying of consciousness described by Vedanta. This process can be seen operating in supermodernity as defined by Marc Augé and in cultural hybridity as defined by Homi Bhabha—both of which are forms of intersubjectivity. Supporting these observations, chapter 3 compares Indian literary theory and deconstruction, illustrating how both approaches point to the silent meaning of an aesthetic work. This meaning, which reception theorists describe in terms of *ostranenie* (Shklovsky), *verfremdung* (Brecht), and gaps (Iser), is attainable as the mind expands toward what Indian aesthetics describes as the transpersonal, transcultural state of witnessing awareness.

Chapter 4, which is pivotal in defining intersubjectivity as an unmediated subject-to-subject communication, should be read before the ensuing chapters. It argues that social drama and stage drama increasingly interpenetrate with the effect that an aesthetics of presence complements and even embraces our everyday experience within a intersubjective unity of differences. Chapter 5 examines how the plays of Beckett and Pinter, in dramatizing the relative, nonuniversal nature of the mind as conceptual content, have the performative effect of expanding the subject's awareness beyond conceptuality altogether. These plays give performers and audience a taste of intersubjective presence after discursive thought has run its course. In chapter 6 I explore how disturbing memories in Vonnegut's *Slaughterhouse-Five* can drive the protagonist and reader toward flashes of being—the pure awareness underlying the social construction of the self and the basis of interconnectedness. Shifting from an historical to a virtual context in chapter 7, I demonstrate how the postindustrial environment-as-electronic-medium in DeLillo's *White Noise* swings our awareness from the physical to the metaphysical, from temporal boundaries to the aestheticized reality of cyberspace. This move takes us from object awareness (mind) to a virtual intersubjectivity. Finally in chapter 8 I bring the above issues to bear in the analysis of the relation between intersubjectivity and the human-machine interface. I conclude that a true intersubjectivity involves the human attributes of volition and ethics, that these attributes are not explainable by any presently known physical laws, and that the posthuman "man-machine" as a material construct may not have access to the full range of intersubjectivity.

The freeplay of postmodern culture with its conceptual indeterminacy and lack of depth can help to free awareness from its objects by allowing attention to slip into the spaces between the mind's conceptual content. This slippage is promoted by intersubjectivity, a process of "relating to the other," whether the other is a human being, a creative inspiration, or a work of art. I suggest that at a certain level the duality of self and other is overcome in an experience of unity. To support this claim, the first part of the book indicates how all knowledge domains—sensory, mental, and contemplative—can be seen as distinct yet integrated. No one sphere can rightfully dominate the others, as in the attempted poststructuralist domination of the subject. That which integrates these domains ultimately is not language or reasaon but consciousness, the all-pervasive ground of knowledge. Access to this ground is enhanced by aesthetic experience and by certain postmodern cultural activities. Because consciousness cannot be explained by sensory or mental empiricism, no theory like poststructuralism can effectively call into question something still beyond our consensual, third-person understanding.

Acknowledgments

I WOULD LIKE TO THANK ASSOCIATED UNIVERSITY PRESSES FOR PERMISsion to reprint chapter 1, "The Science of Mind, Consciousness, and Literary Studies," a modified version of my chapter in *Humanism and the Humanities in the Twenty-first Century*, Bucknell University Press, 2001.

Culture and Consciousness

1
The Science of Mind, Consciousness, and Literary Studies

Introduction

In proclaiming the death of man, god, and meaning, postmodernists have called into question the universality of a liberal humanism. But in the twenty-first century, theories of the self will undoubtedly continue to play an important role in literary and cultural studies. As Howard Mancing discerns, the "vast interdisciplinary activity centered around cognitive science has enormous implications for literary theory and criticism and it will be ignored at our great peril as it continues to form the prevailing mode of discourse of the physical, biological, social, and human sciences in the twenty-first century" (1999, 167). After romanticism the metaphors of the self have steadily devolved outward from the notion of a deep interior. Defined as the soul and the seat of inspiration, creativity, passion, and genius, the romantic self has given way in modernism to an observable and rational self and the metaphor of the machine, and in postmodernism to a fragmentary, relational self devoid of autonomy or essence. As Kenneth Gergen says, "With the spread of postmodern consciousness, we see the demise of personal definition, reason, authority, commitment, trust, the sense of authenticity, and faith in progress" (1991, 228). But given the current boom of research into consciousness in fields ranging from philosophy and cognitive science to quantum physics, the story of the self in Western culture is far from over. Research in the burgeoning field of consciousness studies suggests that when viewed not psychologically as distinct from the Freudian or Jungian unconscious but rather ontologically as distinct from the nonconscious, consciousness is not an epiphenomenon, not reducible to the structure and functions of the physical domain, not a cultural construct (Wallace 1993; Farrow and Herbert 1982). Consciousness understood in this ontological sense has significant implications for literary and cultural studies.

In the "Editors' Introduction" to the inaugural issue of the *Journal of Consciousness Studies*, a journal devoted to controversies on the self in science and the humanities, the editors highlight the need for research into consciousness through "systematic investigative methods" that would "replace the naive, commonsensical Aristotelian-Cartesian" approach (1994, 8), while pointing out that these methodologies need not be developed "entirely *de novo*." "For while development of appropriate procedures has not been the major concern of western culture, eastern cultures, for a variety of reasons, have traditionally given more attention to the problem" (1994, 8). Many eastern methodologies along with their associated physiological and experiential claims have recently begun to be discussed in scientific literature. As the editors of *JCS* suggest,

> If we come to believe that we are all "just a bunch of neurons," then it is fanciful to assume that concepts like the sanctity of human life will survive unaltered. Alternately, if the sort of idealist cosmology espoused by the perennial and contemplative traditions is found to have some scientific basis, then the transformative claims of the meditation procedures associated with these [Eastern] traditions will have to be taken seriously. (1994, 1:8)

What is the relevance of Western research into consciousness for the humanities? One effect of a poststructuralist postmodernism (as opposed to a reconstructive postmodernism suggested by Suzi Gablik [1991], Danah Zohar [1994] and others) has been to blur the distinction between high and popular cultures and in so doing to eliminate the notions of a unified self and universal truth. If perennial notions of the self are found to have a valid empirical basis, then postmodernist claims about consciousness will have to be reconsidered and the bias against humanism reevaluated. Already we see emerging a powerful alternative to the postmodernist view of the self as no more that a social construction or the product of material forces.

This chapter begins with an overview of the concepts of the self in literary theory and traces their development from premodernity through modernity to postmodernity. It then reviews contemporary views on consciousness and its recent history from William James to the current controversies on the "hard problem" of consciousness (why mental processing is accompanied by conscious awareness in the first place). On the basis of these developments we can speculate on the phenomenology of consciousness in the postmodern condition. The final sections compare Eastern and Western, reductive and nonreductive theories of consciousness in light of the difference between mind/body dualism (in the West) and consciousness/matter dualism (in the East)—where matter includes both mind and body. Throughout, I propose a nonreductive theory of consciousness and emphasize the importance to the humanities of a full understanding not only of the mind but also of pure consciousness itself. Theorists who have recently defended humanism include John Ellis (1997), Wendell Harris (1996), and Colin McGinn (1997); my approach adds the dimensions of consciousness and perennial psychology. As Ellis states, "Enlightenment thinkers realize that humane values can prevail only if we identify ourselves as human beings first and foremost" (1997, 112). I will argue the position that consciousness is innate to all human beings and the basis of our common humanity.

The Self in Critical Theory

As the prevailing cultural paradigm in the wake of liberal humanism, postmodernism has made the antihumanist, anti-idealist claim that man (including the author) and unitary meaning are dead—if they were ever more than an illusion to begin with. Ferdinand de Saussure, Jacques Lacan, Roland Barthes, Michel Foucault, Jean Baudrillard, Jean-François Lyotard, Jacques Derrida, and others propose that language and consciousness are not what they appear to be. For Saussure, language as an arbitrary system of signs precedes being and also assumes a vital role in its construction. Barthes, Derrida, and others claim that this conclusion holds regardless of the way we approach the concept of self, whether through phenomenology or deconstruction. Hence if the self is a linguistic construct and language has no tangible reality "out there," no actual referent, then what reality can we ascribe the self? Louis Althusser, with his influential concept of ideology as the "imaginary representation" of real social relations in the world, argues that individuals are socially constructed subjects (1969, 56), subjugated by "ideological State apparatuses" (54). The "individual *is interpellated* [hailed] *as a (free) subject* [by ideology] *in order that he shall submit freely to the commandments of the Subject, i.e. in order that he shall (freely) accept his subjection. . . . There are no subjects except by and for their subjection*" (62; Althusser's emphasis).

Decentered and subjected, the self is no longer considered the source of meaning.

For Barthes, the author is dead and textuality becomes an interplay of codes without origin: "Writing is that neutral, composite, oblique space where our subject slips away, the negative where all identity is lost, starting with the very identity of the body writing" (1977, 142). Even in claiming that "the birth of the reader must be at the cost of the death of the Author" (1977, 148), Barthes gives priority to the sign and its codes over the reader. Similarly, in asking "What Is an Author?" Foucault defines the author not as a unified consciousness but as comprised by "author-functions" or socially determined roles. "The author does not precede the works, he is a certain functional principle by which, in our culture, one limits, excludes, and chooses" (1989, 274). Foucault thus rejects the "philosophies of consciousness" in favor of structuralism and explains human identity in terms of the pressure to conform exerted by discursive practices and the "technologies of power" as they developed through the course of history.

While Barthes and Foucault decenter the reader in the text, Lacan in his "metatheory" of psychoanalysis decenters the self from within, arguing that the unconscious is "structured like a language" (Eagleton 1983, 157). The identity of the self is constituted by relations, like the relation between the sign and referent, subject and world, with the subject dispersed along chain of signifiers in its desire to regain the imaginary fullness of a whole identity, the pre-oedipal unity of signifier and signified, self and world, child and mother (Lacan 1989, 301–20). For Lacan, the loss of unity and the primary repression of the desire for the lost mother marks our entry into the Symbolic Order, which constitutes our self-identity. The speaking subject is thus defined in terms of lack. Terry Eagleton refers to this as a state of "poststructuralist anxiety" (1983, 116).

Whereas Saussure divides the sign from the referent, Derrida divides the sign within itself through the play of *différance*, and thereby further undermines the notion of a transcendental signified or integrated self. For Derrida, "There is nothing outside the text" (1976, 158). Reference becomes self-reference as meaning is created not through a directedness to things or concepts but rather through intertextual play, a play of the world structured within a linguistic system of differences. In deconstructing logocentrism and the Western metaphysics of presence, Derrida argues that the subject is a function of language—of "a retention and protention of differences, a spacing and temporalizing, a play of traces" (1973, 146). He calls into question the notion of a presence or self-presence of consciousness prior to language and the play of traces. In his critique of Husserl, for whom consciousness is a "self-presence, a self perception of presence," Derrida holds that "the power of synthesis and of the incessant gathering-up of traces is always accorded to the 'living present'" (1973, 147). Like J. Hillis Miller, Paul de Man, and other poststructuralists, Derrida regards the self as a social construction that is different in different societies. More recently Derrida has sought a unity with difference, or as the subtitle of John D. Caputo's book on Derrida puts it, a "religion without religion" (1997). In *Politics of Friendship* (1994), Derrida makes an appeal not so much for a greater social integration between individuals as for a fraternity that excludes women. But the unity of friendship remains within, and is ultimately rendered possible by, the movement of difference. Friendship has its roots in the dissymmetrical equilibrium between loving and being loved, knowing and being known (11). In terms of presence and absence, Derrida holds that to speak to a friend, or to an enemy for that matter, is to use a sentence that "simultaneously puts him at a distance or retards his arrival, since it must always ask or presuppose the question 'are you there?' . . . the other is made to come, allowed to come, but his coming is *simultaneously* deferred" (173; Derrida's emphasis).

Modernity adopted the view that reason, unity, and singularity are "good" and disunity and fragmentation are "bad." Deconstructive postmodernity, or what Harris calls "hermetic poststructuralism" (1996, 65–66), conversely rejects unity, singularity, and reason in favor of disunity, fragmentation, irrationality, and undecidability. Postmodernists like Lyotard and Baudrillard claim there can be many viewpoints, all subjective, and many truths, all relative. At the decentered core of postmodernity is the fragmentary self, consciousness splintered by social forces, and a multiplicity of conflicting voices. The political and philosophical grand narratives of emancipation and enlightenment give way to splintering micronarratives. Politics is pervasive and predominates over aesthetics, language is constitutive of reality and the subject, truth is provisional, meaning is contingent if not undecidable, and human nature is an illusion. Hence the postmodern condition often exhibits an aura of exhaustion or "used-upness," with the earlier optimism of linear progress replaced by the despair of relativism and no future. The sense of nothingness outside the "language game" described by Wittgenstein has led some postmodernists to predict "the end of philosophy." Nietzsche had already declared that "God is dead" (1974, 181), and that "facts are precisely what there is not, only interpretations" (1968, 267).

But not all literary and cultural theorists reject the self as a locus of unity and source of meaning. In *Omens of Millennium*, Harold Bloom says, "The self's potential as power involves the self's immortality, not as duration but as the awakening to a knowledge of something in the self that cannot die, because it was never born" (16). In the Eastern tradition this would be the self as pure consciousness. Similarly Jürgen Habermas, who rejects Jean-François Lyotard's notion of the postmodern condition, suggests that the project of modernity is still unfinished. To solve the dilemmas posed by language for the "philosophies of consciousness," he proposes a project of critical theory based on intersubjectivity, emphasizing that the subject has a universal and self-present identity (1987b, 120). Remarkably, as suggested by Derrida's recent work, many of the principles of deconstructive postmodernism—contingency, indeterminacy, and the constructedness of the subject and reality—do not contradict and in fact often complement the principles of humanism as defined in terms of perennial psychology. As I shall demonstrate in the following sections, this complementarity can also be found in Eastern and Western theories of consciousness.

Premodernity, Modernity, Postmodernity: Interior and Exterior Domains

The development of our notions of the self can be traced from the premodern worldview through the modern to the postmodern worldview. The move from the premodern to the modern has resulted in the current division between the interior and exterior realms of experience. The Great Chain of Being of the premodern era, reaching from matter to body to mind to spirit, has been superseded by the modern differentiation of what Ken Wilber refers to as the spheres of cultural value, namely those of art, morals, and science (*Eye of Spirit* 1–36). The modern differentiation between the value spheres has meant that scientists, artists, and scholars can pursue truth in their diverse fields unimpeded by repressive domination by the other spheres. This is the positive side of modernity. The negative side is that differentiation in modernity has gone to the extreme of scientific imperialism, resulting in dissociation, alienation, and fragmentation. In the premodern era the inner and outer domains were not so much integrated as undifferentiated, and in the modern era the dignity of differentiation has turned into the soulless dissociation of monological science.

Wilber, who has written extensively on Eastern and Western philosophy, notes that modern empirical science has (until recently) rejected an epistemological pluralism that would allow for a correspondence between levels of knowing (sensory, mental, archetypal, and mystical) and levels of being (body, mind, and spirit) (1998b). He sees the need for a differentiation and a reintegration of the spheres of knowledge. Huston Smith, who agrees with this view, discerns that "Reality is graded, and with it, cognition," (*Forgotten Truth*, qtd. in Wilber 1998b, 35)—a truth also stated in the Upanishads. Wilber condenses the four levels of knowing into three: the eye of flesh (the "It" of empiricism), the eye of mind (the "We" of rationalism, which includes ethics), and the eye of contemplation (the "I" of mysticism) (1998b, 59–70). Instead of differentiating and then reintegrating these forms of knowing, science asserts the dominance of the It of empiricism or the eye of flesh. The It perspective, which is monological, represses the We perspective, which is dialogical, and the I perspective, which is translogical. Colin McGinn, in *Ethics, Evil and Fiction*, also argues with regard to science that we should be wary of selecting "one sort of knowledge as setting the standard for all the rest; this is apt to be arbitrary and tendentious, not founded on the application of impartial criteria of epistemic value" (35–36). McGinn explains that because moral facts and events, unlike physical facts and events, do not cause our belief in them does not preclude the possibility of ethical knowledge—which he considers a key element of aesthetics. He asserts that "humans enjoy a natural, spontaneous knowledge of ethical truth, which is part of their innate endowment" (45).

Margaret Wertheim, like Wilber, traces the move from a premodern spatial dualism composed of a physical space and a spiritual space, to a modern monism in which physical space takes over, and ultimately to a postmodern cyberspace, which is being "touted as a new realm for the 'self'" (1999, 41). The erasure of spiritual space begins in the Renaissance with perspective art when physical vision supplanted "spiritual vision" (108), and continues with the growth of science and the discovery that the physical universe is infinite. Attempts to integrate science and culture are increasing, particularly in consciousness studies. The encounter between the physical and spiritual generates a transcendental naturalism or a naturalistic transcendentalism, which is best described in terms of consciousness and aesthetic experience.

In contemplating a beautiful object, whether visual or verbal, one may have the experience of freedom from all activity, including the desire or will to do anything but continue in this state of contemplation. The aesthetic object suspends our grasping for anything in the regretted past or anticipated future, opening a clearing for the awareness in the timeless present. This stasis results not from the expressed content of the work of art but rather from the response it evokes through the power of suggestion. This contemplative response is known in Indian literary theory as *rasadhvani*, the flavor of the subtle sentiments leading toward "liberation" or *moksha* suggested by a work (Krishnamoorthy 1968, 26; as discussed in chapter 2). Entering the timeless present suggested by a work of art can bring transpersonal revelations or translogical connections; a flash of truth or a moment of eternity. All forms of empiricism—sensory, mental and contemplative—are encompassed by the theory of *rasadhvani* and by the *Mundaka Upanishad* (Radhakrishnan 1992). Great works of art portray an interrelationship among them: the expressed form and content belong to sensory and mental empiricism, while the suggestion of a timeless freedom belongs to the contemplative. As Thomas Reid puts it, "those who look for grandeur in mere matter, seek the living among the dead" (1969, 778).

Historically in the West the principle of falsifiability, the criterion of scientific validity, has been applied only to sensory empiricism and denied to the other two. In Eastern cultures, falsifiability has also been applied to mental and contemplative empiricism. Through Eastern influence this principle is being applied in the Western philosophy of science. That is, as in sensory empiricism, so in mental and contemplative empiricism one can apply the three strands of valid knowledge: injunction (doing something), apprehension (getting results), and confirmation (testing these results)—or exemplar, data, and falsifiability (Wilber 1998b, 137–75). McGinn shows that not only ethical and aesthetic knowledge but also logic and mathematics "are not causally responsible for our knowledge of them" (1997, 40). He observes, along with John Locke and Bertrand Russell, that "scientific knowledge is conjectural and inherently stretches our natural capacities, but moral knowledge has certainty and universality, and hence admits of demonstration" (1997, 41).

The criteria of science, however, is beginning to be applied in the study of art. V. S. Ramachandran and William Hirstein, in "The Science of Art: A Neurological Theory of Aesthetic Experience" (*JCS* 15–51), explore the relation between aesthetic experience and consciousness. Although "The Science of Art" is reductive to the extent that it links consciousness to the physiology of the brain, unlike poststructuralism it also seeks universal rules and principles. Ramachandran and Hirstein believe that any theory of art should have three components: a logic of art, an evolutionary rationale, and an understanding of the brain circuitry involved (15). In addition they propose five other principles for a total of what they call "eight laws of aesthetic experience" (15). Although Ramachandran and Hirstein have been criticized by peer commentators in both the humanities and sciences for oversimplifying aesthetic experience, they nevertheless offer an alternative to the linguistic determinism and cultural relativism of a deconstructive postmodernism. They are among a growing number of scientists who assert that the phenomenological dimension of great art is of key importance. Although they see art and consciousness in physiologically reductionist terms, they acknowledge that no simple metric or quantification such as galvanic skin response or Birkhoff's aesthetic ratio (Goguen 13) can fully account for aesthetic experience.

Wilber has traced three failed reactions against the domination of monological science: Idealism, Romanticism, and postmodernism. But as I will suggest, even within postmodernism we can see the beginnings of a differentiation that successfully reintegrates art, morals, and science, one based on the transcendental naturalism of aesthetic experience.

Of the three reactions to modernity, Romanticism was the first to understand that the dissolution of value spheres was a disease in need of a cure. But the romantics in Wilber's view made the mistake of trying to de-differentiate the spheres of knowledge rather than transdifferentiate them in a way that would avoid the failure of dissolution. Instead of advancing through modernity, they wanted to go backward, confusing predifferentiation with transdifferentiation (Wilber 1998b, 90–101). Idealism, on the other hand, came the closest to reestablishing the validity of interior knowledge against the flattening influence of science. Immanuel Kant, Johann Fichte, Georg Hegel, and Friedrich Schelling understood that the prerational modes of knowledge existing before modernity may appear to be transrational, but are really only nonrational and therefore can not constitute a ground for valid knowledge. Fallen into the world, slumbering Spirit began a process of ascent to return to itself, that is, to becoming self-reflexively aware. But unfortunately the idealists did not have a practical and effective way to realize the transpersonal and translogical insights of their contemplative vision. They lacked, for instance, the practice of yoga through which Vedanta provides a way to realize the identity of Atman, or the koans through which Zen meditation provides a way to enlightenment. These techniques have been tested for falsifiability through injunction, apprehension and confirmation and proved to be valid means of gaining knowledge.

Postmodernism, the third reaction, attempts the most radical cure for the dissolution or flattening of the value spheres by monological science. While modernity killed two value spheres, aesthetics and morals, postmodernity killed all three, including that of science. By rendering all three spheres equally defunct, postmodernity rejects all foundationalism, essentialism, and transcendentalism. That is, it rejects the myth of the given. All values are replaced by interpretation, which becomes the foundation or essential feature of the universe. The modernist view of the world in which language is representational, "the mirror of nature," gives way to the linguistic turn of semiotics, structuralism, and poststructuralism. This linguistic turn constitutes a shift from modernity to postmodernity. Language becomes opaque and meaning no longer points objectively but becomes undecidable, a network of dialogical and intersubjective contexts. Signifiers are grounded not in natural referents or signifieds but in nothing but power, ideology, prejudice, gender, race, and colonialism. Hence, the sliding chains of signifiers in postmodernity constitute sliding material contexts only, or chains of data alienated from the values of inner life. Modernity at first differentiated the diverse spheres or contexts of knowledge, only to dissolve them into one—displacing the individual and collective interior domains with the exterior domain of sensory empiricism. Postmodernity, in turn, flattened the distinction between the interior and exterior, substituting an infinity of sliding contexts in which the individual's intentionality as a source of meaning is not situated but erased.

Yet in spite of the attempt to reduce the translogical/transpersonal mind to a form of sensory knowing, the interior domain is still with us. Even the mediated data of sensory empiricism in science must finally become unmediated experience at the moment of apprehension, otherwise there would only be mediation without experience.

It may help clarify the nature of the interior domains as the basis of contemplative empiricism, as in aesthetic experience (*rasadhvani*), if we return for a moment to the idealist tradition. As Jonathan Shear notes, on the topic of self-knowledge, Descartes, Hume, and Kant held that this knowledge provided the basis "of all human understanding," but they found that to understand the self was problematic (1998, 673). Descartes concluded on the basis of common sense that everyone has a "clear intuitive knowledge of the self as *single, simple*, and *continuing*," which he expressed through the phrase *cogito ergo sum*, or in modern parlance, "I am conscious, therefore I exist" (1998, 673; Shear's emphasis). Hume, on the other hand, looked within but could find nothing corresponding to Descartes's single, continuing self, which he regarded as nonsense. Kant, however, found that Descartes and Hume were both right. He argued, as Shear puts it, that "we *have to have*" a unified self as posited by Descartes, but that as Hume indicated "there is *no possibility whatsoever* of experiencing it, or indeed of knowing it as anything but an *abstract vacuous cipher*" (1998, 673; his emphasis).

Kant agreed with Hume that we have no overall sense of unity of the self based on the content of our experiences, but he also argued that such an overall unity, which he called "the transcendental unity of apperception," must be presupposed as the underlying principle of all human understanding (Shear 1998, 674). He reasoned that because experience is extended in time and space, it consists of separate parts; but to exist as a single experience, it must have a single experiencer, which for Kant means that a single, simple, and continuing self is the essential precondition for any experience. But Kant also agreed with Hume that we have no concept of or any way of knowing this simple, unified self. As Shear states, one of Kant's "major conclusions about the self is that it cannot have any experiential quality of its own at all. That is, it has to be a 'pure, original unchanging consciousness,' a 'bare consciousness' with 'no distinguishing features' of its own" (1998, 675). This implies that the self is knowable only as a "blank abstraction," necessary to all experience yet unexperienceable and unknowable in itself, a paradox which, as Kant said, "mocks and torments" even the wisest philosopher (1998, 675). He describes the self as a "qualityless pure consciousness"; it has "no distinguishing quality of its own," but as the witness or seer it underlies all of our manifold experience (1998, 675–76). It is the observer of our changing mental content, but is itself devoid of empirical content. Hence, even as our bodies and personalities mutate over time, we still identify them as belonging to us, to the self as a qualityless unchanging witness.

This ungraspable nature of the self, which cannot be known by observing it but only by being it, is the reason for its divination in premodernity and also the apparent ease with which its erasure has been accepted in postmodernity. No solution to the problem of modernity can effectively ignore this unified, transpersonal, translogical self. As a remedy to postmodern fragmentation, the transpersonal self is not difficult to find; if anything it is unavoidable. As discussed in the final section in terms of Eastern thought, the self as qualityless pure consciousness, the witnessing awareness devoid of empirical content, is always already here behind every thought, feeling, and perception. It is the ever-present witness of the mind, body, and socially constructed self.

Paradoxically, postmodernism serves as a kind of Derridean pharmakon for the self, both a poison and a remedy. That is, it denies the self and simultaneously suggests a way to reach it. To begin with, postmodernity flattens the world to mere surfaces, eliminating values, depth, and the need to search for meaning below the surface. Meaning is determined by its contexts, and contexts are infinite and ultimately unmasterable. Similarly, the qualityless self of Kant and Eastern cultures is also a kind of surface phenomenon, one that extends beyond conceptual content such as language. But for Derrida, even though meaning is undecidable, it is nevertheless a linguistic undecidability. He is not able to "pole-vault" beyond language as a system of difference into the realm of pure witness. In his essay "Edmund Jabès and the Question of the Book," Derrida claims that in Judaism one does not find God or Being intuitively or directly, as through the Book: "Being never is, never shows *itself*, is never *present* . . . outside difference" (1978, 74; his emphasis). Harold Coward notes that in Derrida the real is experienced only "when the opposites of language are maintained in dynamic tension . . . through a continual deconstruction of first one and then the other" (1992, 210). Derrida attempts to undermine the Western logocentric tradition by arguing that we never reach a moment of presence or pure consciousness, but only its trace in the linguistic flickering of presence and absence held in tension.

Nevertheless, the gaps between the pairs of opposites in the pendulum swing of deconstruction, as the traces of presence, need to be understood in terms of the witnessing experience of such moments of (non)presence. These gaps evoke Kant's "qualityless pure consciousness," that witnessing awareness that has "no distinguishing quality of its own" (Shear 1998, 675–76). Derrida argues that the silence between words, as between the words of God's voice, is pregnant with desire and intentional meaning. He gives sensory attributes to that which belongs to contemplative empiricism. But if the gap or silence between words is by definition empty of empirical content, then to experience silence suggests not intentional objects but the ever-present witnessing awareness, as noted by nondual mystics from Plotinus and Eckhart in the west to Shankara and Nagarjuna in the east. As Kant pointed out, moreover, we have no concept or way of knowing this unified witnessing self. We cannot think the gap; we can only be it. The deconstructive movement of difference attempts to undermine the unity of presence; but in designating empirical gaps and promoting our continual experience of them in the oscillation between pairs of opposites, it simultaneously suggests the silence of pure awareness—the simple, qualityless, ever-present witness of all empirical difference and its gaps. Otherwise, for whom would the mediation of difference be an object of experience? Would it be another mediation in an endless series, with no experiencer ever at hand? Even in postmodernity, then, literary and cultural studies and the human sciences suggest that the various domains of knowing can remain distinct yet complementary, integrated on the basis of consciousness.

The Existence of Consciousness

The attempt to reintegrate the value spheres has received a boost from consciousness studies as a discipline, even though the opposition found in the humanities between materialism and metaphysics can also be found in the scientific literature on consciousness. In *The Astonishing Hypothesis*, Francis Crick, Nobel laureate, defines consciousness reductively by eliminating the notion of conscious experience altogether in favor of a neurobiological account for consciousness. He says that "consciousness is associated with certain neural activities" (1994a, 251), probably related to "visual awareness" (252). On the other hand, the physicist Roger Penrose, in *The Emperor's New Mind* and *Shadows of the Mind*, invokes the mechanism of quantum coherence in an attempt to explain the unified nature of conscious experience. He defines consciousness as something separate, more than the sum of the parts, "some sort of global capacity which allows us to take into account the whole of a situation at once" (1994a, 20). Because quantum mechanics is incomplete, however, he thinks we can't really look to it for an explanation of consciousness; we need to go beyond it (21).

In his book *The Large, the Small and the Human Mind*, Penrose continues his argument on the noncomputability of consciousness and the need to go beyond our monological sensory worldview to better understand the relation between the subjective and physical realms. Of great interest to him are what he calls the three worlds or three mysteries and their interrelationships: the physical world, the mental world, and the Platonic or mathematical world. "The more we understand about the physical world," he says, "and the deeper we probe into the laws of nature, the more it seems as though the physical world almost evaporates and we are left only with mathematics" (1997, 3). In an interview he says that physical matter we now understand "as much more of a mathematical thing . . . much more of a mental substance" (1994a, 24). He thus attempts to integrate the monological (sensory) perspective of science with the dialogical and translogical (rational and contemplative) perspectives. He finds problematic the notion that the mental world emerges out of the physical world, that our feelings, sense of color, and happiness could arise out of physics, with its concern for particles, massive objects, energy, space, and time (1997, 94). In terms of the differentiation of the domains of knowledge—as well as the virtualization of reality in the postindustrial age (discussed in chapter 7)—it is anachronistic and indeed untenable for postmodernist and Marxist critics still to hold it on faith that consciousness is a materialist product.

The physicist Jean Burns, in "Volition and Physical Laws" (1999), points out that volition, an aspect of consciousness and the basis of ethical choice, "is not a part of presently known physical laws and it is not even known whether it exists—no physics experiments have ever established its presence" (27). Burns defines free will in philosophical terms as "an influence on physical events which corresponds with mental intention and causes a physical change which would not otherwise occur in identical physical circumstances" (29). But whether volition and consciousness are considered physical or nonphysical, she demonstrates that the physical effects of volition cannot be explained by "presently known physical laws because these laws encompass only determinism and quantum randomness" (32), which are not what is indicated by consciousness or volition.

The astrophysicist Undo Uus, in "The Libertarian Imperative" (1999), also argues that free will, defined "as the ability to select one actuality from several possibilities," is "incompatible with causal determinism" (51). Linking free will with consciousness, he says that "the empirically grounded science of phenomenal consciousness is possible only if the physical world as conceptualized by modern materialistic science is causally open" (50), a view that at present does not prevail and that requires "denying the causal completeness of physics" (51). Science has discovered no laws that account for ethics and free will, which are either illusions or not physically determined. To characterize phenomenal consciousness as an epiphenomenon, a product of the physical, would be to exclude the possibility of ethics and volition. These are not explainable by any known conceptual discourse or determined by any presently known laws of physics.

Penrose observes that even though it cannot be said that any of the three worlds simply emerges out of the others, the physical world seems to obey mathematical laws in an extremely precise way (1997, 95). He notes that "there is a small part of the Platonic world which encompasses our physical world" (1997, 97). This observation in physics has radical implications for the poststructuralist notion that language precedes meaning and that the self is a linguistic construct. Saussure's claim that language is an arbitrary system of differences together with Derrida's movement of *différance* cannot account for the way the Platonic world of mathematics seems to encompass the physical world. As Shear explains in terms of philosophy:

> The discovery and articulation of mathematical structures has led time and again directly to the discovery of previously unperceived and unsuspected structures and phenomena of nature. And many of these previously unsuspected structures and phenomena have turned out to be identifiable and even perceivable (laser light, atomic lattices, telecommunication phenomena, moons and rings orbiting planets, etc.) completely independently of the abstract mathematical considerations that originally led to their discovery. That is, it is clear that our mathematically oriented physical sciences have regularly uncovered objective structures and phenomena which exist and function independently of both our perceptions and our theorizing. (1990, 190)

Contrary to poststructuralist claims about the lack of a natural connection between sign and thing, the language of mathematics indicates that referents accessible to conscious experience do seem to exist prior to and independently of the language system. Derrida's decentering of metaphysics and logocentrism is thus problematized by mathematical laws.

Physicists such as Penrose (1994a, 1994b, 1997), Paul Davies (1983), Nick Herbert (1985), Fritjof Capra (1977), John Hagelin (1987), and theorists such as Katherine Hayles (1984) have observed parallels between consciousness and quantum physics. It has also been suggested, however, that quantum theory has a need for consciousness, not the other way around. Euan Squires states that "the main reason why quantum theory is relevant to consciousness is that the theory cannot be completely defined without introducing some features of consciousness" (1994, 201). Whereas books on classical mechanics deal with "what is and the way things are," books on quantum mechanics deal with "what is observed" (1994, 202). The significance of quantum theory for research into consciousness does not involve any ability on the part of theory to explain consciousness, but rather the role of consciousness in providing "a concept of what it means to 'know'" (1994, 203). The hermeneutic circle here is that we can't explain consciousness in terms of physics because we can't fully understand physics without consciousness. Arguably, the same circle would apply in a deconstructive understanding, which deals with "what is observed" in the act of reading, and therefore cannot do without firsthand conscious experience. For deconstructive postmodernism to deny consciousness is a performative contradiction. Any theory of what it means to "know" would depend on the light of awareness, unless we associate epistemology with a state of darkness.

The History of Consciousness

Consciousness has been defined in many ways throughout the history of Western philosophy, from Plato and Plotinus to Descartes, Kant, the German Enlightenment, Hegel, Husserl, Heidegger, Sartre, and Derrida. As Güven Güzeldere observes, Sartre and others have used two possible meanings of consciousness: "the state or faculty of being conscious, as a condition and concomitant of all thought, feeling and volition [as distinct psychologically from the Freudian/Jungian unconscious]"; and "the state of being conscious, regarded as the normal condition of healthy waking life [as distinct ontologically from the nonconscious]" (1995a, 34). The former sense corresponds with Descartes's usage of consciousness as "consciousness of," the awareness of our mental states, a transitive usage that also implies intention. The latter is something more basic, an intransitive usage that implies a state of consciousness by itself, as in the experience of nonintentional, pure consciousness in the tradition of Eastern cultures. Güzeldere notes that consciousness can also be defined in terms of its two faces, "two major, equally attractive, pre-theoretic intuitions" (1995a, 35). The first is "consciousness is as consciousness does," and the second "consciousness is as consciousness seems" (36). The former intuition is causal and associated with third-person observation (theory), and the latter is phenomenal and associated with direct, first-person experience (praxis). While poststructuralist postmodernists would deconstruct phenomenal intuition, there is a growing consensus in consciousness studies that the two aspects of conscious experience are not mutually exclusive but complementary.

The modern Western history of the study of consciousness begins with the early work of William James. As psychology broke from philosophy and started to develop into a scientific discipline in its own right, one of its first offspring was introspectionism, a study of the phenomenology of the human mind (Güzeldere 1995a, 38–49). James began by saying that introspection was so obvious it hardly needed to be defined. When we look inward, "*Every one agrees that we there discover states of consciousness*" (1950, 185; James's emphasis) Later he denounces consciousness, saying it "is the name of a nonentity" (1971, 4). Gradually in its bid to become classified among the natural sciences, psychology was shaped by positivism, and behaviorism replaced the study of introspection. In this shift psychology moved from phenomenal intuition, or first-person experience, which did not seem to fit with scientific methodology, to causal intuition or third-party observation, with the emphasis on publicly observable behavior. Reducing first-person experience to observable behavior came about largely due to professional anxiety among psychologists. As Julian Jaynes aptly notes, "Off the printed page, behaviorism was only a refusal to talk about consciousness" (1976, 15).

Cognitivism, the next phase in psychology, was inspired by computational models. Consciousness is here defined in terms of information processing, as in computer science. The taboo on the study of consciousness began to disappear, but not until the current boom of neuropsychological research, which started in the 1970s, did consciousness begin to reclaim the spotlight. As Güzeldere notes, "In cognitivism, cognition needed defense over behaviorism no longer, but consciousness over cognition still did" (1995a, 43). Because information-processing models were so successful in explaining functions such as memory, learning, and problem solving—almost everything except consciousness—the unexplained phenomenon of consciousness began to call for greater attention. The various models of consciousness in cognitive psychology, including models of the unconscious in Freud and cognitivism, always seemed to leave something out. To remedy this, new research paradigms on consciousness started being developed that take into account the subjective, experiential aspect of mental phenomena.

The contemporary paradigms of consciousness have had to deal with a puzzle: namely, the epistemic factor that consciousness can be approached from different points of view—first-person or third-person, phenomenological or physicalist. The latter we know only through external reports, while the former we know intimately through the phenomenology of aromas, sights, sounds, tastes, and other contacts that enrich our daily lives—known as *qualia* (see Chalmers 1996, 249–75). This puzzle includes the fact that in our study of consciousness the object and the means of study are the same. The dilemma here parallels that of the deconstructive attempt to undermine logocentrism by means of a language inextricably invested in metaphysics. But if phenomenology seeks the basis of experience in the light of consciousness, deconstruction would apparently place it in the dark.

The experience of qualia constitutes an individual's mode of being, or in Thomas Nagel's famous phrase, "what it is like to be" that individual (1974, 435–50). In an effort to explain this phenomenon, scientists have formulated two aspects of the study of consciousness: the "easy problems of consciousness," how the brain processes sensory stimulation and integrates information used when we report on subjective states; and the "hard problem: Why is all this processing accompanied by an experienced inner life?" (Chalmers 1996, xi–xii)

The Hard Problem of Consciousness

In "Facing Up to the Problem of Consciousness," David Chalmers elaborates on the hard problem and how it stems from the inability of cognitive science to explain consciousness nonreductively:

> What makes the hard problem hard and almost unique is that it goes beyond problems about the performance of functions. To see this, note that even when we have explained the performance of all the cognitive and behavioral functions in the vicinity of experience—perceptual discrimination, categorization, internal access, verbal report—there may still remain a further unanswered question: *Why is the performance of these functions accompanied by experience?* . . . This further question is the key question in the problem of consciousness. Why doesn't all this information-processing go on "in the dark," free of any inner feel? (1995, 203; Chalmers's emphasis)

Chalmers suggests that a full theory of consciousness would explain why and how the information globally accessible to us rises into conscious experience. He finds that current strategies for solving the hard problem and formulating a full theory have proved inadequate. Deconstruction, as if content to operate "in the dark," would reduce the self to a function of difference.

For Chalmers and an increasing number of others philosophers, no purely physical or functional account can explain mental phenomena. The result is an "explanatory gap" between these mainly reductive accounts and consciousness itself (1996, 47). Chalmers proposes what he calls a psychophysical theory of consciousness that would bridge the explanatory gap between the mental and physical without being reductive. This theory, which he calls a "naturalistic dualism" (1996, 168–71), postulates properties that exist above and beyond those described in physics. Physics characterizes entities only in their extrinsic relations, leaving out their intrinsic properties. While some scientists have argued that the intrinsic or phenomenal doesn't exist, Chalmers notes that this creates the problem of a world of "primitive differences" in a "causal flux" with no properties being causally related. "If physics is pure information," he says, "there will be nothing to distinguish instantiations of the two information spaces" (1996, 303). Phenomenal properties, however, can ground these information spaces. "We might say that phenomenal properties are the internal aspect of information (1995, 217). This is one way that quantum physics (as in Squire's suggestion mentioned earlier) has a need for consciousness. The phenomenal approach to the hard problem of consciousness, then, though stretching the limits of our present understanding of physics, has supporters in a variety of disciplines.

In "Neurophenomenology: A Methodological Remedy for the Hard Problem," Francisco Varela defends Chalmers's basic point that subjective, first-person experience is irreducible (1996). He also argues in favor of cooperation or "mutual constraints" between the two basic approaches to the field of phenomena: the experiential and the cognitive sciences. This cooperation would allay the fears among psychologists working in the experiential about the rigor of their scientific research. In developing his theoretical model, Varela distinguishes four basic approaches to consciousness in the ongoing resurgence of interest in mental phenomena: reductionism, functionalism, mysterianism, and phenomenology. Reductionists (like F. Crick, P. S. Churchland, and C. Kock) try to eliminate phenomenal experience in favor of neurobiological accounts; functionalists (D. Dennett, B.

Baars, and G. Edelman) try to assimilate conscious experience to behavior or function; mysterians (like T. Nagel and C. McGinn) find the hard problem unsolvable due to the limitations in our means of understanding mental phenomena; and phenomenologists (Penrose, Chalmers, Varela, Searle, and Shear) define firsthand consciousness as irreducible. This last group, emphasized here, seems to offer the greatest hope for understanding consciousness, and ultimately one suspects for human survival.

In the sustained evolution of phenomenology—which unlike most theories has thrived uninterruptedly on a global scale since its inception—Varela attempts a rigorous methodology and pragmatics based on the style of thinking known as "phenomenological reduction" inaugurated by Edmund Husserl. Rejecting our habitual attitude toward things as existing independently of the subject, phenomenological reduction puts things "in brackets" in order to examine them reflexively as being posited or intended by consciousness. Although phenomenology has been criticized as a form of transcendental idealism, Husserl's famous dictum, "Back to the things themselves" (Varela, 1996, 336), represents a return to the primacy of firsthand experience. Based on the experience of openness, phenomenology is not an authoritarian theory as some critics have argued (Eagleton 1983, 57). This label would better characterize the closure of a third-person objectification, although even this finally comes down to a theorist giving a firsthand epistemic account.

Through a neurophenomenological approach, which integrates phenomenal experience and cognitive science, Varela hopes to avoid some common misconceptions about phenomenology. The first takes phenomenology as merely uncritical introspectionism. But introspection involves "seeing inside," while phenomenological reduction gives us insight into the phenomenal world. As Wilber would say, it differentiates and then reintegrates. Varela notes that this reflexive phenomenal move goes beyond the duality of subject-object and "opens into a field of phenomena where it becomes less and less obvious how to distinguish between subject and object (this is what Husserl called the 'fundamental correlation')" (1996, 339). Penrose confirms this point in his theory of the three worlds, with mathematical laws found at the basis of the physical world. In another misunderstanding, intuition is taken for something "fluffy," a "will-o'-the-wisp inspiration." Varela refutes this misconception with an example from mathematics: "ultimately the weight of a [mathematical] proof is its convincing nature, the immediacy of the evidence which is imposed on us, beyond the logical chains of symbolic reasoning" (339). The decisiveness of intuitive evidence stems less from argument than from a convincing clarity.

Rather than deconstruct binary oppositions such as reason-intuition, subject-object, phenomenology finds their fundamental correlation in consciousness. Consciousness transcends the split between the subjective and objective through its phenomenal link to the external world. In Husserlian language, consciousness in this sense is "transcendental." That is, rather than being restricted to private, internal events, it encompasses the external world that, though apparently nonconscious, may possibly as Chalmers believes embody phenomenal properties. In spite of the Derridean notion of difference, consciousness seems to follow certain structural principles that lead it beyond duality. There is intuitive and empirical evidence for this move—as well as the record of Eastern cultures. Although poststructuralists question conscious experience for being strictly personal, Varela notes that this "does not mean it is private, in the sense of some kind of isolated subject that is parachuted down on a pre-given objective world" (1996, 340). This phenomenal experience radically differs from Anglo-American empiricism with its concern for private inspection. Instead consciousness is linked to the phenomenal world, and in its transcendental state comprises the basis for the empathetic web of human existence, or what Husserl and Jürgen Habermas call intersubjectivity. Varela and his coauthors, in *The Embodied Mind: Cognitive Science and Human Experience*, emphasize the importance of the concrete and embodied, but also of the Buddhist notion of self as being no essential self—as awareness in the sense of pure consciousness. The self realizes itself as part of an unbounded whole that encompasses the world.

Ultimately, Varela's working hypothesis for neurophenomenology calls for reciprocal restraints between firsthand accounts of the structure of conscious experience (praxis) and the accounts of cognitive science (theory). Phenomenological accounts turn out to be important for two reasons: first, without them the direct quality of our experience disappears or becomes a mystery; and second, they monitor empirical observations indispensable to modern science (1996, 343). The interconnection between human experience and cognitive science (which can be said to include critical theory) may also help to open up new aspects of firsthand experience not readily available before (like those recorded in Eastern cultures).

The Phenomenology of Consciousness

Even though consciousness can only be known firsthand, people tend to agree on certain external accounts of its characteristics. We all know, for example, that "what it is like to be" conscious involves the experience of qualia, or empirical phenomenological qualities, and that our thoughts can freely range across the boundaries of space and time. Colin McGinn investigates the lack of extension and other spatial properties in consciousness first postulated by Descartes (1991). He notes that once we acknowledge the nonspatial character of consciousness, then the notion of mental causation, or "how conscious events cause physical changes in the body," becomes problematic (1995, 223). And as we have seen, Burns and Uus have pointed out that consciousness as the basis of ethical choice is not accounted for by any presently known physical laws, that at a certain point the mental exceeds physical causation. For McGinn, this nonspatiality involves radical implications for the origin of consciousness. Although critical theorists complacently define the self as a social construction, a product of material forces, science and philosophy have yet to find the real source of consciousness.

McGinn relates consciousness to the theory of the big bang. In the consensual view, space was created during the big bang, before which it was nonexistent. But McGinn asks, how can space come from nonspace? (1995, 224). He suggests that the big bang may not have been the beginning of all existence. In terms of consciousness, the brain seems to reverse the effect of the big bang through the nonspatial dimension of thought, erasing the spatial rather than creating it: "This suggests the following heady speculation: that the origin of consciousness somehow draws upon those properties of the universe that antedate and explain the occurrence of the big bang. If we need a prespatial level of reality to account for the big bang, then it may be this very level that is exploited in the generation of consciousness" (224). McGinn recognizes that we are spatial beings par excellence, that the brain has spatial properties, and that thoughts appear to be spatial because of their link to the spatial framework of our perceptions. But he asserts that this appearance does not nullify the nonspatial conception of consciousness—the experience that consciousness is not a thing.

The difficulty we have in fathoming the nature of consciousness and formulating a theory about it, McGinn concludes, stems from the lack of an adequate fit between consciousness, which is nonspatial, and thoughts, which through our visual perceptions are tied to the notion of time and space. "We can form thoughts *about* consciousness states, but we cannot articulate the natural constitution of what we are thinking about. It is the spatial bias of our thinking that stands in our way (along perhaps with other impediments)" (1995, 229; McGinn's emphasis). As Wertheim observes, the dominance of physical space over the past three and a half centuries has made it difficult for spiritual space to be appreciated (1999, 31).

C. J. S. Clark also argues that the awareness of visual percepts linked to space makes our thoughts appear spatial, when in fact they are nonspatial. The spatial dimension is not inherent in the mind but originates from outside. He argues that even the brain is not entirely spatial, that "there is a perfectly good place for the non-spatial in physics" (1995, 231). Clark is among the many mathematicians who find that conscious experience, while related to the structure of brain processes, is fundamentally separate from it. He accounts for the nonlocality of the brain associated with consciousness through "quantum logic" (1995, 239), an approach that takes into consideration the total quantum state of the brain. Clark's account of nonlocality resembles Penrose's notion of the mind's global capacity—his view that "matter itself is now much more of a mental substance" (1994a, 24).

Related to nonlocality, as we have seen, is the generation problem (generating consciousness out of matter) addressed by McGinn, Chalmers, Nagel, Burns, and Uus. For Nagel, emergence is impossible and reduction is nonsense. Chalmers proposes that consciousness emerges from or is somehow linked to the physical, but is not reducible to or dependent for its functional description on it. As mentioned earlier, he also suggests that consciousness may be inherent in information and therefore a basic feature of the "material" world. Bluntly stated, as William Seager observes, what is at issue here is panpsychism, the doctrine that "all matter, or all nature, is itself psychical, or has a psychical aspect" (*OED*; qtd. in Seager 1995, 279). Although objections to panpsychism go back to James (see his notion of "the combination problem," 1950, 160), Seager emphasizes how quantum theory highlights "the ineradicable incompleteness of a purely physical picture of the world" (1995, 283). This perception of incompleteness seems plausible from a phenomenal (intuitive) perspective even without quantum mechanics. When confronted with the generation problem in 1874, for example, W. K. Clifford argued that the theory of evolution does not account for an event in the line of physical development where consciousness emerged (Seager 1995, 280). Seager concludes "that one can postulate with at least bare intelligibility that consciousness is a fundamental feature of the universe" (282).

EAST/WEST

Western philosophy of mind has traditionally made a basic distinction between dualists and monists. Dualists include substance dualists, who think the mind and body are two separates kinds of substance, and property dualists, who think the mental and physical are merely two properties of the same substance—as in the case of the psychophysiology of a human being. Like dualists, monists also come in two categories: idealists who believe the world is ultimately mental, and materialists believe it is ultimately material. Most researchers in the philosophy of mind are monists of the materialist bent who try to get rid of the mental by rejecting dualism. But the problem materialists have is that after describing the material facts of the world they are still left with a lot of unexplained mental phenomena. The materialist Crick, for instance, defines consciousness reductively through a neurobiological account: "Consciousness is associated with certain neural activities" (1994a, 251), probably related to "visual awareness" (252). But the quantitative and objective description of neuron firings does not explain our qualitative, subjective experience. As Searle says, "How, to put it naively, does the brain get us over the hump from electrochemistry to feeling?" (1997, 28).

K. Ramakrishna Rao, in "The Two Faces of Consciousness," defines several possible meanings of consciousness and then places them into two categories: "object awareness" and "subject awareness" (1998, 309). As their names imply, "object awareness" predicates awareness on an object, while "subject awareness" is the awareness of awareness itself or one of its aspects. Object awareness is the phenomenal or intentional domain of consciousness, and subject awareness is the transcendental or nonintentional domain. Further, object awareness as the intentional aspect of consciousness is associated with the West, and subject awareness as the nonintentional aspect is associated with the East. Because different cultures have different notions of consciousness, one's preference here usually depends on one's cultural background. As Rao puts it, "In the western tradition the dominant perspective is one of *rational* understanding of what consciousness is. In the eastern tradition the approach is one of developing practical methods for *transforming* consciousness in specific ways for specific purposes" (310, emphasis added).

In terms of Advaita (nondual) Vedanta, the philosophical tradition founded by Ṣhankara, one of India's most influential philosophers, the indeterminate, transcendent Absolute (Brahman) comprises the "content" of the nondualistic experience of pure consciousness (atman). Though without attributes, Brahman is traditionally characterized as *sat* (infinite being), *chit* (consciousness), *ananda* (bliss). Brahman is the truth of the universe, and atman is the truth of the self. "All this is, verily, *Brahman*. This self [Atman] is *Brahman*. This same self has four quarters" (*Mandukya Upanishad*, verse 2; Radhakrishnan 1992, 695). The four quarters refer to the three ordinary states of consciousness—waking, sleeping, dreaming—and a fourth (*turiya*) state of pure consciousness without qualities or content. As the ever-present witness (atman), the fourth state (*turiya*) underlies all mental phenomena manifested in the three ordinary states of consciousness.

Unlike Western epistemology in which knowledge is based on language, the *Mundaka Upanishad* distinguishes "two kinds of knowledge [which] are to be known, as, indeed, the knowers of *Brahman* declare—the higher as well as the lower. . . . Of these, the lower is the *Rig Veda* [plus the other three Vedas and assorted Vedic texts]. . . . . And the higher is that by which the Undecaying [Brahman] is apprehended [directly]" (I.1.4; Radhakrishnan 1992, 672). Lower knowledge corresponds to the three ordinary states of consciousness and to sensory and mental empiricism, and higher knowledge to the fourth state of pure consciousness (*turiya*) and to contemplative empiricism. Advaita (nondual) Vedanta refers to these two aspects or modes of Brahman as *saguna* and *nirguna*. As Eliot Deutsch explains, "*Nirguna* Brahman—Brahman without qualities—is just that transcendent indeterminate state of being about which ultimately nothing can be affirmed. *Saguna* Brahman—Brahman with qualities—is Brahman as interpreted and affirmed by the mind from its necessarily limited standpoint" (1973, 12). Since higher knowledge or consciousness (*nirguna*) is latent within the lower (*saguna*), the different knowledge spheres of modernity can be said to be distinct on one level yet integrated on another. To flatten this differentiation monologically into empirical science or discursive reason would be to deny the higher level of knowledge, just as to nondifferentiate by collapsing everything to the metaphysical would be to deny legitimacy to the full evolutionary range of human experience. The two kinds of knowledge are thus complementary. As exterior and interior domains, they can be integrated through aesthetic experience (*rasadhvani*) in which the sensory and mental dimensions of a work lead the awareness back to itself as timeless witness through the contemplation of the beauty of art. In this way the naturalistic transcendentalism of art constitutes a unity of opposites.

As Deutsch observes in his lucid account of Shankara's Vedanta, "The central concern of Advaita Vedanta is to establish the oneness of Reality and to lead the human being to a realization of it" (1973, 47). This realization occurs through the "experience" of consciousness in its unified or irreducible state as witness or seer, single, simple, and continuing. Atman however is beyond "experience" in the usual sense of a division of subject and object found in the three ordinary states of consciousness. It is "self-shining," "spaceless," and "not-different from Brahman" (Deutsch 1973, 48–49). In the words of Shankara, "The knowledge of the Atman iş self-revealed and is not dependent upon perception and other means of knowledge" (*Brahmasutrabhasya*; qtd. in Deutsch 1973, 49). A work of art or literature does not create this state but only helps one to recognize it as an ever-present reality. Aesthetic experience facilitates our letting go of the boundary between subject and object.

In "'I' = Awareness," Arthur Deikman further distinguishes awareness as the ground of experience (Atman) and the objects of awareness—thoughts, sensations, images, moods, emotions, and memories (1996). The difference here, as we have seen, is between a psychological interpretation of consciousness (as distinct from the Freudian or Jungian unconscious), and an ontological interpretation of consciousness (as distinct from nonconscious experience). Most psychology texts deal with the contents of awareness, the sensations of the body and memories of our social identities, and not with "awareness as a phenomenon in its own right" (Deikman 1996, 352). While the pronoun "I" usually signifies the ego, Deikman intends the "I" of awareness to signify the witnessing faculty and not an object of observation as in ordinary experience. It is "the experiencer, prior to all conscious content" (350). "Experiencing" the "I" or Atman solves the problem of infinite regress, since "we know the internal observer not by observing it but *by being it*" (355; Deikman's emphasis). As the ever-present witness it is unavoidable, yet our recognition of it is heightened during aesthetic experience. The ultimate reality of the world or a text is not something perceived, but rather witnessing awareness or the seer. Because it is neither this nor that, you cannot see the seer; you can only be it. The self as witness does not have to be searched for; it is always present and constantly functioning in our spontaneous awareness of everything around us. All the events of the past and future occur for the witness now in the present, which is all we ever know. Timeless, spaceless, causeless, beginningless, and endless, the pure and simple witness that we always already are is the radical emptiness into which arise all manifestations of thoughts, sensations, emotions, and perceptions. The recognition of this ever-present witness—to varying degrees of fullness—is what aesthetic experience brings us through its suggestive power (*rasadhvani*) as we transcend the subject and object duality in our identification, for example, with a fictional character.

In a recent exchange between Henry W. Sullivan and Howard Mancing in the journal *Cervantes* (1999), Sullivan argues that a fictional character, while not a real person, can still be the subject of psychoanalysis, as in a Lacanian analysis of Don Quixote de la Mancha. To support this argument Sullivan proposes a distinction between body and "organism," the latter defined in Lacanian terms as a linguistic and psychological being. He claims that the human biological animal (body) is not the same thing as a human linguistic and psychological being (organism), and questions the assumption that the "real person" means exclusively a human biological mammal "who has, or had, a historical existence" (1998, 12). In this way Sullivan makes a case for "the virtual psychic reality of personae in literature whose life extends beyond the time of their literary creation into an indefinite future posterity" (12). The organism—defined through the Lacanian notions of the Imaginary, the Symbolic order, and the Real through which the subject is constructed—constitutes the essence of fictional personae, serving to "'debiologize' the human subject" (14). With the concept of organism Sullivan also intends to undermine the mind/body dualism that cognitive scientists increasingly find to be untenable.

Mancing, however, questions Sullivan's definition of organism as a concept distinct from body and accuses him of positing "an absolute (Cartesian) mind-body dualism as the cornerstone of psychoanalytic theory" (1999, 158). He does not accept the notion of an organism as a culturally constructed virtual psyche, condemning it as a reaffirmation of Cartesian dualism, and instead espouses reductive concepts in cognitive science such as the "embodied mind," "the body in the mind," and "the mind-brain" (162). He quotes Richard Restak's assertion that consciousness is "a very special *emergent* property of the human brain . . . made possible by a sufficient number of parallel interacting modules" (163). Sullivan, however, is amazed by Mancing's misunderstanding of his use of organism, which he intended to overturn an absolute Cartesian dualism. Organism as a "third term" was meant to provide a "solvent" to binary dualisms by replacing them with the notion of a mind/body *distinction*. Hence the title of Sullivan's response to Mancing: "Don Quixote and the 'Third Term' as Solvent of Binary Dualisms" (1999).

For Sullivan, then, a "mind/body *distinction* is not the same as a mind/body *dualism*," for the "mind is *inseparable* from the brain, but *distinct* from it" (1999, 192; Sullivan's emphasis). He attempts to deconstruct binary thinking by identifying the third term responsible for creating dualisms in the first place. Yet however much Sullivan and Mancing may agree or disagree about their definitions of dualism in the context of cognitive science, they both differ from the notion of dualism in Eastern thought, for which the mind and body are both material. In the tradition of Samkhya-Yoga, which like Vedanta belongs to the six systems of Indian philosophy, the structure of reality consists of twenty-five components in a firm dualism.

As Lloyd Pflueger explains, in Samkhya-Yoga "there are two irreducible, innate, and independent realities in our universe of experience: 1. consciousness itself (*purusha*); 2. primordial materiality (*prakrti*)" (1998, 48). In these copresent and coeternal realities, primordial materiality (*prakrti*) contains twenty-three components, including intellect (*buddhi*, *mahat*), ego (*ahamkara*), and mind (*manas*) (Pflueger 1998, 48). The intellect, ego, and mind together with thought, feeling, and perception are as Pflueger notes "all seen as merely different forms of nonconscious matter. . . . This is not the garden variety of mind/body dualism encountered in Western philosophy! Here both body and mind are seen as unequivocally material. Even so, Samkhya-Yoga cannot reduce the universe of experience to the nonconscious permutations of matter alone" (49). As in Vedanta, the material content of experience related to the intellect, ego, and mind are "only half the equation of experience—[for] our experience necessarily involves the element of consciousness" (49). That is, in addition to the twenty-four material components of experience, there is also *purusha* [or atman in Advaita Vedanta], "the principle of consciousness itself" (49).

From this perspective, the Western mind/body dualism is really a monism, for the mind and body comprise the material building blocks of experience as distinct from the witnessing faculty (*purusha* or atman) that "illuminates" this experience (Pflueger 1998, 50). Samkhya-Yoga dualism consists on the one hand of *purusha* or consciousness itself, and on the other hand of *prakrti* or matter, which includes all "psychological faculties: intellect, ego, mind, sense capacities, and action capacities; and subtle elements, gross elements, and material objects" (51). *Purusha* is contentless pure consciousness "without which even mental processes *know* nothing" (51; Pflueger's emphasis). The mistake of the intellect is to identify the intellect, ego, and mind with consciousness. Even though the intellect seems to know, the knowing or witnessing faculty belongs to consciousness alone. As a material linguistic construct, the intellect has no light to shine on experience and cannot answer Chalmers's question, "Why doesn't all this information processing go on 'in the dark,' free of any inner feel?" (1996, 203). The answer lies with consciousness, the immaterial witness of language, and all other objects of awareness. No subject/object duality obtains in consciousness, which is not a process of knowing, as in self-consciousness, but a state of being, as in knowingness. As Pflueger puts it, "Consciousness is eternally free of . . . objects, infinite, immaterial, and awake. The sensations and judgments assembled by the intellect are mere permutations of matter, *prakrti*, without consciousness of any kind" (55).

For Vedanta and Samkhya-Yoga, which combine theory and direct experience, consciousness is not apprehended by faith or any other mental construction. It is not a material product like the notion of organism in Sullivan or mind in Mancing and cognitive science. Sullivan's third term is only a synonym for the other two terms in a nondual or monist materialism: mind-body. When Sullivan accuses Mancing of collapsing the mind-body distinction on the side of body instead of accepting the notion of organism, he is merely accusing him of unintentionally recognizing what Samkya-Yoga already posits: namely, that mind and body, or mind-body in its various permutations belongs to the material realm. The concept of organism does not save the distinction except insofar as mind and body are different aspects of the same material process. By disassociating mind from its (mis)-identification with pure consciousness, which can be achieved only through direct experience, Eastern thought would transform human suffering into a freedom from bondage to the material realm. As an innate experience, pure consciousness entails liberation from "all concepts, all thinking, all words, all feeling, all memory, and all perception" (Pflueger 69–70).

It is important to remember, then, that Eastern thought distinguishes between consciousness and mind, whereas Western thought identifies the two. The Eastern tradition regards consciousness as completely noncorporeal, the witnessing aspect of awareness, and mind, which is a form of matter, albeit subtle, as related to the content of consciousness. The mind is the link between the phenomenal world of sense impressions and the realm of qualityless pure consciousness, defined as the experience of awareness itself without intentional content. A key significance of the difference between mind and consciousness, as we shall see in chapter 4, is that it underlies the distinction between two kinds of intersubjectivity: one based on reason and language, and one that includes but goes beyond language and the intentional mind. Rao explains that the Western definition of consciousness in terms of intentionality means that consciousness is always "*of* or *about* something" (313, Rao's emphasis). John Searle also holds that intentionality, which requires that consciousness be of something—an object—is the essence of mind or consciousness (1983), as does Edmund Husserl. Understanding consciousness in terms of intentionality and its identity with the mind is central to a phenomenology that does not accommodate the subject as pure awareness, or communication apart from conceptual content.

The Western tradition, positing an identity between consciousness and mind, considers intentionality the defining characteristic of consciousness, and lacks any practical means of applying an understanding of consciousness toward improving the human condition. In contrast, the Eastern tradition distinguishes between mind and consciousness, posits the existence of pure consciousness or awareness as such, and has developed methods such as yoga and meditation for accessing pure consciousness and thereby achieving tangible benefits and specific goals. "Whereas the western perspective is focused on the phenomenal manifestation of consciousness, the eastern tradition pays special attention to the transcendental aspects of consciousness through its concern with pure consciousness" (Rao 317).

In deconstructive postmodernism, of courses, being, presence, and consciousness are flattened out of existence by an external viewpoint. The notion of an "experiencer prior to all conscious content" falls prey to Derrida's distinction between speech and writing. Traditional humanism favors the "phonocentric," which permits a first-person experience of the unity of voice and meaning. Derrida's third-person theory of *différance*, on the other hand, extends the freeplay of the graphic text over the entire field of signs, including speech. But as Harris has aptly demonstrated, Derrida relies heavily on (among other fallacies) equivocation and the ambiguities that make it possible

(1996, 54–58). In terms of the possibility of preverbal meaning, Eastern philosophy provides a language theory that accounts for the experience of meaning in relation to different levels of consciousness; these levels correspond to the two kinds of knowledge in the *Mundaka Upanishad* (Ramachandran 1992). Robert Forman, moreover, points out that no one "has ever explained how language and its background are actually part of a mystical experience" (1994, 41)—part of witnessing awareness.

Conclusion

The post-Saussurean theories of language that allegedly undermine the unity of self and text through the notion of difference relate at best to the ordinary states of consciousness; they do not fathom *turiya* (pure awareness), nor communication based on *turiya*. But even for the ordinary waking and dream states—whose content consists of qualia—third-person accounts are rarely indisputable. Although deconstructive postmodernism may apply to mental phenomena, it does not apply to witnessing awareness as a state of being. One might therefore suggest that rather than being dead, man is but momentarily out of focus or lost from sight. The revival of humanism and the humanities in terms of consciousness may only take a shift in our perspective away from a monological theory toward a greater comprehensiveness of theory and practice.

The conjunction of theory and praxis in Eastern cultures can provide a model for the cooperation that Varela proposes between phenomenology and cognitive science (1996). This model may help us shift our perspective toward a new humanism through which all knowledge domains—sensory, mental, and contemplative—are seen as distinct yet integrated, with no one sphere dominating the others, as in the poststructuralist domination of the subject. Since consciousness remains a mystery to sensory and mental empiricism, it is hard to see how deconstruction, or any critical theory for that matter, can effectively call into question something still beyond our consensual, third-person understanding. Could it be that critical theory has reached a closure on the humanities, shut the doors of perception even as other disciplines advance in their explorations on the final frontier of human awareness? Through a greater openness to and recognition of consciousness in its irreducible condition, the humanities would be better poised to participate in a renaissance of the self and a reenchantment of humanity.

2
Models of the Self

Introduction

ALTHOUGH POSTMODERNISTS HAVE JETTISONED THE UNIVERSALISM OF liberal humanism and new theories of the subject continue to emerge, in some cases the new may only be a transformation of the old. Gergen notes that "the social saturation brought about by the technologies of the twentieth century, and the accompanying immersion in multiple perspectives, have brought about a new consciousness: postmodernist" (1991, 228). More recently in *How We Became Posthuman* (1999), Hayles observes that we live in conditions of virtuality and cybernetics where the self has nearly become disembodied, a function of informational patterns rather than material structure. The posthuman subject, for whom "the biological substrate is seen as an accident of history" (2), is an amalgam, "a material-informational entity whose boundaries undergo continuous construction and reconstruction" (3). But postmodern and posthuman perspectives of the self, as of anything, are avowedly limited and do not exhaust the unboundedness of phenomenal states. As Robert Forman notes, "Human capacity includes more epistemological modalities that is generally imagined" (1998b, 196).

As Searle says in *The Mystery of Consciousness*, "This era is at once the most exciting and the most frustrating for the study of consciousness in my intellectual lifetime: exciting because consciousness has again become respectable, indeed almost central, as a subject of investigation in philosophy, psychology, cognitive science, and even neuroscience; frustrating because the whole subject is still plagued with mistakes and errors I thought had been long exposed" (1997, xi). The study of consciousness today increasingly suggests that its nature cannot be adequately characterized in physical terms, nor in terms of mind-body duality. Moreover, in the Western tradition, the "constructivist" or relative understanding of consciousness is being forcefully challenged by the "decontextualist" or universal understanding. Constructivists or Neo-Kantians such as Steven Katz consider consciousness to be a social construct, while decontextualists such as Robert Forman, who prefer to be called "perennial psychologists" (1998a, 27), believe in the unity or identity of consciousness across cultural and historical boundaries. The comeback of consciousness in the West and the complementarity of Western and Eastern (or transcultural) viewpoints on the self have significant implications for literary and cultural studies.

Searle, in *The Rediscovery of the Mind*, suggests that "Consciousness and intentionality are intrinsic and ineliminable, and computation—except for the few cases in which the computation is actually being performed by a conscious mind—is observer relative" (1992, xiii). Computation here includes the third-person observations of consciousness made by poststructuralists. While Searle, as a Western philosopher, identifies consciousness with the intentional mind, he nevertheless asserts that no convincing evidence supports the argument that phenomenological first-person experience can be reduced to third-person observation. Forman, taking the Vedanta-inspired view, defines self-identity as an experience of consciousness through what he calls "knowledge-by-identity." Unlike "knowledge-by-acquaintance" or "knowledge-about," which as defined by William James have intentional objects, "knowledge-by-identity" is a third form of knowledge that does not have an intentional object and through which "the subject knows something by virtue of being it. . . . I *know* my own consciousness, and I know that I am and have been conscious simply because I *am* it" (1998a, 20–21). Foreman and colleagues argue that pure consciousness accessible through "knowledge-by-identity" is an innate capacity (1998a passim).

The Range of Consciousness

Forman, in "What Does Mysticism Have to Teach Us?" (1998b), describes several nonordinary states of consciousness documented by people around the world. He discusses these states within the context of mysticism, which he calls a "somewhat unusual but increasingly accepted field" (185). Part of my thesis in this book is that incipient stages of these (mystical) states are apparently becoming more prevalent in contemporary life, as suggested by the quality of experience found both in the postmodern and post-postmodern condition, or what the French anthropologist Marc Augé calls supermodernity (1995, 29)—discussed later in this chapter. In *The Innate Capacity*, Forman and colleagues put forward the hypothesis that the experience of pure consciousness results from an innate human capacity and not "from a learned, socially conditioned constructive process" (1998a, viii). Forman notes that in large-scale studies, David Hay "concludes that nearly *half*—43 percent of all Americans and 48 percent of all British people—have had one or more mystical experiences. These experiences are not confined to the uneducated; more that half of all college graduates have had such experiences" (1998a, 3, Forman's emphasis).

Drawing on cognitive science, phenomenology, and Eastern philosophy, Forman describes the simplest form of consciousness in a manner analogous to the way biologists seek to describe a complex phenomenon through a simple gene, and the way "Freud and Durkheim both used totemism, which they construed as the simplest form of religion, to understand the complexities of life" (1998b, 185). This simplest form of consciousness, as we have seen, is widely known as pure consciousness, the experience of that Forman calls the "pure consciousness event," or PCE (1998b, 186). In this state, consciousness is by itself without the intentional content of discursive thought. The experience of pure consciousness or PCE he calls "just the least complex encounter with awareness *per se* that we students of consciousness seek" (1998b, 186). Shear, in "The Hard Problem: Closing the Empirical Gap," refers to pure consciousness as "consciousness *devoid of all its discrete activities and* contents," which in Eastern traditions, such as Hinayana Buddhism and nondual or Advaita Vedanta, "is properly regarded as a 'higher' state of consciousness" (1996a, 64–65). The Upanishads, recall, refer to this state as *turiya*, the "fourth" condition.

Pure consciousness is systematically explored in Eastern cultures through experiential procedures such as yoga or meditation. Although the various traditions of meditation have their differences, they widely agree, as Shear notes,

> that the surface phenomena of consciousness emerge from deeper structures of consciousness which can be experienced directly, and that these deeper structures in turn emerge from an underlying "ground" of consciousness which is also experienceable. This ground, moreover, is regularly described as . . . consciousness *devoid of all its discrete activities and contents*. Thus, as the Yoga *Sutras* [of Patanjali], the central text of Yoga,

> puts it, it is qualityless "pure consciousness," . . . consciousness alone by itself in a state of "objectless *samadhi.*" (1996a, 64, Shear's emphasis)

Pure consciousness, as the *Yoga Sutras* indicate, can be attained through yoga, defined as "the inhibition of the modifications of the mind" (I. 2; Taimni 1986, 6). Patanjali, moreover, defines pure consciousness (*purusa*) as the unified observer: "The Seer is pure consciousness but though pure, appears to see through the mind" (II. 20; Taimni 1986, 185). For Vedanta, as Dasgupta notes, the identification of the self (awareness) with the mind, body, and senses "is a beginningless illusion" (1975, vol. 1, 435). As a Western mystic who has described the experience of pure consciousness, W. T. Stace says that "the introverted mystics—thousands of them all over the world—unanimously assert that they have attained to this complete vacuum of particular mental contents . . . a state of *pure* consciousness—'pure' in the sense that it is not the consciousness *of* any empirical content. It has no content except itself" (1960, 85–86; Stace's emphasis). Because pure consciousness is not a typical object of awareness, it is described in Vedanta as being "self-luminous" and without form (Dasgupta 1975, 444). As Forman observes, a PCE (pure consciousness event) is an innate capacity accessible to everyone, whether through meditation, certain kinds of aesthetic rapture, or in spontaneous introspection.

Considering the widespread reports of PCEs from diverse eras and cultures—which corroborate texts like the Vedas, Upanishads, and *Patanjali's Yoga-Sutras*—we can draw several implications about the nature of human consciousness. To begin with, as Forman and colleagues suggest, consciousness does not seem to be an historical or cultural construct, as constructivists and poststructuralists would claim. Further, since consciousness can be experienced by itself, "stripped of all psychological contents and objects" (Stace 1960, 86), it is not dependent on, nor an epiphenomenon of, perception, action or thought, nor is it identical to the functions of bearing information or controlling behavior. And as Searle argues, the mind is not a computer limited by computation. You can't teach a computer what it's like to be conscious, Forman notes, "since the knowledge of being conscious seems available only to someone who knows consciousness by virtue of being conscious" (1998a, 32). Moreover, as recorded by William James in *The Varieties of Religious Experience*, during a PCE the subject senses the continuity of awareness; after the event the subject will know intuitively that awareness, even without remembered content, tied itself together (1902/1983, 409). While in ordinary waking states the mental content that comprises our sense of self may be fragmentary and the roles we play in society forever changing, consciousness itself persists as a unified state of inner silence. As Forman puts it:

> to the question How do I know this continuity of consciousness, I think we should say I know it not because I have learned about it through words or analysis but because I am directly acquainted with it by virtue of being it. I know my awareness per se as a unity, tying itself together as it ties memories and thoughts together with present stimuli because I do this. I know it as a unity that can become aware of a thought, perception, or what have you because I am this unity. (1998a, 23)

This knowledge of unity or oneness is not a "knowledge-about" something of the intentional mind, but a "knowledge-by-identity" of nonintentional consciousness; "in *turiya* one comes to employ knowledge-by-identity alone" (1998a, 26).

The experience of pure consciousness may come spontaneously, or it may be evoked in various ways, either through aesthetic rapture (see Haney 1998) or, as I suggest below, through a transformation of awareness in the world of supermodernity and even postmodernity. More typically, pure consciousness is associated with traditions of long-term meditation or yoga that lead to advanced states known as *moksa* or "enlightenment." That is, through continual PCEs, which are transitory, the awareness gradually reaches what Forman calls "a deep shift in epistemological structure," with a distinct change in "the experienced relationship between the self and one's perceptual objects" (1998b, 186). As Forman observes,

> These long-term shifts in epistemological structure often take the form of two quantum leaps in experience; typically they develop sequentially. The first is an experience of a permanent interior stillness, even while engaged in thought and activity—one remains aware of one's own awareness while simultaneously remaining conscious of thoughts, sensations and actions. Because of its phenomenological dualism—a heightened cognizance of awareness itself plus a consciousness of thoughts and objects—I call it the dualistic mystical state (DMS). The second shift is described as a perceived unity of one's own awareness *per se* with the objects around one, an immediate sense of a quasi-physical unity of self, objects and other people. States akin to this have been called "extrovertive-" or sometimes "nature-" mysticism; but I prefer to call it the unitive mystical state, UMS. (1998b, 186)

While the PCE is transitory, Forman's dualistic mystical state (DMS) and unitive mystical state (UMS) are the permanent experience of pure consciousness. First the silence of inner wholeness is in the background along with mental activity (DMS), and then it gradually extends out from the self and permeates the field of perception (UMS). The DMS and UMS are the stages of *turiya* (pure consciousness) becoming fully established. But as Forman is the first to concede, phenomenal first-person reports of higher consciousness, whether by authors of the Upanishads, Meister Eckhart, Teresa of Avila, or others, do not constitute scientific proof. And yet, as a growing number of scientists tell us, these experiences are "unusually wise" (1998b, 188). Since no reason compels us to deny the reality of higher consciousness or the implications of their reports, common sense tells us to keep an open mind and see what comes. The alternative would be to prejudge consciousness through the external third-person observation of the intentional mind, which would only lead to further unconvincing arguments such as those many literary and cultural theorists would have us believe.

To facilitate the ongoing development of a scientific theory of consciousness through an integration of third-person theory and first-person experience, Forman proposes three sets of terms for the different facets of consciousness. "Awareness" and "consciousness" for consciousness aware within itself, "which may persist even without intentional content"; "awareness of" and "consciousness of" for the experience of being intentionally aware of something; and "pure awareness" and "pure consciousness" for awareness devoid of intentional content (1998b, 192). We cannot through introspection observe pure consciousness, we can only be it, for it is a state in which the subject and object are united. This unity describes pure consciousness, the simplest form of awareness, but the situation changes in the more advanced DMS and UMS, where pure consciousness is maintained along with thoughts and then extended into the field of perception (see Forman for a detailed description, 1998b, 192–200).

In the dualistic mystical state (DMS), then, which Freud referred to as an "oceanic feeling," the experience of pure consciousness as the silence of inner stillness is no longer transitory but becomes a permanent condition, persisting throughout all activity and thought. This state, as I will suggest, resembles an aspect of "supermodern" or post-postmodern subjectivity. An example of the DMS is recorded by Teresa of Avila, who writes of herself in the third person:

> However numerous were her trials and business worries, the essential part of her soul seemed never to move from [its] dwelling place. So in a sense she felt that her soul was divided. . . . Sometimes she would say that it was doing nothing but enjoy[ing] itself in that quietness, while she herself was left with all her trials and occupations so that she could not keep it company. (Peers 1961, 211)

In Teresa's experience, pure consciousness and daily activity coexist on a permanent basis. Here is Forman's description of his own experience of this state:

> It was and is as if what was *me*, my consciousness itself, was (and is) now this emptiness. The *silence* was now me, and the thoughts that have gone on inside have not felt quite in contact with what is really "me," this empty awareness. "I" was now silent inside. My thinking has been as if on the outside of this silence without quite contacting it: When I say, felt or heard something, that perception or thought has been seen by this silent consciousness, but it has not been quite connected to this interior silence. (1998b, 194, Forman's emphasis)

In Buddhism and Hinduism, the silence of inner emptiness is called by several names, such as *sunyata* and *samadhi* respectively. The permanent coexistence of pure awareness and daily experience is also known as cosmic consciousness or, as Eliot Deutsch lucidly explains in his book on advaita Vedanta, *nirvikalpa samadhi* (1973, 62–63). Even though pure awareness is without attributes or content, " 'something persists' in this contentlessness, and that is consciousness itself" (Forman 1998b, 191). In Teresa of Avila's and Forman's dualistic experience, "the fullness of emptiness" defined as consciousness devoid of attributes or content is maintained permanently along with intentional content: "consciousness is aware of itself through knowledge-by-identity and simultaneously is perceiving thought or language intentionally" (Forman 1998a, 27).

Forman lists several implications of the experience of pure consciousness during activity. Here consciousness is not something separate, not a new awareness, but rather a "becoming more *immediately* cognizant of the awareness" we've always enjoyed (1998b, 196). In the DMS, "Awareness itself is experienced as still or silent, perceptions as active and changing" (1998b, 197). In this cosmic phenomenology, moreover, consciousness is not limited to a point but begins to extend beyond the body. It is "encountered as something more like a field than a localized point, a field that transcends the body and yet somehow interacts with it" (197). The mind may be nonlocalized, therefore, with experience arising through "some sort of interplay between non-localized awareness and the localized brain" (197). This phenomenon leads to two possible theories about consciousness as a field rather than the product of a bunch of neurons. The brain may be like a magnet that "'produces' a field which extends well beyond its own physical borders . . . [or] the brain may be more like a receiver or transformer for the field of awareness than its generator: less like a magnet than a TV receiver" (197).

It is reasonable to hold that a first-person experience of this field transcends the deconstructive third-person critique of consciousness as being divided within itself through the play of *différance*. While post-structucturalist theories may apply to ordinary waking consciousness and its content or attributes, they apparently do not apply to consciousness itself. In fact, postmodernity and supermodernity may actually increase the accessibility of nonintentional states of self-presence, states devoid of subject/object duality and prior to language and the play of traces. The prevalence through history and around the world of mystical states suggests a basic human psychophysiological structure, which has led Forman to propose that mystical states comprise a *psychologia perennis* or "perennial psychology" (*Innate* 27–28). Language may determine the intentional content of the mind, but it is absent in nonintentional awareness as such, which is devoid of attributes. As Forman explains,

> consciousness itself is not linguistically formulated. Just the reverse is true. This can be seen very simply. For a child to learn any language at all, he or she must be conscious. Being aware, or having consciousness, is presupposed by language acquisition, not the other way around. Awareness per se must be present not only before someone can learn the word "consciousness"; it must be present before one can learn the meaning of any word at all. For it is only by virtue of being conscious that we have the capacity to understand any speech acts at all. (*Innate* 23)

As an epistemological prerequisite for the mind's intentional content, language drops away in the experience of consciousness itself. If knowledge of awareness by identity is nonlinguistic and nonconceptual, it must also be nonpluralistic. People in different cultural and historical contexts would have similar direct experiences of a PCE, even though after the fact they may describe them differently according to their own mystical traditions. Forman calls this the "nonpluralistic phenomenon," which may bring "an answer to the postmodern problem of incommensurability" (1998a, 32–33). That is, the nonpluralistic phenomenon suggests that the differences among recorded descriptions of pure consciousness in different traditions are accidental, that they all refer to the same phenomenon.

R. L. Franklin, in "Postconstructivist Approaches to Mysticism," proposes a way to allow for differences in the experience of universal consciousness from different mystical traditions. As a way of meeting the constructivist challenge that culture shapes all our mental activity, he observes that theistic, advaitan, and Buddhist mystical experiences all involve three characteristics: transcending the "boundaries of ordinary discursive thought"; experiencing a "feeling-tone" of bliss, joy, or rapture; and leaving conceptual distinctions for "a state of *nonseparateness*" (1998, 231–33; Franklin's emphasis). In defining the state of nonseparateness, Franklin admits to "conced[ing] to constructivism more than some postconstructivists might like: that there are flavors of nonseparateness, such as theistic, advaitan, or Buddhist ones" (234). Franklin's purpose is to capture the underlying oneness of mystical states while doing justice to their diversity. People are different, but nonseparate. Forman's "forgetting model" as a deconditioning of experience in the PCE also applies in Franklin's "stripping off of boundaries in nonseparateness" (240). Franklin's point here is that our innate capacity remains even if a residual flavor of our original learning persists. The relevance of this point for my argument in this book is that however distant our ordinary experience of "self and consciousness may be from unbounded nonseparateness," the phenomenon of oneness (or what Franklin calls identification) shows that seemingly ordinary experience may be "less bounded than we usually allow" (239).

In a similar vein, Diane Jonte-Pace, in "The Swami and the Rorschach," concludes from her analysis of Rorschach literature that meditative practices from different cultures do strip away perceptual categories and lead to mystical consciousness. But while the Rorschach literature offers "a valuable paradigm for a cross-cultural psychology" of nonordinary experience proposed by Forman, it does not completely resolve the conflict between constructivists and decontextualists; instead it suggests "the necessity of acknowledging both innate elements and cultural elements in nonordinary experience" (Jonte-Pace 1998, 153, 55). It seems to me that the decontextualist view applies more to the higher states of consciousness of the Eastern tradition, while the constructivist view applies more to the incipient stages of these states—as measured by diagnostic tools such as the Rorschach test or in anthropological studies of supermodernity.

CONSCIOUSNESS AND SUPERMODERNITY

Some literary and cultural theorists, such as the American philosopher Richard Rorty, suggest that we should get rid of the term *postmodernism* because no one knows what it means. It's not an idea so much as a word that pretends to be an idea. The French anthropologist Marc Augé suggests that the contemporary world has moved beyond postmodernism. Indeed, postmodernist principles such as the illusion of progress and the collapse of both grand narratives and the division between high and low culture are not unique to the twentieth century, for the crisis of European consciousness goes back to much earlier times. Augé proposes a concept that would replace postmodernism. In *Non-Places: Introduction to an Anthropology of Supermodernity* (1995), he uses the term supermodernity to describe a new cultural construct of global proportions. Augé defines the supermodern in terms of excess: excessive information and events in time, excessive space on a shrinking planet, and excessive individuation of references, or the renewed status of individual consciousness.

The excess of time stems not from any collapse of a sense of progress or grand narratives but rather from an overabundance of events in the world we live in, which gives us the impression of "history snapping at our heals (almost immanent in each of our day-to-day existences)" (Augé 1995, 30). This overabundance of events in time, which coincides with disappointments in socialism, liberalism, and other social aspirations, creates "a positive demand for meaning" among individuals. The crisis of meaning in a world of excessive information is, as it were, continually compelling us to abandon third-person representations of the world for our own phenomenal firsthand perspectives. In other words, individuals seem to be divesting themselves of their socially constructed selves at a rate that would alarm a staunch constructivist or poststructuralist. The ideological State apparatuses described by Althusser have proliferated to the extent that they have ironically lost their power to interpellate the subject into submitting freely to subjection. In this phase of supermodernity, the individual is reclaiming control over the intentional content of awareness, which no longer seems fully to dominate awareness in itself.

In the excess of space, the second characteristic of the supermodern, distances shrink due to the Internet, mass media, satellites, and other advanced technologies. Through spatial excess, broadcast images of news, advertising, and fiction "assemble before our eyes a universe that is relatively homogeneous in its diversity" (1995, 32). Homogeneity here is key, suggesting a background unity of consciousness amidst a diversity of individuals. The concrete result of what Augé calls "the spatial overabundance of the present . . . involves considerable physical modifications: urban concentration, movements of population and the multiplication of what we call 'non-places'" (1995, 34), the supermodern site of homogeneity. Nonplaces include supermarkets, suburbs, airports, hotels, motorways, TVs, computers, and cash machines. Globally profuse, these nonplaces contribute to our sense of living in a world that is "relatively homogeneous in its diversity." And homogeneity, interpreted as a diminishment of the difference of mental content, impels the subject toward the emptiness of nonintentional (pure) awareness.

The third and perhaps most significant characteristic of supermodern excess concerns the figure of the ego, the individual. As Augé writes, "never before have individual histories been so explicitly affected by collective history, but never before, either, have the reference points for collective identification been so unstable. The individual production of meaning is thus more necessary than ever" (1995, 37). Individuals today, particularly in the West, are ensconced in the excesses of supermodernity in the form of nonplaces. On a daily basis we live in the nonplaces of supermarkets, suburbs, airports, hotels, motorways, TVs, computers, and cash machines, all of which through their homogeneity tend to disburden the mind of its intentional content—which in an age of interpretation is created by ourselves. As Augé observes, in modernism the place constitutes an anthropological space involving relation, history, and cultural identity. The nonplaces of supermodernity, on the other hand, are mostly devoid of cultural content. Rather than integrate earlier, historical space, the nonplace empties space of its historical baggage. It is in nonplaces "that we are most likely to find prophetic evocations of spaces in which neither identity, nor relation, nor history really make any sense; spaces in which solitude is experienced as an overburdening or emptying of individuality" (Augé 1995, 87). In modernity the two different worlds of past and present coexist; in supermodernity, while the past is not entirely absent, the nonplace has the effect of "turning the individual back on the self, a simultaneous distancing of the spectator and the spectacle" (92), as the spectator lives more in the immediate present. Unlike postmodernism, which defines the self as differential, fragmentary, and saturated by multiple voices, modernism allows for epiphanic moments of self-presence, as in the works of James Joyce and Virginia Woolf. The modern and supermodern selves share an affinity for presence.

In supermodernity the transient experience of nonplaces bears a remarkable resemblance to the experience of a pure consciousness event (PCE), as if they were two sides of the same coin, the external/internal, objective/subjective. This resemblance moreover seems to be empirical, not just metaphorical. In supermodernity, as in the aesthetic dimension of modernism, the individual in the realm of an anthropological space undergoes an empirical "emptying of the consciousness" (Augé 1995, 93). Supermodernity, says Augé, "subject[s] the individual consciousness to entirely new experiences and ordeals of solitude, directly linked with the appearance and proliferation of non-places" (93). But this subjection, unlike that of Althusser, involves emptying or deconditioning the mind rather than instilling specific content. Furthermore, certain conditions must be met for this encounter.

The individual's concrete relation to nonplaces is based on contractuality, insofar that nonplaces can be defined partly by words, as in the signs of a motorway, labels in a supermarket, or data on a computer. To enter a nonplace, one needs to fulfill a contract, to prove one's "innocence" (Augé 1995, 102) (as in the quest for the Holy Grail): obey the traffic laws, present a ticket to enter the departure lounge of an airport, insert your bank card in a cash machine. In this way the nonplace creates a shared identity among its passengers or customers; they momentarily empty their minds of burdensome content and are free to live nonintentionally on a more fundamental level of being—however fleetingly. Forman, in *The Problem of Pure Consciousness*, describes forgetting as "an event in which thought ceases," which he defines as a PCE (1990, 31). As Eckhart writes, mystical experience stems from a process in which "you are able to draw in your [intellectual and sensory] powers to a unity and forget all those things and their [mental] images which you have absorbed" (qtd. in Forman 1990, 30). Augé describes forgetting or emptying of the mind in nonplaces:

> No doubt the relative anonymity that goes with this temporary identity can even be felt as a *liberation*, by people who, for a time, have only to keep in line, go where they are told, check their appearance. As soon as his passport or identity card has been checked, the passenger for the next

> flight, *freed* from the weight of his luggage and everyday responsibility, rushes into the "duty free" space; not so much, perhaps, in order to buy at the best prices as to experience the reality of his momentary availability, his unchallengeable position as a passenger in the *process of departing*. (1995, 101; emphasis added)

Augé does not imply that nonplaces lead toward pure consciousness per se, which he does not discuss, but he does find in supermodernity a similar process of emptying the mind of intentional content.

The nonplaces of supermodernity seem to have two implications for human consciousness. First, nonplaces enhance the process of emptying the self; they effect an "identity-loss" (Augé 1995, 102), compelling the individual to let go and move toward a taste of nonseparateness or pure awareness. Secondly, nonplaces suggest the condition Forman calls the dualistic mystical state (DMS), that of enjoying inner silence, a kind of eternal present, while engaged in activity, thought, and perception. As Augé observes, what reigns in nonplaces "is actuality, the urgency of the present moment" (104), characterized in an airport, for instance, by a flood of commercial images, together with the experience of an emptier self-awareness: "the passenger in non-places has the simultaneous experience of a perpetual present and an encounter with the [emptier] self" (105). To encounter the perpetual present and the (nonintentional) self while simultaneously within activity is to step virtually out of time; for as Forman puts its, "awareness per se simply ties past and present together as one single continuous awareness. It transcends our time experience" (1998a, 24). Hence place and nonplace, "intertwine[d] and tangle[d] together," are like ordinary awareness and pure awareness—the latter always latent within the former: "The possibility of non-place is never absent from any place" (Augé 1995, 107). I would speculate that the intertwining of place and nonplace, mind and consciousness seems to evoke what Franklin, as mentioned earlier, would call a "flavor" of the dualistic mystical state (DMS): the simultaneity of a knowledge-by-identity (of witnessing awareness) and a knowledge-about the contents of awareness. The relation evoked here between the self as it moves toward its simplest form in qualityless pure awareness, and the nonplace, while in a sense metaphorical, may also be empirical and of real practical benefit, though this benefit must be left for individuals to assess for themselves.

Supermodernity, then, rather than producing fragmentation like postmodernism, seems to encourage the expansion of consciousness toward the unity of higher states. The outward flow of attention balanced by an emptying of consciousness in nonplaces may promote a PCE or even a DMS. But whatever the residual flavor of one's subjected conditioning may be in a nonplace, the move toward a state of nonseparateness (as described by Franklin) is clearly evident. In the nonplace, the normally active individual finds that the activity of intentional consciousness begins to be stilled as the awareness moves toward a nonintentional interiority—nonintentional because it does not depend on knowing an object.

One nonplace Augé does not discuss, but which is possibly the ultimate nonplace, is the virtual reality of cyberspace, an increasingly prominent feature of supermodernity. William Gibson famously defines cyberspace as a "consensual hallucination" (*Neuromancer* 51), suggesting the ephemeral nature of any mental content compared with consciousness itself, which is more fundamental than perceiving or thinking. Erik Davis makes a connection between cyberculture and gnostic illumination. He traces the history of the hermetic imagination in "the magical art of memory, demonic cryptography, and Gnostic cosmology" (1994, 31), which emphasize that humanity has the potential "to discover within itself the mystical knowledge of god and cosmos" (32). Through the virtual nonplaces of cyberspace and its artificial memory, one may undergo an ecstatic expansion of consciousness and acquire universal knowledge. The dream of hermetic gnosticism, "to know everything instantaneously and thereby, presumably, to know God" (Davis 42), is also the dream of the New Age movement and possibly the whole of Cyberia, as Douglas Rushkoff points out in his book by that title. Benjamin Woolley, in *Virtual Worlds*, says of cyberspace, "The power of this realm comes from its connectedness. It is a continuum, not a series of discrete systems that act independently of each other" (1993, 133–34).

Nonplaces, whether physical or virtual, reveal the interrelatedness or nonseparateness of the distinction Mircea Eliade makes between the sacred and the profane. Indeed, as Eliade says, "It follows that *every construction or fabrication has the cosmogony as paradigmatic mode*" (1959, 45; original emphasis). Mark Taylor quotes Paul Virilio on the effects of cyberspace: "Curiously, telecommunications sets in motion in civil society the properties of divinity: ubiquity (being present everywhere at every instant), instantaneousness, immediacy, omnivision, omnipresence. Every one of us is metamorphosed into a divine being here and there at the same time" (1999, 139). Nonplaces also represent an environment increasingly aestheticized as well as virtualized. As Taylor notes, "just as the death of God is not a simple negation but a complex process in which the divine becomes incarnate when the profane is grasped as sacred, so art ends not because it disappears but because it appears everywhere. Art dies when everyone becomes an artist and the world is finally transformed into a work of art" (1999,. 189). Nonplaces like the hotel "New York, New York, Las Vegas" are a form of popular art that can virtualize or disburden awareness of its phenomenal content.

Ultimately, to know everything instantaneously must be understood as first to know the self beyond time through knowledge-by-identity, the basis of all knowledge-by-acquaintance and knowledge-about. Even without subscribing to gnosticism, one can imagine that the aesthetic, philosophical, and scientific transformations of supermodernity will continue to modify subjectivity in unforeseen and perhaps unbelievable ways (as discussed further in chapters seven and eight). The flux of these transformations of identity is particularly noticeable in the postmodern world of cultural hybridity, where the possibility of glimpsing consciousness per se offers the practical benefits of increased stability and freedom for culturally mixed or displaced people around the world. My assertions about nonplaces and hybridity are speculative by necessity, for as Burns and Uus have pointed out, consciousness is not explainable by physical laws: "no physics experiments have ever established" a relation between consciousness and physical change, as in the case of volition (Burns 1999, 27).

Consciousness and Cultural Hybridity

If the nonseparateness found in supermodernity seems too much the privilege of the developed world, we can also find evidence of it in the postcolonial world. In contrast to the "nonpluralistic phenomenon" described by Forman, poststructuralist and postcolonial theorists emphasize ethnic and cultural diversity against the universalist claims of the Western tradition of liberal humanism. Postcolonial criticism, emerging in the 1990s out of deconstruction, poststructuralism, feminism, and other postmodernist theories, argues that we have to resist the rationale of universalism because of the terrible experiences of destruction perpetrated in its name over the past millennia, and particularly over the past century. Its ancestry can be traced to Frantz Fanon's 1961 classic *The Wretched of the Earth*. Fanon initiated a "cultural resistance" to colonial empires, particularly French Algeria, arguing that the first step for a postcolonial perspective was for the colonized to reclaim their past. Subsequent steps by postcolonial writers have highlighted the cultural difference in literary texts and the need to explore the complex relation between culture and identity. Postcolonial critics such as Gayatri Spivak (*In Other Worlds*), Bill Ashcroft (*The Empire Writes Back*), Homi Bhabha (*Nation and Narration, The Location of Culture*), and Edward Said (*Orientalism: Culture and Imperialism*) have justifiably exposed the long-standing Eurocentric practice of using timeless and universal cultural and aesthetic concepts to demote, suppress, or exploit regional, cultural, or national differences.

They argue that all universalist literary or cultural claims are veiled attempts to impose white, Eurocentric norms and practices on the colonized. All gender, ethnic, regional, or racial minorities are classified as the "Other" and thus marginalized. In *Orientalism* (1979), Said criticizes Eurocentric universalism as part of a tradition of elevating European or Western culture and demoting the East to the inferior status of the "Other." This European cultural perspective toward the East Said identifies as "Orientalism," an ironic nomenclature considering how much the East has to teach the West that is rejected by postcolonial critics—like the universalism of Vedanta. Yet despite its insights, postcolonial criticism casts only a partial light on the nature of identity and its relation to culture. As suggested by Forman's perennial psychology, the concept of "Other"—not to mention culture in general—is a feature of the intentional content of the thinking mind; it complements a more fundamental aspect of human identity beyond ratiocination, namely consciousness itself as shared by people of all nations and cultures as an innate capacity. I would suggest that postcolonial hybridity, as analyzed by Homi Bhabha and others, seems to constitute a breach in the boundaries of cultural difference and an opening of human awareness to a realm similar to that partially opened through the nonplaces of supermodernity. Decontextualists or perennial psychologists like Forman and Shear are universalists who argue not for a unity of intentional constructs, but for a unity or identity of nonordinary, nonintentional experiences across cultural and historical boundaries.

Since the 1950s postcolonial writers have gone from the cultural resistance of reclaiming their past to living a life of double identity. *In Things Fall Apart*, Chinua Achebe writes about African villagers from the perspective of a writer educated in Europe. His identity is divided between European civilization and African tribal community. Similarly in his "Byzantium" poems, William Butler Yeats, as Said notes (1994, 265–88), orientalizes the East, projecting an image of Istanbul that mythologizes his own ideals as an Irish Protestant who identified with Irish nationalism. Yeats expresses a longing to relieve Ireland's colonial burden in his desire to be gathered into the artifice of eternity represented by Byzantium, a process that albeit incomplete Said calls "a major international achievement in cultural decolonization" (1994, 288).

Going from fixed to hybrid identities, postcolonial writers gradually evolved from accepting European models and norms, to modifying these forms, then creating original forms and finally producing cross-cultural texts. As evidenced by the work of Spivak and Bhabha, the divided or fluid identities of postcolonial writers and their cross-cultural works lend themselves to poststructuralist analysis. As a deconstructive postcolonial critic, Bhabha shows how the "polyvalent," shifting, contradictory currents of textual meaning reflect cultural hybridity. He particularly focuses on states of plurality, "Otherness," and maginality. These states, as I will attempt to show, seem to constitute gaps in the mind's stream of intentional content capable of yielding partial or fleeting access to consciousness itself, if not as a PCE then at least as an incipient flavor of nonseparateness.

Bhabha, in *The Location of Culture*, investigates the articulation of "border lives" in the "in-between spaces" of cultural differences: "These 'in-between' spaces provide the terrain for elaborating strategies of selfhood—singular or communal—that initiate new signs of identity, and innovative sites of collaboration, and contestation, in the act of defining the idea of society itself" (1994, 1–2). Bhabha throughout *The Location of Culture* elaborates indirectly on what he means by new signs of identity, which he never explicitly defines. One reason for this is that his deconstructive approach precludes ultimate or stable concepts. Another reason may be that the postcolonial "in-between" identity is not only "in-between" cultures, the linguistically determined manifestations of the mind's intentional content, but also "in-between" the mind and consciousness per se—a space that, if not beyond language, is at the border of linguistic indeterminacy. In relation to any specific culture, the new postcolonial identity is a nonordinary experience. This identity may extend beyond the realm of conceptuality or mind into the realm of nonordinary consciousness. The subject's awareness apparently flows through the gaps between the hybridity and polyvalency of cultural identities to and fro a qualityless nonintentional state. Bhabha's deconstructive account of the history of postcolonial migration and the narratives of the social/political diaspora, which create "the demography of a new internationalism" (1994, 5), intimates without confirming or rejecting the possibility of transcending conceptual content. The reason he can only half formulate this process is that consciousness is not an object of observation but a state of being in the perpetual present.

> It is in this sense that the boundary becomes the place from which *something begins its presencing* in a movement not dissimilar to the ambulant, ambivalent articulation of the beyond that I have drawn out: "Always and ever differently the bridge escorts the lingering and hastening ways of men to and fro, so that they may get to other banks. . . . The bridge *gathers* as a passage that crosses." (1994, 5, with paraphrase of Heidegger's *Poetry, Language, Thought* 152–53; Bhabha's emphasis)

This transformation in the (extrovertive) realm of culture, like Victor Turner's redressive or liminal phase of life experience (1998), resembles and perhaps evokes what Forman describes as a move from one modality of consciousness to another, from an ordinary to a perennial psychological state. It is a "stripping or letting go of concepts, attachments, and pictures of one's self and others. This allows one to separate what is inherently 'within' from what is not. By this means one can shift from the constructed modality into something closer to the utterly unconstructed one" (Forman 1998a, 30).

Bhabha's cultural hybridity is a state beyond the culture of both the colonizer and colonized; it is an ever-present in-between state in the margins or borderlines through which identity is continually renewed. This process reflects the movement to and fro between mind and consciousness referred to in Zen as the "pathless path." Stepping outside of authoritative, cultural norms, one moves toward a state beyond temporal boundaries, as in a process Walter Benjamin refers to as "establishing a conception of the present as the 'time of the now'" (qtd. by Bhabha 1994, 4). This time of the now evoked by culture and history may, it seems reasonable to say, have its basis in the innate capacity for perennial psychology. In terms of Advaita Vedanta, postcolonial hybridity is like the *neti neti* (not-this, not-that) of transcending conceptuality, a *via negative* (Deutsch 1973, 10–11) from polyvalency toward a "nonpluralistic phenomenon," whether conceived in terms of a PCE or a flavored state of nonseparateness.

In exploring the semiotics of this hybrid cultural identity, Bhabha again intimates a modality of consciousness that is nonintentional and nonlinguistic. Here he discusses cultural hybridity in terms of Barthes's idea of being "outside the sentence" (1994, 180):

> If you seek simply the sententious or the exegetical, you will not grasp the hybrid moment outside the sentence—not quite experience, not yet concept; part dream, part analysis; neither signifier nor signified. This intermediate space between theory and practice disrupts the disciplinary semiological demand to enumerate all the languages within earshot. (181)

Referring to a space that poststructuralism speaks of in "varied voices," the nonsentence is nevertheless "not *before* the sentence but something that *could have* acceded to the sentence and yet was *outside* it (181; Bhabha's emphasis). For Bhabha, the displacement of the sentence in the semiotics of cultural hybridity is where "the individuation of the agent occurs" (185). Bhabha seems to imply that the subject is not entirely a product of language. He speaks of the return of the subject from outside the sentence, outside fixity, from a space of contingency that is intersubjective. As proposed here, the most fundamental intersubjective field would be that of perennial psychology. Bhabha's subject is not the transparent subject of liberal humanism, insofar that this definition of the subject is suspected (probably rightly) as being essentialist in the sense of a conceptual construct. The subject as a conceptual (or linguistic) construct differs from the cultural hybrid and the perennial self, which as a nonpluralistic phenomenon is devoid of attributes or content. Bhabha oscillates here between theory (or intentionality) and practice (or nonintentionality), as if in fear of collapsing the latter into the former. In postcolonialism, as a new internationalism, the hybridity of cultural and personal identity seems to take the subject to the liminal space between the intentional mind and nonintentional consciousness. This space for Bhabha is neither the one nor the other; if anything it is a kind of "pathless path" or bridge linking the two. The poststructuralist indeterminism and unexpectability of the nonsentence, which for Bhabha is "neither 'pure' contingency or negativity nor endless deferral" (181), resembles the nonplaces of supermodernity, which is neither fully place nor nonplace, but the two intertwined and tangled together. Hybridity and the nonplace both have affinities with intersubjectivity, as defined in chapter 4.

The paradox of the culturally hybrid individual in the new age of postcolonial internationalism is that he or she would presumably feel at home in virtually any cultural context, particularly in the age of supermodernity. Augé says that "a foreigner lost in a country he does not know (a 'passing stranger') can feel at home there only in the anonymity of motorways, service stations, big stores or hotel chains" (1995, 106). But for someone who is culturally hybrid this feeling of being at home may extend from nonplaces to nearly anyplace in the postmodern or postcolonial world. Nonplaces may act as an external catalyst for emptying consciousness of its intentional content, but cultural hybridity, which seems to characterize an increasing number of people in the modern world, carries its own internal nonplaces in the gaps between cultural identities. On the one hand the intentional mind serves to link the sensory world to the background of nonintentional consciousness, while on the other hand consciousness serves as a bridge for crossing the gaps between cultural perspectives. The bridge of awareness also links together all of one's viewpoints to create a continuity of self-identity. In a postcolonial context, one would know this nonseparate self in the gaps between cultural identities through a knowledge-by-identity of awareness, which is nonlinguistic and nonconceptual. As Forman puts it, "Our knowledge of our consciousness and our awareness that we have remained conscious is, in general, more fundamental than any thinking or perceiving" (1998a, 34).

Conclusion

Perennial psychology tells us that a profound acquaintance with consciousness comes through a knowledge-by-identity. But as suggested here, a significant acquaintance with consciousness may also come through the quotidian experience of supermodern excesses and the gaps of hybrid identities, both of which give rise to a sense of nonseparateness as a perpetual presence. Any process of realizing consciousness unmixed with intentional content involves letting go or forgetting the language, sensations, and other attributes of human experience. As Forman points out, we have the innate capacity not only to know things intentionally through discursive thought but also "to remain conscious when content drops away" (1998, 34). Consciousness is innate to all people regardless of their cultural differences. This claim has two implications: that consciousness itself is an all-pervasive ground to intentional knowledge; and that access to this ground is not only an innate capacity but also promoted by the excesses of a world that compel us to let go of our fixed attachments. Ironically, the hybridity and supermodernity of the world, instead of merely producing ever greater complexity, may also be taking us toward the realization of simplicity: that of a nonpluralistic phenomenon—open not only to the individual but also collectively to the intersubject.

3

Deconstruction, Indian Literary Theory, and Consciousness

The question of unity

In response to structuralism and the entire Western tradition of "the metaphysics of presence," Derrida deconstructs all theoretical models that would explain the diversity of human experience in terms of the ideals of unity or universality. Modernists such as Virginia Woolf and T. S. Eliot have expressed nostalgia for an age of faith and wholeness; postmodernists, who John Ellis refers to as race-gender-class critics (1997 passim) and Wendell Harris as hermetic critics (1996, 20–50), celebrate fragmentation as liberating and even exhilarating. And yet it is arguable that deconstruction—as a sort of emptying-out of the meaning of a text—corroborates a certain kind of unity: namely, that conceptual emptiness associated with aesthetic rapture and the self as pure awareness. In pointing to a realm anterior to the categories and concepts of thought, deconstruction in practice points to a type of unity or oneness that may best be understood in terms of consciousness, even though in theory it undermines oneness, consciousness, and presence. By removing all fixed points or absolutes and thereby decentering our conceptual universe, deconstruction inadvertently initiates us into a virtual frame of reference, that supplement of conceptuality—awareness itself.

Deconstruction is a term that been generalized ad absurdum. Although much in deconstruction is systematic and general, it is best understood as a singular, situated response to an individual text—with text referring not only to language or graphic signs but to all possible referents. As a method of oppositional reading or, as Terry Eagleton says, of reading the text against itself (1983, 132), deconstruction attempts to show that a text is characterized by fragmentation rather than unity. Derrida defines fragmentation as a function of the "freeplay" of language that "excludes totalization" or the wholeness of meaning and thereby leads to an indeterminacy (1978a, 239). Even in his recent work, like *Politics of Friendship,* Derrida still adheres to the principle of difference. Expressed in terms of a "human and finite *cogito,* this gives the formula: I think, therefore I am the other; I think, therefore I need the other (in order to think): I think, therefore the possibility of friendship is lodged in the movement of my thought in so far as it demands, calls for, desires the other, the necessity of the other, the cause of the other at the heart of the *cogito*" (1997, 224). But thinking here merges with feeling in a move from duality to a greater coexistence of opposites. Far from saying "anything *against* the brother or against fraternity," Derrida says, "In my own special way, like everyone else, I believe, I no doubt love, yes, in my own way, my brother, my only brother" (1997, 305; original emphasis). And love, in bridging the gap between self and other, is considered in eastern philosophy to be the basis of oneness, or glue of the universe.

As we saw in the discussion of Forman in chapter 2, pure consciousness is devoid of the subject-object duality found in mental content, yet even mental content can approach nonduality to a greater or lesser degree. The measure of the unity of concepualization would be the degree to which pure consciousness infuses the contents of awareness, which would differ for each individual. Ordinarily in the experience of conceptual content, unity consists of the information from perception, memory, and thought being integrated into a whole. In the ordinary experience of a watermelon, for instance, our sense impressions form the contents of consciousness that "hang together" as a succulent fruit. In extraordinary aesthetic experience, the unity of our conceptual content increases through an integration between subject and object induced by the aesthetic medium. Figurative language has the effect of opening the mind beyond the familiar objects of consciousness to represent truths incommunicable by other means. In the process of the mind settling down through the interiority of reading, the physiology also settles down. This process resembles the experience described in Eastern texts, such as the Upanishads and *Patanjali's Yoga Sutras*, of the mind moving from the boundaries of conceptuality toward pure awareness, which is associated "with a uniquely settled metabolic state, characterized by . . . reduced pulse . . . and complete suspension of respiratory activity" (Shear 1996a, 65).[1] We find a comparable settled state of mind and body occurring in the well-known lines of Wordsworth's "Tintern Abbey": "Until, the breath of this corporeal frame / And even the motion of our human blood / Almost suspended, we are laid asleep / In body, and become a living soul" (1973, 147).

The expansion of meaning toward ever larger unities or "pictures" also seems to expand the frame or container of meaning, consciousness itself. That is (as proposed in greater detail below), the expansion of conceptual meaning toward its infinite possibility, as through the freeplay of the signifier, can take consciousness to the boundary between subject and object, consciousness and mind, *purusa* and *prakrti*. From this junction point, the awareness may momentarily go beyond not only referential meaning, but all mental content for a glimpse of nonintentional pure awareness. As McGinn says, given the nonlocal or nonspatial nature of consciousness, "to represent consciousness as it is in itself—neat, as it were—we would need to let go of the spatial skeleton of our thought" (1995, 229). At this point we would need to let go of the expressive form of art, which would have served its purpose.

The attempt to deconstruct the unity of consciousness is made problematic by the pure consciousness event (PCE) being without any conceptual content to be deconstructed. This discrepancy between the nature of consciousness and its alleged deconstruction may account for the discrepancy between what deconstruction claims in theory and what seems to follow through its critical praxis.

Like deconstruction, constructivism as expounded by Steven Katz and colleagues holds that "our language, background, concepts, culture, dreams, and dreads all shape and determine our experiences" (Forman 1990, 40). Constructivists claim that mystical experiences, like ordinary experience, "are subject to the formative and constructive processes of language and culture" (Forman 1990, 39). But perennial psychologists such as Forman, as we have seen, observe that no causal connection has ever been shown to exist between linguistic or cultural training and mystical experiences, that in fact these experiences occur even without cultural preconditioning. Forman, in discussing language and the *via negativa*, asserts that "the key process in mysticism is not like the horse of language pulling the cart of experience, but more like *unhitching* the experience-cart from the language horse. . . . Mystical experiences . . . [result] from the *un*-conditioning of language and belief" (1994, 42). Similarly the *Maitri Upanishad* states that "when a knower has restrained his mind from the external, and the breathing spirit (*prana*) has put to rest objects of sense, thereupon let him continue void of conceptions" (6.19; Hume 1931, 436).

Commenting on Forman's notion of the *via negativa* aspect of decontextualism, Bruce Mangan argues that it "gives the linguistic approach, however 'negative,' far more importance for the study of mysticism than it deserves" (1994, 250). The obsession with language in poststructuralism reflects the limitations of knowledge-about or knowledge-by-acquaintance. Mangan advocates an approach to language that places a stronger emphasis on the knowledge-by-identity of consciousness, the unmediated sense of an all-pervading oneness. Deconstruction as an act of reading, I would suggest, parallels in its deconceptualization the effect of yoga and the experience of unity described in the *Maitri Upanishad*. Both involve direct first-person experience, a withdrawal from the familiar world of sense experience, and a move toward a world of self-referral. A deconstructive reading of a literary text seeks to defamiliarize the text rather than to gain permanent access to conceptual truth. The emphasis on individual response as opposed to systematic and programmable meaning indicates that for deconstruction the text has no conceptual essence; reading as a direct experience resists philosophical conceptuality. Derek Attridge, commenting on this transverbal aspect of deconstruction, says that "what deconstruction is concerned to show is that a verbal artifact can never close upon itself, and the other that summons us from literature is not confined within language in the narrow sense" (1992, 20). In leading toward a transverbal nonseparateness, deconstructive readings both determine and simultaneously subvert the notion of the postmodern self—as I will illustrate in a later section through a reading of Toni Morrison's *Beloved*.

The Practice of Deconstruction

In deconstructing Western philosophy, Derrida critiques the notion of presence, as in the self-presence of language and consciousness. He argues that the metaphysical notions of truth, being, and reality are intended to repress difference and absence for the sake of stability, whether ontological or political. Difference and absence are associated with the secondary representation of writing, and unity and presence are associated with the immediacy of speech. The historical repression of writing and difference in "logocentrism" or "phonocentrism" is linked to a belief in a logos or self-present word constituted by the presence of the human voice (1978a, 278–82). Derrida undermines presence by dispensing with the covert hierarchy of binary oppositions, such as presence/absence, inside/outside, nature/culture, speech/writing, in which the left side of the equation is privileged over the right. He argues that the boundaries between these (metaphysical) oppositions are unstable, that the order and values implied are questionable, and that meaning in language is ultimately indeterminate. Speech loses its priority over writing, and both writing and speech are characterized by disunity rather than unity.

But it would be a mistake to overgeneralize, as the tendency is in "American deconstruction," and say that all meaning is indeterminate, all presence illusory, all theme or intention irrelevant, all reference a fiction (see Attridge 1992, 12). That a text for Derrida, especially a literary text, is always situated, read and reread in a specific place and time, makes it "iterable" or repeatable, the same but always different, and therefore never reducible to an abstraction by theoretical contemplation (1977b, 172–97). A text is unique and repeatable, concrete and abstract simultaneously. This coexistence lies at the heart of deconstruction and parallels the connectedness of subject and object in the pure consciousness event (PCE), as well as in the DMS discussed in chapter 2.

Yet in subverting any experience of unity, Derrida famously theorizes what he calls the movement of *différance* (1973, 129–60), a pun on the meaning of two French words, "to differ" (in space) and "to defer" (in time). Derrida extends Saussure's division of sign and referent, signifier (sound) and signified (meaning) by following through on the radical implications of these divisions. Through the play of *différance*, the signifier infinitely defers and differs from the signified, which in turn becomes a signifier in an endless chain of signifiers, thereby precluding the possibility transcendental signified. The sign, which exists for Derrida under "erasure," derives and confers meanings through its "trace" in relation to other signs and not through its relation to the world itself (1973, 154–58; 1978a, 292). In deconstruction, "pure difference, which constitutes the self-presence of the living present, introduces into self-presence from the beginning all the impurity putatively excluded from it" (1973, 85). Derrida claims that the "privilege accorded to consciousness thus means a privilege accorded to the present; and even if the transcendental temporality of consciousness is described in depth, as Husserl described it, the power of synthesis and the incessant gathering-up of traces is always accorded to the 'living present' " (1973, 147). For Derrida, then, presence is always divided from within itself by difference. But this view of presence is incomplete, a product of thought or the duality of mental content. The virtual difference of a PCE, where the self is identified with awareness beyond the duality of subject and object, is a different kind of presence—as Forman and colleagues suggest (1998a, 24, passim).

The movement of *différance*, with a spatio-temporal gap between sound and meaning that endlessly defers ultimate meaning, no doubt applies to the surface structures of language and consciousness. We apprehend the written or spoken word first as a sound and then as a concept. The gap between sound and meaning leads different people to attach different meanings to the same sound. Yet despite the heavy presence of difference in deconstruction, the gap between sound and meaning is distinctly more pronounced in outward speech and less so in inward speech or thought, as we shall soon see in the discussion of Indian literary theory.

Through the freeplay of the signifier, deconstruction postpones the ultimate meaning of language (the transcendental signified), yet retains the auditory content or sound (the signifier), and therefore does not completely empty the awareness of its content. That is, the awareness is not void of conceptions insofar as it still observes the object of sound. In theory, then, deconstruction does not allow a nonintentional state of witnessing awareness, which according to Indian literary theory is necessary to experience a "transcendental signified." But in practice the deconstructive freeplay of the signifier as a function of the temporal mind seems to mediate between pure awareness and its contents—expanding that content toward unity in a manner similar to aesthetic rapture.

Indeed, the valorizing of rhetorical play by deconstruction as a philosophy has led to a debate over its compatibility with the ideals of logical accountability. Richard Rorty, among others, has accused Derrida of confusing literature and theory (1991, 119–28). But Derrida claims that he always tries to do justice to a text by emphasizing the relation between singularity (or rhetoric) and generality (or theory). This relation belongs to the (anterior) movement of writing (or *arche-writing*), which Derrida describes with terms such as "re-mark" and *différance*, a movement of repeatable singularity (re-mark) that keeps a text open to new contexts and, for literary texts especially, to new ways of emptying-out conceptual meaning. In terms of unity, then, the difficulty with deconstruction as a theory is that it contradicts itself in practice by mixing two ontological modes: reason (associated with the contents of awareness) and aesthetics (associated with the tendency of awareness to move toward the oneness of its own being). On the one hand, the fact that deconstruction in its application subverts itself illustrates the *différance* of verbal discourse, the apparent gap between language and reality. But on the other hand the deconstructive claim that the speaking subject is always different from the subject spoken of has less to do with the supposed *différance* of verbal discourse than with the difference between witnessing awareness and its contents. The direct experience of pure awareness differs from its subsequent description. In describing a pure consciousness event, which is nondual, the speaking subject must articulate this description from within the duality of logical discourse after the PCE has passed. The deconstruction of this description therefore does not touch the actual experience being described.

Consciousness and Aporia

The *Maitri Upanishad* describes the stages in the experience of pure consciousness. Through the "restraint of the breath" and the "withdrawal of the senses," the mind settles down and the awareness flows inward until it becomes absorbed in itself, and we experience a "void of conceptions," "that which is non-thought, [yet] which stands in the midst of thought" (6.19, Hume 1931, 436). The awareness flows from diversity to "the One." This One is an indeterminacy in the sense of encompassing all possibilities, a non-thought that is yet the basis of all thought and all points of view. In practice deconstruction seems to defy its theoretical stance on the nature of consciousness and approach the experience of the mental procedures of eastern cultures, though it of course also has real differences from these procedures and their psychophysiological effects.

And yet to some extent psychophysiology is certainly involved as the play of *différance* takes us from binary oppositions—surface/depth, signifier/signified—toward all possibilities. The senses are divided from the world of reference, the mind is focused over time by a sign whose meaning is dispersed along a chain of signifiers, and the awareness comes to an indeterminate state emptied of concepts at least in the sense of an ultimate meaning or transcendental signified. This indeterminacy results in a logic of paradox or a logical impasse—the "aporia." As Derrida argues, a "movement of supplementarity" so heightens rhetorical play—with signs replacing each other in a chain of signifiers, each adding something more, a surplus—that it precludes the totalization of meaning and results in aporia (1978a, 287). For a deconstructive postmodernism, aporia precludes unity and ultimate meaning and increases fragmentation and the multiplicity of relative truths.

A reconstructive postmodernism or perennial psychology, on the other hand, offers a different though related response to aporia. From this perspective a logical impasse is a junction point between the ordinary waking and fourth states of consciousness (*turiya*)—where the mind borders, as we have seen, on being "void of conceptions." But according to deconstruction, no signified, much less a transcendental signified, ever attains the status of a presence. Even the tools of deconstruction—such as *différance*, trace, and supplementarity—are implicated in the strategies of deconstruction. As Derrida says, "the *supplement* is neither a plus nor a minus, neither an outside nor the complement of an inside, neither confusion nor distinction, neither identity nor difference" (1981b, 43). These terms never reach conceptual presence and thus problematize deconstruction as a logical enterprise, adding to the experience of aporia. Yet the graphic sign in deconstruction loses its depth in such a way that the signifier (sound) becomes the signified (concept) in a kind of virtual unity that parallels the unity of the *logos* between sound and meaning, name and form. The awareness, if not the physiology, is here poised at the juncture between two ontological modes (the mind and consciousness) without (necessarily) transcending into the fourth state (*turiya*). But this juncture itself seems to be invoked by the deconstructive move toward aporias, which resemble the doctrine of voidness that Madhyamika Buddhists and Shunyavadis express by the phrase, "neti-neti," not this–not this, or neither this, nor that (see Shear 1996a, 67).[2] The proliferation of the signifier leads to the border of the conceptual "void," but unlike eastern procedures not necessarily beyond, certainly not in a systematic way designed to produce a settled metabolism.

The two ways of interpreting aporia (increased difference versus a conceptual void or juncture with *turiya*) correspond to different ways of understanding self-referral. In poststructuralism, self-referral is defined as the play of language that leads to increasing relativism, fragmentation, and indeterminacy. But as proposed above, the move toward indeterminacy also results in a self-referral of consciousness, a narrowing of the gap between consciousness and mind, awareness and its contents. The praxis of deconstruction leads consciousness beyond ordinary thinking toward nonthought, the voidness of "neti-neti." But for perennial psychology conceptual emptiness is induced by the language of the *via negativa*, which "seems designed to project the subject outside the limits of his or her linguistic system. Language here functions more like a rocket pushing a capsule beyond Earth's gravity than a horse drawing a cart" (Forman 1994, 45).

This negative referentiality is rejected by Derrida, who claims that "there is nothing outside the text" (1976, 163). Since we know the world only through its representation by language as a (self-referral) system of differences, our knowledge is "always already" an interpretation rendered by the movement of supplementarity. It is never of the thing-in-itself. For Derrida, since the basic feature of the text is not the graphic sign but the mark, a "general text" goes beyond what is usually understood by text. As Derrida clarifies,

> What I call the "text" implies all the structures called "real," "economic," "historical," socio-institutional, in short: all possible referents. Another way of recalling once again that "there is nothing outside the text." That does not mean that all referents are suspended, denied, or enclosed in a book, as people have claimed. . . . But it does mean that every referent, all reality has the structure of a *differential trace*, and that one cannot refer to this "real" except in an *interpretive experience*. (1988, 148; emphasis added)

Derrida further comments: "I never cease to be surprised by critics who see my work as a declaration that there is nothing beyond language, that we are imprisoned in language; it is, in fact, saying the exact opposite. The critique of logocentrism is above all else the search for the 'other' and the 'other of language'" (1984, 123). In a sense, the self-referentiality of the text that seeks the "other of language" implies a field of consciousness at the basis of knowledge. Recall Homi Bhabha's deconstructive interpretation of cultural hybridity discussed in chapter 2. Knowledge of fragmentation or the "differential trace," though radically different from knowledge-by-identity, can still lead to its threshold and even spill across it. After all, what other platform except duality is there for reaching nonduality? If the general text is everywhere, then the possibility of experiencing aporia as the other side of language, a voidness on the border with *turiya*, is by implication also everywhere. If there is nothing outside the text, and the text oscillates between presence and absence, fragmentation and aporia (as a flavor of voidness), then the opposition between a deconstructive and a reconstructive postmodernism would seem to collapse toward the reconstructive. Like cultural hybridity and the nonplaces of supermodernity, deconstructive aporia also illustrates how the everyday blurs into the extraordinary, boundaries into boundlessness, language on this side into awareness on the "other" transverbal, transpersonal side. This is no longer a purely "interpretive experience" but suggests a state of being anterior to thought.

Practical Consequences

Deconstructive analysis purports to undermine, expose, undo, or demystify the so-called traditional ideas, authoritative readings, consensus, or referential meaning of a text, whether fiction or nonfiction. Yet through a double stance of being both inside and outside of philosophy, Derrida conceives of deconstruction as effecting real changes in the institutional structures of knowledge and power. As he says in an interview, "My central question is: how can philosophy as such appear to itself as other than itself, so that it can interrogate and reflect upon itself in an original manner?" (qtd. in Norris 1987, 26). How can philosophy be itself and simultaneously go beyond itself and thereby transcend conventional meaning?

Many believe we have no way of "getting down to the self as it is" beyond conventional meaning. They question the assumption that any such state can be found beneath the accumulated layers of thoughts, memories, emotions, sensations, and images. But the act of questioning as such hardly proves anything. And yet the idealist self has given way to a postmodernist self defined in terms of lack, or as Barbara Johnson would say, "a presence whose lack has not been preceded by any fullness" ("Introduction" to Derrida 1981a, xii).

Being overpopulated with conflicting voices makes us shift constantly from one conception to another without ever dwelling on any one conception for any length of time—as Bhabha suggests in his analysis of cultural hybridity and the nonsentence. This bewildering sequence of conceptions is interspersed by a series of gaps—like the condition of nonthought associated with pure consciousness. Immersion in multiple perspectives therefore is only one side of the story, the other side being the gaps of nonthought or silences between perspectives. As deconstruction tells us, the conceptual underpinnings of our perspectives are tenuous, and the mind forever finds itself faced with new aporias. But these logical impasses, which break up the flow of our thought and general experience of the world, seem to verify the continuum of consciousness, which even as our thoughts and experiences of the world come and go remains a constant.

The freeplay of postmodern culture and its lack of conceptual depth combined with the nonplaces of supermodernity help to liberate the self from the field of difference, causing it continually to fall back on the conceptual void in the spaces between perspectives. The constant alternation between the steady onslaught of perspectives and the conceptual breaks between them suggests the possibility of our awareness shifting from the ordinary structures of mind toward the structure of pure consciousness and back. As understood through Eastern philosophy and meditation, this shifting may have the effect of culturing the experience of "higher" consciousness. Although the extent to which this experience is promoted by postmodern culture remains speculative, Gergen, Davis, Gablik, Zohar, and others have commented on the potential of postmodern culture for counteracting the anti-idealist impact of a deconstructive postmodernism.

Because the postmodern posture invites all possible options for human experience, the difference between a deconstructive and reconstructive postmodernism (and supermodernity) may largely be a matter of theory—a metanarrative. In practical terms, cultural forces seem to impel the individual to reconnect with the nonintentional self on a quotidian basis. Rorty's pragmatism, which rejects the notion of ultimate truth and goodness (1991, 317), may differ from an idealist pragmatism, but idealists and realists both believe that local truths and goodness have the potential to enhance the harmony of the larger dance of life.

Deconstruction and Indian Literary Theory

Because deconstruction in practice seems to evoke a field of pure possibility at the basis of language, one can say that deconstruction bears a resemblance to Sanskrit poetics or Indian literary theory. Central to Indian philosophy is the distinction between theory and practice—which is basically that between knowledge-by-acquaintance and knowledge-by-identity. Like Indian philosophy, Sanskrit poetics holds that unity and diversity are not mutually exclusive, that in a virtual sense diversity is unity, and that nature, consciousness, and language are inwardly akin. The similarity between Indian literary theory and deconstruction can be seen by comparing Derrida with two Indian philosophers, Bhartrhari and Shankara.

This comparison lends credibility to the suggestion that pure consciousness is not an illusion, nor restricted to high art, but is commonly available through cultural experiences such as reading, transiting a nonplace, or finding oneself defamiliarized as a cultural hybrid. Deconstruction and Indian literary theory, like the philosophy of yoga, expand the boundaries of mental and emotional states. Indeed, modern life at almost every turn blends two apparently incompatible domains: locality and globalization, boundaries and unboundedness.

The basic principles of language, consciousness and meaning found in Indian literary theory derive from the sacred texts of the Vedas (*Veda* means knowledge), which are the direct cognitions (*shruti*) of Vedic Seers. Dasgupta notes that the dates of the Vedas have been variously set between 4000 and 1200 B.C. (1988, vol. 1, 10). The body of Vedic literature evolves from and explicates the four basic Vedas—*Rig-Veda*, *Sama-Veda*, *Yajur-Veda*, and *Artharva-Veda*—and includes the Upanishads, *Brahmanas*, *Ithihasa*, and *Puranas*. The *Ithihasa* consists of the well-known epics *The Ramayana* and *The Mahabharata*, which contains the *Bhagavad-Gita*, considered one of the most authoritative texts of Indian philosophy. Valmiki, the author of the *Ramayana*, is credited with being the first poet as well as first theorist of poetic form. Sanskrit served as the lingua franca of the Vedic tradition, and because classical Indian literature consists of Sanskrit poetry, India literary theory deals primarily with poetic expressions analyzed through various schools of Sanskrit poetics. Emerging in antiquity, the tradition of Sanskrit poetics extends from its Renaissance in the eighth century A.D. to 1800. The first mention of the relation between consciousness and language, which forms the basis of Panini's grammar and the structure, rhythm and effect of Sanskrit poetry, is in the *Rig-Veda* (Coward 1980, 130).

The *Mundaka Upanishad* is among the Vedic texts that distinguishes intentional and nonintentional states (as described by Forman): "Two kinds of knowledge must be known . . . , the higher and the lower knowledge. . . . The lower knowledge is the *Rig-Veda* [and other Vedic literature]; but the higher knowledge is that by which the Indestructible (Brahman) is apprehended" (Müller 1962, 27–28). What is articulated here is a clear distinction between knowledge-by-acquaintance (conceptualization) and knowledge-by-identity (direct experience) of pure witnessing awareness (*turiya*).[3]

The Bhagavad-Gita also distinguishes levels of knowledge in chapter II, verse 45, which describes pure consciousness (*turiya*). The modern Hindu teacher and mystic Maharishi Mahesh Yogi translates verse 45 in part as, "Be without the three gunas, / O Arjuna, freed from duality / . . . possessed of the Self" (1969, 126). He explains that Arjuna is told "that there are two aspects of life, perishable and imperishable. The perishable is relative existence, and the imperishable is absolute Being" (1969, 128). This difference corresponds to the two kinds of Brahman referred to in the *Maitri Upanishad*: "sound and non-sound," the lower and the higher, quality and qualityless, or *saguna* and *nirguna* (Radhakrishnan 1992, 833).

Central to Indian literary theory is the special quality of poetic integration, which is based on the unity of language and accessible through the knowledge-by-identity of nonintentional consciousness. The absolute unity of sound and meaning found naturally at the basis of language is also a key attribute of poetry and underlies the experience of aesthetic rapture. G. H. Tarlekar explains that aesthetic rapture (*rasa*), as distinct from ordinary emotion, is defined as the flavor of a permanent emotional mode (*sthayibhava*) represented through the imagination of the poet (1991, 56). T. P. Ramachandran notes that *rasa* gives "a foretaste of the bliss of *moksa* [liberation]" (1979, 111), or as S. K. De puts it, *rasa* "transcend[s] the limitation of the personal attitude" (1963, 13).

Deconstruction, which as Robert Magliola writes is "on the verge" of another way of "knowing" (1984, 124), points in the same direction as the Vedic tradition. Though, as I have suggested, deconstruction can only intimate in practice the process of transcending into a fourth state (*turiya*). The withdrawal from all mental, sensory, and emotional experience without loss of awareness is the beginning of several higher states of consciousness. The fourth state (*turiya*), when temporary, is also known as *savikalpa samadhi* (Forman's PCE). When permanent it results in the fifth state or *nirvikalpa samadhi* (Forman's dualistic mystical state [DMS] and unitive mystical state [UMS]). Each state corresponds to a unique physiological style of functioning, as scientists such as David Orme-Johnson and C. T. Haynes have demonstrated (1981), as have Michael Murphy and Steven Donovan in *The Physical and Psychological Effects of Meditation* (1997).

Bhartrhari, Shankara, Derrida

In the language theory developed by the fifth-century Indian grammarian Bhartrhari, different levels of consciousness correspond to different levels of language. The mind, ordinary waking consciousness, corresponds to the temporal sequence of language in its two aspects:

outward speech (*vaikhari*) and inward speech or thought (*madhyama*); pure consciousness corresponds to the two higher levels of language beyond ordinary experience: *pashyanti* and *para* (Coward 1980, 126–37). The two higher levels of language, *pashyanti* and *para*, constitute a unity sound and meaning without temporal sequence or phenomenal differentiations. As Bhartrhari notes, they are accessible through the temporary and permanent experiences of pure consciousness respectively—the first in *savikalpa samadhi* (PCE) and the second in *nirvikalpa samadhi* (DMS and UMS). This distinction is also made both in the *Rig Veda* and by Shankara's nondual or *advaita* School of Vedanta. Coming a century after Bhartrhari, Shankara further explains that *pashyanti* corresponds to the junction point between the ordinary waking state and pure consciousness, whereas *para* corresponds to pure consciousness (*turiya*) itself (see Chakrabarti 1971, 176; Maharishi 1972). Only a temporary unity of language occurs in a temporary PCE, in which the awareness is not yet stabilized but crisscrosses the junction point between consciousness and its mental content.

As Subramania Iyer points out, *para*, the highest level of language, is said to be ever present and eternal and belonging to pure consciousness or Brahman (1969, 144–45). A further distinction between *pashyanti* and *para* is that in the former the unity of sound and meaning has the impulse toward manifestation whereas in the latter it does not. A word spoken or thought in the ordinary waking state is only a partial expression of an eternal meaning or transcendental signified. Unlike the deconstructive notion of an absolute conceptual closure, *para* for Shankara is a level of infinite possibilities in language only accessible through a fully realized state of pure consciousness (*turiya* or *nirvikalpaka samadhi*). Because meaning here belongs to the transcendent and is not a human product, it is not a temporal effect and therefore not perishable. (To avoid unfamiliar terminology for the levels of language and consciousness, I will use the terms outward speech for *vaikhari*, inward speech or thought for *madhyama*, the unity of language for *pashyanti*, and the absolute unity of language for *para*.)

Coward, in *Derrida and Indian Philosophy*, analyzes the parallels between Derrida's deconstruction and the two schools of Bhartrhari and Shankara. He notes that Bhartrhari regards language and consciousness as corresponding to the field of temporal sequence, constituting "the dynamic becoming of reality itself" (1990, 148). Like Derrida, Bhartrhari sees difference, or the sequencing of time, as the nonlogocentric, nontranscendental originary state of language. Shankara on the other hand has a more inclusive theory of language. Although Coward construes Shankara as separating language from the real or Brahman (1990, 81–98), in fact Shaṅkara's notion of Brahman can be understood as encompassing all aspects of language and indeed the entire field of diversity.

As Dasgupta writes, in Shankara's nondual Vedanta "the ultimate and absolute truth is the self, which is one, though appearing as many in different individuals. The world also, as apart from us the individuals, has no reality and has no other truth to show than this self. All other events, mental or physical, are but passing appearances, while the only absolute and unchangeable truth underlying them all is the self" (1988, 439). Shankara, in *Vivekacudamani*, writes that "Brahman is plenary, without beginning or end, beyond comprehension, changeless; one only without a second. There is no manifold there"; and, "Qualityless, without parts, subtle, without change, without blemish, Brahman is one only, not dual" (1988, 439, 441). Brahman and Atman (*turiya*) are ultimately one and the same. As I will suggest, Shankara's nondual Vedanta provides a more complete description of the link between language and consciousness than does Bhartrhari's theory of difference.

Coward interprets Shankara as holding that Brahman or the real is separate from the differential structure of language, and that difference constitutes ignorance (*avidya*) and therefore obstructs the real. But the *Rig-Veda* refers not only to the unity of language (*pashyanti*) discussed by Bhartrhari, which has an impulse toward manifestation; it also refers to an absolute unity of language (*para*) that lies at the basis of Shankara's nondual Vedanta. Shankara's notion of Brahman includes the full range of language, both its unified and differential aspects.

Shankara states that "Brahman is the real; without a second; compacted of pure intelligence; free from defect; serene; without beginning and end; actionless; of the nature of unremitting bliss; free from all differences wrought by maya; permanent; unchanging; pure; beyond the faculty of reasoning; formless; subtle, without name; immutable; such an effulgence, Brahman, shines" (1988, 254). It is inaccurate to suggest as Coward does that for Shankara language and the real are separate, for Brahman does not, simply speaking, transcend history but rather encompasses all levels of reality, both absolute and relative. In Shankara's nondualism, Brahman is by definition one with the universe, encompassing language in all its unity and diversity. Even in the absolute unity of language (*para*), diversity exists in the virtual triad of name, form, and relationship. So Shankara, emphasizing unity, expounds on *para*, while Bhartrhari, emphasizing difference, does not.

Derrida as a Western philosopher does not distinguish between mind and consciousness. Hence for Shankara, Derrida's description of language and the real as a function of difference would be correct for the lower level of reality associated with mind, which to Derrida would encompass our "whole" experience of the real. On the one hand, deconstruction undermines the transcendental signified as a conceptual closure and thereby unmasks totalizations based on mental content. On the other hand, for Shankara the unity of language as an absolute meaning is not a conceptual closure based on the mind, but rather a knowledge-by-identity of the word or logos—that is, of *pashyanti* and/or *para*. This identity is a revelation or eureka experience through which we gain instantaneous knowledge beyond space, time and logical discourse. Here the unity of language does not fit under the "logocentric" notion of a transcendental signified understood as conceptual closure.

Whereas Derrida emphasizes play within the field of difference, Shankara integrates unity and difference through a level of language and consciousness that subsumes duality in virtual form. The true transcendental signified consists of an unbounded conceptualization apprehended through knowledge-by-identity. This as Indian literary theory tells us is associated more with the feelings or emotional modes than with the intellect, insofar as it touches the heart of consciousness and remains elusive to the language of logic. These emotional modes constitute the experience of *rasa* evoked by aesthetic images that lift us beyond our finite sentiments (Chakrabarti 1971, 40–43). *Rasa* is analogous to the catharsis of classical tragedy and to the expanded states evoked by West African ritual drama.

While in theory deconstruction purports to undermine logocentrism, in practice as I have suggested it produces an effect that approaches the experience described by Shankara's nondual Vedanta: the transcendence of conceptual content. Derrida deconstructs unity and consciousness with rational discourse or outward speech, and yet his theory of grammatology implements a mechanics of extending knowledge-by-acquaintance to the threshold of a knowledge-by-identity.

Bhartrhari, like Derrida, conceives of the real (difference) and language as being one and the same. But as we have seen, for Shankara the unity of language (*pashyanti*) boarders on two dimensions, both of which contribute to its makeup: ordinary waking consciousness, which determines its manifestation; and pure consciousness, which determines its nonsequenced unity of sound and meaning. In theory Derrida rejects the latter, but in practice deconstruction seems to expand the intellect almost to the point of transcendence, paradoxically providing a taste of the unity of sound and meaning. The rhetorical freeplay of deconstruction, by extending the meaning of a word or sentence toward indeterminacy, can expand the reader's awareness to the extreme limit of the mind's powers of rational comprehension. We can either resist this expansion and remain within the limits of the rational mind, or take it as it comes and move toward the threshold of pure consciousness. These alternatives correspond to two kinds of infinity: that of deconstructive dissemination, of unlimited extension within space and time; and that of pure consciousness and the unity of meaningness beyond space and time.

Stretching the intellect through deconstruction points, then, to nonintentional consciousness. Derrida's notions of *différance* and the trace (defined as "not a presence but a simulacrum of a presence that dislocates, displaces, and refers beyond itself" [1973, 156]) are theoretically not privileged as absolute signifieds but conceived as ordinary signifiers. Derrida uses these terms "under erasure" and seems to define them as if they belonged neither to inward speech, the temporal level of language, nor to the unity or absolute unity of language, a transcendental signified, but to a gray zone somewhere in between—a junction point, an "aporia" or gap like that Homi Bhabha finds in the in-between of cultural hybridity.

For Indian literary theory, the unity of sound and meaning, name and form is represented by the suggestive power of figurative language (*dhvani*) (Chakrabarti 1971, 176; Coward 1990, 37, 43). Suggested meaning (*dhvani*), in which the sign is united both with consciousness and within itself, does not precede language, which Derrida would condemn as logocentric; rather, language, reality and consciousness are interconnected and coterminous. As Chakrabarti notes, "*dhvani*, the suggested meaning par excellence, is also a transformation, i.e. another state, of the Eternal Verbum" (1971, 43)—the *logos*. Access to this experience is gained through aesthetic rapture (*rasa*). As S. K. De puts it, the awareness, "transcending the limitations of the personal attitude, is lifted . . . above pain and pleasure into pure joy, the essence of which is its relish [*rasa*] itself" (1963, 13). The implication here is that there is nothing outside of consciousness—a reconstructive interpretation of Derrida's claim that "there is nothing outside the text."

Theory and the Text

Franklin as we saw in chapter two characterizes degrees of unity as "flavors of nonseparateness." These flavors have "an incipiently conceptual aspect" but "also affect the feeling-tone of joy or bliss" (1998, 234), also known as aesthetic rapture (*rasa*). A deconstructive reading of Toni Morrison's novel *Beloved* will help to illustrate how its play of *différance* can move the reader toward a taste (or *rasa*) of nonseparateness. Deconstruction undermines the mimetic function of language, claiming that the narrative structure of the novel has no parallel structure in the physical universe. In *Beloved*, Morrison's magical realism can be said to accentuate the division between signifier and signified, text and reality. Yet in blurring the distinction between the real and magical worlds, *Beloved* questions our understanding of them and undermines their differential status. After Sethe kills one daughter out of love to save her from the living death of slavery, she and her other daughter, Denver, accept the presence of the poltergeist in their house on 124 Bluestone Road as the dead daughter and sister returned. Later they also accept the appearance of "Beloved" as a physical manifestation of the dead baby. Deconstructionists might argue that the novel calls both worlds into question, but as Brendal Marshall observes, "the supplement of magic to the realism of slavery and its effects was a strategy for survival" (1992, 181). Morrison in an interview says, "One of the things that's important to me is the powerful imaginative way in which we deconstructed and reconstructed reality in order to get through" (qtd. in Marchall 1992, 181). Homi Bhabha, placing *Beloved* in a "new" internationalism, finds that Morrison's "contemporary fable of a woman's history" projects "an affective, historic memory of an emergent sphere of men and women alike" (1994, 5). What distinguishes Morrison's narrative for Bhabha is that her metaphors, in moving from the specific to the general, represent not a smooth transition but a "'middle passage' of contemporary culture, . . . a process of displacement and disjunction that does not totalize experience" (1994, 5)—totalization here referring to conceptual closure as opposed to witnessing awareness.

The murderous rituals in *Beloved*—infanticide, dispossession, possession, and self-possession—reflect a moral and psychic ambiguity. This ambiguity is part of a strategy of survival within a wider context of political disjunctions. From the perspective of consciousness studies, it also involves for reader and characters a shift of awareness from the expressed form of the narrative to its suggested meaning—as distinguished from its conceptual content. This suggested meaning (*dhvani*), specifically the ghost "Beloved," metaphorically represents a field of all possibilities accessible to intuition, or knowledge-by-identity, and reached through the gaps in the text's rational content. Sethe's memory of her murderous act is riddled with gaps, "the holes—the things the fugitives did not say; the questions they did not ask . . . the unnamed, the unmentioned" (1988, 170).[4] They suggest a meaning grasped beyond conceptual closure, an intuitive wholeness encompassing the binary opposites of the real and magical. Here awareness moves from the intentional content of the mind toward nonintentional consciousness. For Bhabha, the narrative gaps belong to "an 'in-between' temporality that takes the measure of dwelling at home, while producing an image of the world of history" (1994, 13)—again a joining of opposites. The suggested unity of the material and psychic elements in *Beloved* corresponds to the unity of the sensible and intelligible (suggested) aspects of language in *pashyanti* and *para*. As a ghost who enters the phenomenal world, "Beloved" herself symbolizes the novel's magical unity, and the reader's awareness shifts from her realistic to her magical dimension and back. "Beloved" constitutes an aesthetic image that induces in the reader an experience of *rasa*, the aesthetic rapture of awareness opening toward the wholeness of language. This unity, realized to different degrees by different people, goes beyond the limits of the personal attitude and thereby eludes the conceptual form of language (*madhyama*) and knowledge-by-acquaintance, which would yield a mere conceptual closure.

Bhabha quotes Emmanuel Levinas on the twilight or "in-between" nature the aesthetic image: images of art as "the very event of obscuring, a descent into night, an invasion of the shadow" (1994, 15; Levinas 1987, 1–13). For Levinas, the images of fictional discourse reveal "an interruption of time by a movement going on the hither side of time, in its interstices" (*ibid.*). These interstices or gaps in the text, while remaining on this side of time, by implication point beyond time to a nonseparateness or intersubjectivity. Likewise, as Bhabha notes, the "undecipherable languages of the slave memory" this side of time simultaneously obscures the narrative of infanticide and "articulate[s] the unspoken: that ghostly discourse that enters the world of 124 'from the outside' in order to reveal the transitional world of the aftermath of slavery in the 1870s" (1994, 15). The image creates an opening through what Levinas, via Robert Bernasconi, calls an "externality of the inward . . . introducing into the heart of subjectivity a radical and anarchical reference to the other which in fact constitutes the inwardness of the subject" (15). The magical realism of "seeing inwardness from the outside" (16) constitutes the suggestiveness of language (*dhvani*). For at the hither side of transcendence (as in *pashyanti*, which borders ordinary waking and pure consciousness), aesthetic language both constitutes and is constituted by the in-between state of subjectivity. This state, a flavored state of nonseparateness, has "an incipiently conceptual aspect" that "also affect[s] the feeling-tone of joy or bliss" (Franklin 234). Sethe as slave mother sees inward to her in-between hybridity through the outside of the ghostly return of "Beloved." She sees her double: "she is the laugh and I am the laughter. I see her face which is mine" (*Beloved* 213).

The real and the magical, the social and the aesthetic, the ordinary and the extraordinary in *Beloved* interpenetrate in a manner reminiscent of the nonplaces of supermodernity. That is, the "externality of the inward" in *Beloved* resembles the inwardness of the external in the experience of the nonplace. Morrison's characters in their cultural hybridity pierce the boundary between two kinds of knowledge or empiricism—intentional and nonintentional, mental and contemplative—while on the hither side of time. The African-American experience shows us how even when steeped in the drama of life and the boundaries of time and space, one intuits the boundless.

A deconstruction of subjectivity in *Beloved* blurs the distinction between the self and other, a process that Marshall claims "reinforces the concept of the subject as both constituted and constituting" (1992, 181). The subject is both a cause in its own right and an effect of outside causes, dispersed along a chain of signifiers as "a narrative restatement of intertextuality" (1992, 182). Sethe cannot distinguish between herself and her children, and Baby Suggs, her mother-in-law, feels that "a sadness was at her center, the desolated center where the self that was no self made its home" (*Beloved* 140). For Lorna Sage, the example of Sethe and Baby Suggs "suggests that to be human is precisely to experience your self as divided" (1992, 184). But in terms of the relation between language and consciousness, the aesthetic images in *Beloved* of in-between hybridity, or the interstices of self and other, suggests that the division of the self has two aspects, both related to the apparent division of mind and consciousness. That is, the self is divided in that the mind or contents of awareness belong to the field of difference; and the self as mind is divided from pure consciousness as a state of nonseparateness.

Furthermore, that Sethe and Baby Suggs are dispersed intertextually through citations, echoes and references to their personal and racial pasts does not inevitably make them decentered subjects. *Beloved* is also a novel of self-making in which a verbal power serves to retrieve the ghosts of a collective past. As the characters become hybrid/whole through an aesthetics of re-membering themselves, the reader's awareness also shifts beyond the limitations of their personal attitudes and experience. As Arnold Weinstein notes, "By writing it [the novel] the way she has, as the generic and multivalent speech of mothers and daughters, Morrison has underscored its status as language, as the binding speech of 'join,' of speech itself as the vehicle and fabric of 'join,' yoking together by its very plaint and polysemousness the fissured lives and bodies it commemorates" (1993, 287). Morrison's speech of "join" with its intertextual play has an effect analogous to that of the unity of language in Sanskrit poetics. Both forms of language collect the pieces of human experience into a hybridity that transcends logic and the limitations of past, present, and future. The reader may undergo the aesthetic rapture (*rasa*) of the self realizing its inherent nonseparateness—an experience evoked by the generalizing, suggestive power of language through which individual suffering can be purged.

Like deconstruction, psychoanalytic criticism also questions the unity of the self, as in the famous debate between Derrida and Lacan (see Muller 1988). The poststructuralist anxiety of the subject is supposedly induced by the fact that "the unconscious is structured like a language" (Lacan 1978, 20). Arguably, however, this anxiety stems not from language itself but rather from the incomplete apprehension of language in the form of outward speech or thought (*vaikhari* or *madhyama*). Anxiety springs from duality, as in the temporal gap between sound and meaning found in the lower levels of consciousness and language. As deconstruction reveals, the subject seeking fulfillment in the finite temporal field of mind and language is always vulnerable to the pitfalls of "logocentrism," as defined conceptually. On the other hand, the subject who flows with suggested meaning (*dhvani*), even as induced by the play of the signifier, can move toward a taste of the self (*rasa*) in its condition of nonseparateness beyond conceptuality, whatever its residual historical flavor may be.

Conclusion

From the perspective of Shankara's nondual Vedanta, the unity of self-presence—whether in language, consciousness or the material world—already encompasses an unmanifest spatial/temporalizing movement of *différance* that characterizes the deconstructive model. Deconstructive free-play, as a rhetorical or metaphorical experience of language by the ordinary waking mind, not only uncovers the sedimentation of signifiers in temporal speech; it also tends to expand the mind through a spontaneous abstraction of thought toward the non-thought of nonintentional consciousness.

The centrifugal self-referral of the text that pushes the reader toward a general meaningfulness seems to produce a corresponding centripetal self-referral *within* the reader that pulls toward the Self (*turiya*). This reciprocal self-referral of reader and text may provide a taste of an ultimate signified, an experience of aesthetic rapture (*rasa*). In this way, while ostensibly decentering the subject, deconstruction also locates a reference point beyond the duality of the relative and absolute. What it obscures in theory is that the transcendental signified does not have to be separate from language, that unity and difference in language can coexist, and that *différance* can lead toward the transcendental. From the perspective of the nondual tradition, a silent or suggested meaning (*dhvani*) can be glimpsed as the mind expands through literature toward unbounded consciousness (Pandey 1963, 728–32). This experience constitutes the ground of being of the true intersubjectivity described in chapter 4 (and supported by the three preceding chapters). The everyday experience of unboundedness in the modern world, though not immediately apparent, seems to be on the rise in the drama of living. Social and aesthetic domains overlap considerably, with the aesthetic not being confined to high art but rather permeating the drama of living. By uncovering the social forces behind the production of literary meaning, cultural studies do not displace transcultural truths or aesthetic values, but rather discover them at the very heart of popular culture.

4

Intersubjective Phenomenology and Performance

Introduction

Postmodern drama theorists have reexamined the notions of essential form, the plural identity of the dramatic work, and its embeddedness in social and historical contexts. This chapter further explores the relation between text and performance, presentation and representation, original and simulacrum. In what sense might a performance present rather than re-present, and what is the nature of presence? Is it full or is it empty? While postmodern theorists claim that theater is a fictional representation, I will suggest a way in which it is not only a derivation or a fiction but something closer to the drama of living. Instead of merely living, people now perform their lives, and life as cultural performance is said to hold a mirror up to art. This mirroring of art results from the interrelation between social drama, or the "drama of living," and aesthetic drama, particularly stage drama as defined by Antonin Artaud and theorists influenced by him, such as Jerzy Grotowski, Peter Brook, Eugenio Barba, and Richard Schechner.

As we enter the new millennium, stage drama and social drama increasingly interpenetrate. The transformational structures of social drama that have always influenced stage drama have proliferated and intensified, and the numinous supernatural aspect of ritual drama has penetrated a wider range of cultural practices. The distinction between presence and absence, presentation and representation, subject and object begins to fade.

As Victor Turner says:

> social drama feeds into the latent realm of stage drama: its characteristic form in a given culture, at a given time and place, unconsciously, or perhaps preconsciously, influences not only the form but also the content of

> the stage drama of which it is the active or "magic" mirror. The stage drama . . . is a metacommentary, explicit or implicit, witting or unwitting, on the major dramas of its social context (wars, revolutions, scandals, institutional changes). (1998, 67)

Turner describes the interrelation of the drama of living and stage drama as not exactly a mutual mirroring but an exchange: something old exits and something new appears; we learn through experience, casting off the old and gaining the new. In this exchange, as distinctions dissolve, social drama and other forms of cultural experience manifest the aesthetic forms of stage drama, including ritual, dance, and music. Life and dramatic art are becoming indistinguishable as cultural performances. And yet for Turner, "cultural performance, whether tribal rituals or TV specials, are not . . . simply imitations of the overt form of the completed social drama" (1998, 64–65)). Rather they emerge from what he calls the redressive, reflexive phase of the drama of living, a liminal or threshold stage dominated by the "'subjunctive mood' of culture, the mood of maybe, might-be, as-if, hypothesis, fantasy, conjecture, [and] desire" (65).

Intersubjectivity

To help explain the connection between life and theater, I will use Ken Wilber's four quadrant model of integral psychology and Christian de Quincey's comments on this model. Wilber describes the world, including human beings, as consisting of two domains, exteriors and interiors, which come in two forms, individual and communal. Now imagine a square divided into four quarters. The horizontal axis is divided into interior and exterior, and the vertical axis is divided into singular and plural. In the upper left quadrant of individual-interiors, we have the domain of individual subjects. In the lower left quadrant of communal-interiors, we have the domain of intersubjectivity. In the upper right quadrant of individual-exteriors, we find the domain of individual objects; and in the lower right quadrant of exterior systems, we find the domain of interobjectivity. Wilber calls this his ontological mandala:

> So we have four major perspectives (the inside and the outside of the singular and the plural): I, it, we, and its. Since the objective dimensions (the outside of the individual and the outside of the collective) are both described in third-person it-language, we can reduce the four quadrants to

> just three: I, we, and it. Or first-person, second-person, and third-person accounts. Or art, morals, and science. Or the beautiful, the good, and the true. (2000b, 164)

Wilber's integral theory contains two other factors, evolution and spirit. The four quadrants are coevolving from the lowest to the highest, the simplest to the most complex forms. With each quadrant coevolving simultaneously, no one quadrant can operate in isolation. This integral map brings us to another aspect of Wilber's integral psychology: the idea that everything consists of *holons*, a term borrowed from Arthur Koestler (1969). A holon is a whole that is simultaneously part of another whole, which in turn is in turn part of a greater whole—as in word, sentence, paragraph—in widening concentric circles. The part-whole relation of a holon in one quadrant necessarily partakes of the other three quadrants, so that nothing is exclusively interior (or exterior), individual (or collective), but individual parts embedded in larger systems. If we take two individual subjects, then each individual consists both of interior domains of subjectivity and intersubjectivity, and of exterior domains of objectivity and interobjectivity. Or I, We, It, and Its.

The upper left quadrant in Wilber's model is the domain of consciousness, including pure consciousness—the "culture-independent core component of the self" (Shear 1996b). But the experience of this level of self, which is transconceptual, nonlinguistic, and transcultural, always occurs within the context of the other quadrants: the "We" of culture, morals, and good, and the "It" of science and objective truth. If the individual-interior reaches all the way down to a pure subjectivity of the transpersonal, the question then becomes, how does communication occur in the lower left quadrant of intersubjectivity—the cultural domain that includes art, literature, and aesthetic experience? That is, how does one experience intersubjectivity as a "We" domain distinct from the world of "It"?[1] If subjectivity involves the internal experience of one in relation to oneself, then intersubjectivity involves the internal experience of one in relation to others.

To begin with, the individual-interior at its highest or deepest level of evolution has affinities with Shankara's Advaita (nondual) Vedanta, discussed in chapters 1 and 2. As Eliot Deutsch writes, "The central concern of Advaita Vedanta is to establish the oneness of Reality and to lead the human being to a realization of it" (1973, 47). This realization occurs through the "experience" of consciousness in its unified or irreducible state as witness or seer, single, simple and continuing. In this state, we recall, the transcendent Absolute (Brahman) comprises the "content" of the nondualistic experience of pure consciousness (Atman). "All this is, verily, *Brahman*. This self [Atman] is *Brahman*. This same self has four quarters" (*Mandukya Upanishad*, verse 2; Radhakrishnan 1992, 695). The four quarters are the waking, sleeping, dreaming states, and a fourth (*turiya*) state of pure consciousness without qualities or content. *Turiya* or atman underlies all mental phenomena manifested in the three ordinary states and is beyond "experience" in the usual sense of a division of subject and object. The experience of atman belongs to Wilber's individual-interior upper left quadrant. In becoming atman, however, the individual disappears off the grid of Wilber's four quadrant model, but she knows she has experienced atman upon reentering the boundary of the upper left quadrant. This boundary, moreover, is shared in the intersubjective lower left quadrant in the case of a group experiencing atman together—and as I will suggest in the aesthetic experiences described by drama theorists. While atman occurs within the cultural and material context of the other quadrants, then, it is not reducible to this context, for ultimately it transcends space, time, and causality.

So individual and communal interiors come in different levels. In proposing an experiential approach to anthropology, C. Jason Throop clarifies this by distinguishing two kinds of subjectivity: cognition, which is culture-specific; and noncognitive direct experience, which is transcultural. Whereas anthropology tends to collapse all subjectivity into the cognitive camp, including preconceptual emotion, Throop proposes that "pure experience" is a type of nonconceptual awareness corresponding to pure consciousness. He says that "while both pure experience and pure consciousness can be considered types of nonconceptual awareness, pure experience as a pre-conceptual awareness corresponds to a view of consciousness that focuses on describing the initial 'stages' of sensation and perception from one moment to the next, while pure consciousness as a trans-conceptual awareness points, on the other hand, to different 'levels' of consciousness that may transcend culturally conditioned conceptual awareness" (2000, 48).[2] Preconceptual "pure experience" occurs in the initial stages of perception or sensation before the cognitive function of the mind kicks in with interpretation. Throop suggests that most people are familiar (if only unconsciously) with the preconceptual glimpse of an object of perception—that is, of an object before the cognitive faculty begins to interpret it. With pure experience, we begin to move from the domain of individual-interiors to the domain of intersubjectivity, the interrelation between subject and other—whether another subject or a work of art.

A work of art or literature can induce a pure experience (the preinterpretive stages of perception) or pure consciousness (noncognitive awareness). It helps us to recognize awareness as an ever-present reality, transcultural and transpersonal. Devices in a text that facilitate pure experience for the reader include originality, figurative language, beautiful imagery, and interpretive resonance. Aesthetic experience frees us from the culturally constructed images and symbols of language and facilitates our letting go of the boundary between subject and object. Understood in terms of nondual Vedanta, art transforms "raw emotion" (*bhava*) into an aesthetic emotional experience (*rasa*), a taste or "aesthetic leap" to a higher state of consciousness described as "pure contemplation, characterized by a total absence of conceptual thought" (Dehejia 1997, 57).

The aesthetic leap induced by literature occurs in the consciousness of the subject through the intersubjective space between subject and text. To clarify this, we need to reexamine the nature of intersubjectivity. De Quincey criticizes Wilber's intersubjective quadrant as being empty because it depends on or is reducible to the physical domains of science or "It" (2000, 185). Describing intersubjectivity in his book *Integral Psychology*, Wilber says, "You, as subject, will attempt to understand me as a subject—as a person, as a self, as a bearer of intentionality and meaning. You will talk to me, and interpret what I say; and I will do the same with you" (2000a, 161). As de Quincey observes, Wilber's notion of intersubjectivity depends on *interpretation* as a necessary means for getting at interiors. "There is no unmediated, *direct* experience of the other. Wilber's 'interpretive circle,' he makes clear, is identical to the 'hermeneutic circle'" (186; original emphasis).[3]

De Quincey distinguishes two basic meanings of intersubjectivity, the standard one used by Wilber, and an experiential one which he subdivides into weaker and stronger. Of the experiential interiors, the weaker is a "*psychological intersubjectivity* relying on nonphysical presence," and the stronger is an "*ontological intersubjectivity* relying on cocreative nonphysical presence" (187–88; original emphasis). The difference is between Wilber's "intersubjective agreement" on the one hand, and "intersubjective participation" (weak experiential interiority) or "intersubjective co-creativity" (strong experiential interiority) on the other, which de Quincey calls "true intersubjectivity"

(188). The problem with Wilber's definition of intersubjectivity is that it excludes feeling, the felt component of this domain. It also seems to exclude the nonlinguistic, transconceptual dimension of the subject, although Wilber does include this dimension in the upper left quadrant of subjectivity. In de Quincey's view, "It is not the case that only via language can intersubjectivity occur, but that actually only via intersubjectivity can language carry and exchange meaning. In other words, intersubjectivity is not 'linguistically generated,' it precedes language, and is its ground of being, its context of meaning" (189–90).

Nevertheless, language is not altogether dispensed with. As de Quincey says, "Actually there is direct interior-to-interior engagement even when contact is made via language—in fact, that's the *only* way people can share meaning and understand each other. But the point is that the actual sharing of meaning is not accomplished by linguistic exchanges, but by the accompanying *interior-to-interior participatory presence*—by true intersubjectivity" (188, note 13; original emphasis). This view is supported by Indian literary theory and Vedanta discussed in chapter 3. In *turiya* (pure awareness), as induced through literature by *rasa* (aesthetic rapture), we experience language in the unified level of *pashyanti* or *para*, beyond space, time, causality. On this level language has no spatio-temporal gap between signifier and signified, sign and referent and therefore participates in the creation of an intersubjective wholeness.

To support this view, de Quincey distinguishes two meanings of subjectivity. Subjectivity-1 "means, essentially, a capacity for feeling that is intrinsic, or interior, to the entity under consideration—a what-it-feels-like-from-within" (186). It is a first-person accounting or feeling of its own being. Subjectivity-2 "means an isolated, independent, self-sufficient locus of experience" (186). It is the private Cartesian ego, the "monad" of Leibniz. The difference is that subjectivity-1 can "be either interior and *shared*, or interior and *private* . . . [while the second Cartesian] subject is not only interior, it is self-contained and private" (186; original emphasis). As de Quincey asserts: "With subjectivity-1, interiority or feeling can be 'intersubjective' and precede individual subjects; in subjectivity-2, interiority is *always* private, and intersubjectivity, if it occurs, is always secondary" (187; original emphasis). Subjectivity-1 thus includes subjectivity-2, but not vice versa. Subjectivity-1 and de Quincey's "true intersubjectivity" (psychological and ontological) correspond to the liminal or threshold experience in theater described by Artaud, Turner, and others, as well as to Bhabha's notion of hybridity or in-betweenness and Augé's notion of non-places discussed in chapter 2.

In contrast to Wilber and de Quincey, Habermas in defining intersubjective agreement rejects the "paradigm of consciousness." He favors instead a paradigm of "communicative action" in which, as Thomas McCarthy explains, "the decentered subject remains as a participant in social interaction mediated by language" (1987, xvi). Language use, which conforms to reason, is oriented to validity claims redeemed through intersubjective recognition. As Habermas says,

> Agreement arrived at through communication, which is measured by the intersubjective recognition of validity claims, makes possible a networking of social interactions and lifeworld contexts. Of course, these validity claims have a Janus face: As claims, they transcend any local context; at the same time, they have to be raised here and now and be de facto recognized if they are going to bear the agreement of interaction participants that is needed for effective cooperation. The transcendent moment of *universal* validity bursts every provinciality asunder; the obligatory moment of accepted validity claims renders them carries of a *context-bound* everyday practice. (1987a, 322; original emphasis)

In rejecting the paradigm of consciousness, Habermas attempts to integrate the context-bound with the universal on the basis of language and reason, which he sees as underlying intersubjective recognition. De Quincey on the other hand recognizes that true intersubjectivity can *include* language and reason, which are aspects of the mind, but also *extend* to consciousness. Habermas, Wilber, and de Quincey all accept the importance of intersubjectivity, but have different definitions. (They do not however include in their discussion the *pashyanti* and *para* levels of language associated with *turiya* as mentioned earlier.) The ultimate integration of universal validity and context-bound practice as it pertains to intersubjectivity, it seems to me, must include both mind and consciousness, the exterior and interior realms. In terms of Indian literary theory, language spans these opposite poles, thereby bridging the gap between linguistic agreement and a true intersubjectivity.

In describing panpsychism in the context of intersubjectivity, de Quincey points out that "whether you call in 'interior,' 'experience,' 'feeling,' 'prehension,' or 'consciousness,' the fact remains that ontological type must go all the way down [to the atomic and subatomic levels] if we are even to begin to have a coherent, rational solution to the mind-body problem" (199). Panpsychism corresponds to true (especially ontological) intersubjectivity, in which the interiority goes all the way down, as in direct subject-to-(other)subject, I-to-(other)I communication—unmediated by the exterior quadrants of "It." (As you go all the way down, of course, there is no duality, whereas subject-to-subject, I-to-I implies duality.) Stage drama and the drama of living, as Turner says, entail not so much a mutual mirroring as an exchange, which I will explore in terms of true intersubjectivity.

In-Betweenness

As an anthropologist and comparative symbologist, Turner identifies four phases of the completed social drama reminiscent of Joseph Campbell's monomyth: breach or breaking a rule, crisis, redressive or reflexive action to remedy the crisis, and reintegration if the remedy succeeds or schism if it fails. The world of theater and performance has roots in the third phase of redressive rituals that are either "prophylactic" or "therapeutic" (1998, 64). This liminal third phase, a phase of in-betweenness like Bhabha's cultural hybridity, constitutes the point of exchange between life and drama. It is the channel connecting self and world, subject and object, old and new. In-betweenness is a process of breaking boundaries, of disidentifying with one phase of life and beginning the transformation to another phase. Richard Schechner, who like Turner also explores the liminality or threshold between life and performance, describes in-betweenness as a collapse of the difference between presenting and re-presenting. He finds that liminality has both a cultural and a metaphysical dimension (1973, 5–36). In terms of my argument in this book, the cultural side of in-betweenness is the conceptual content of awareness and the metaphysical side is pure awareness itself as found in the gaps between concepts. In-betweenness therefore constitutes an intersubjective space that begins with conceptual content (Wilber's intersubjective agreement) and then moves beyond that to a nonphysical presence (de Quincey's true intersubjectivity). Liminality or in-betweenness, which underlies the cultural oppositions of the crisis phase of Turner's social drama, has to be experienced directly as a true intersubjective space for a crisis to be redressed in the transformation to levels of greater unity, harmony, or integration.

In any social drama, moving through a crisis to its remedy, exchanging the familiar for the unknown, or crossing the threshold from one phase of existence to another more integrated phase can bring ambiguity. Stage drama portrays the in-between identity of the individual or society in the drama of living through ambiguous symbolic types. These symbolic types are metaphysical figures inherited from preindustrial ritual and include androgynes, angels, mermaids, centaurs, and monsters. Theater intertwines these ambiguous figures with music, dance, body languages, body painting, chant, drinking, burnt offerings, and the "enacting of mythic and heroic plots" that manifest a universal drive to be cosmocentric and immortal beyond material boundaries. As modern leisured society has expanded in complexity and scale, ritual drama has also expanded to encompass entertainment genres, as well as the nonplaces of supermodernity described by Augé: highways, airports, hotels, supermarkets, and malls. The move from archaic social drama to modern performance may have weakened the numinous supernatural aspect of liminal transformations. But in compensation for this loss of intensity, the on-going exchange between life and art has allowed the aesthetic power of theater to interpenetrate social drama. Performance art gains from "the subjunctive, liminal, reflexive, exploratory heart" of the drama of living through which we evolve toward ever greater states of wholeness (Turner 1998, 66). This cultural process is in turn continually modified by the metacommentary of performance. Hence, as de Quincey would say, the linguistically generated intersubjectivity enhances and in turn is heightened by a prelinguist intersubjectivity that constitutes its ground of being and context of meaning (2000, 190).

Text and Performance

As Artaud, Derrida, Worthen, and others have pointed out, the liminal or threshold experience in theater is not dependent on the dramatic text or its author. For Artaud, true theater, the theater of cruelty, signifies an interpenetration of the self and world in which the self transcends the opposition between subject and object. "When this happens in performance," Turner writes, "there may be produced in the audience and actors alike what d'Aquili and Laughlin call in reference to ritual and meditation a 'brief ecstatic state and sense of union (often lasting only a few seconds)'" (1998, 66). The ecstatic union of performance art achieved by working through a crisis to its remedy constitutes a true intersubjective space beyond language and interpretation; it involves the same process through which the self in the drama of living undergoes a transformation of identity toward greater wholeness. This remedy and transformation can be an individual (private) or cultural (intersubjective), an ontogenetic or phylogenetic experience. Ken Wilber equates the development through different structures of identity with disidentification and transcendence, whether spontaneous or aesthetically induced (1996, 120–29). The self ceases to identify exclusively with one stage of development and undergoes a transformation to a more integrated stage. In drama as in life, transcendence toward remedy or ecstatic union includes yet goes beyond language, as in the language of a text, for as Artaud indicates, in performance the verbal is itself transcended.

In *Theater and Its Double*, Artaud writes, "The question, then, for the theater is to create a metaphysics of speech, gesture and expression in order to rescue it from its servitude to psychology and 'human interest'" (1958, 90). Artaud believed that theater should abandon the Western style of speech with its abstract conventions and parasitic dependence on the text and instead adopt the concrete Eastern style of speech that integrates mind and body. When he describes "the language of the stage" in terms of the language and symbolic gestures of dreams where objects and the human body have "the dignity of signs," and when he draws inspiration from hieroglyphic characters "that are precise and immediately legible," Artaud suggests the integration of form and content, sound and meaning that Indian theories of language describe as attainable through aesthetic experience. He describes a unity of form and content reminiscent of that found in *pashyanti* (the unity of sound and meaning) and experienced through aesthetic rapture (*rasa*)—an ontological intersubjectivity. The theater of cruelty for Artaud signifies not sadism or bloodshed but "implacable intention and decision, irreversible and absolute determination" (1958, 101). It is a determination not to reflect the world or text but to produce change through its own force as a metaphysical embodiment, for "it is through the skin that metaphysics must be made to re-enter our minds" (99). Theater changes the world not only through its illocutionary force, enacting a shift of conceptual categories, but also through its perlocutionary effect of integrating mind and body, actor and spectator. In this process performance enacts a letting go of the boundary between subject and object, sound and meaning in both actor and spectator as they co-create an intersubjective space.

While Turner explores the interrelation between drama and life, suggesting how stage drama produces change by engaging the liminal or in-between phase of social drama, Artaud describes a similar interrelation between the actor and the text. Actors as well as spectators enter what Artaud calls a "communication with pure forces" (1958, 82). This subject-to-subject communication produces "a purification" or sublimation (82), a liminal experience beyond conceptual agreement. The actor achieves this not by adhering to the formal manifestations of the text. Artaud, who calls for an end to masterpieces, says of the dramatic text that we should

> recognize that what has been said is not still to be said; that an expression does not have the same value twice, does not live two lives; that all words, once spoken, are dead and function only at the moment when they are uttered, . . . and that the theater is the only place in the world where a gesture, once made, can never be made the same way twice. (1958, 75)

The fact that the action of drama "is never made the same way twice" displays the iterability of dramatic language and action; the same words and actions repeated in different contexts have different meanings (Derrida 1977a, 249). In the theater of cruelty the actor does not read the text, but interprets it and in the process goes beyond its exterior tokens. As Derrida puts it, the actor participates in "the end of representation, but also original representation, the end of interpretation, but also an original interpretation that no master-speech, no project of mastery will have permeated and leveled in advance" (1978b, 238). The theater of cruelty resembles the theater of the absurd in its effect of enacting a liminal condition outside textual representation in the performative present of the intersubject. Representation and interpretation come to an end as they fulfill their purpose in the subject's enactment of the threshold stage of in-betweenness. Life and art, culture and aesthetics intersect through a cosmocentric experience of heightened awareness evoked through the presence-ing of in-betweenness in performance—an unmediated space in which interpretation has run its course.

Performativity

In "Drama, Performativity, and Performance," W. B. Worthen notes that "performing reconstitutes the text; it does not echo, give voice to, or translate the text. Performance does not cite the text any more than [the statement] 'I do' [declared in a marriage ceremony] constitutes the force of marriage. Instead, performance produces the text within a system of manifestly citational behavior" (1998, 1097).

The citational elements of drama—such as acting style, scenography, and conventions of directing—"transform texts into something with performative force" (1098). Worthen adopts the term "surrogation," introduced by Joseph Roach to define dramatic performance "as an alternative or a supplement to textual mediation" (qtd. 1101). But Worthen uses the term in a modified sense to mean "an understanding of the text [that] emerges not as the cause but as the consequence of performance" (1101). Through surrogation, performance interrogates the text and thereby deconstructs it. This deconstruction releases a perlocutionary forçe that, as I have argued throughout this book, leads beyond space, time, and logical discourse.

But how does performance in fact produce the effect described by terms such as *surrogation, sublimation*, and *liminal transformations*. Taking the negative approach, Derrida defines the theater of cruelty in terms of what it is not. It is not "non-sacred theater"; it is not "theater that privileges speech"; it is not "abstract theater," "theater of alienation," "nonpolitical theater," or "ideological theater" (1978b, 243–45). It is devoid of presence insofar that performance does not represent a presence or logos that exists somewhere else, namely in the dramatic text. Nor is performance even present in front of the audience. Derrida considers Artaud's work ultimately a losing battle against logocentrism. "Artaud," he writes, "knew that the theater of cruelty neither begins nor is completed within the purity of simple presence, but rather is already within representation, in the 'Second time of Creation,' in the conflict of forces which could not be that of a simple origin" (1978b, 248). "Presence, in order to be presence and self-presence, has always already begun to represent itself, has always already been penetrated" by difference (249). Derrida however is describing what Indian philosophy designates as the lower level of language, reality, and consciousness. Yet as Turner suggests, the connection between life and art blurs the divide between presenting and re-presenting, presence and difference, high and low, subject and object.

Derrida says that "Cruel representation must permeate me. And nonrepresentation is, thus, original representation" (1978b, 237). But to permeate me with what? Language? Probably not. For one thing, language in poststructuralism is subject to the play of *différance* and thus unable to permeate the self established beyond difference or at least in a liminal phase. For another thing, the cause and effect of performance in its totality is not strictly verbal (it does not privilege speech) but transverbal. The transverbal is distinct from the Freudian preverbal in that it has gone through and beyond the verbal stage—it is not regressive—just as a transpersonal ecstatic union is distinct from the Freudian prepersonal (Wilber 1996a, 117–29).

Drama theorists such as Grotowski, Brook, Barba, Schechner, and Yarrow have attempted a phenomenological understanding of the transverbal, transpersonal nature of performance and the relation between performer and spectator, which I am describing in terms of true intersubjectivity. Grotowski tries to answer the question of "what takes place between the spectator and actor" (1998, 204), which he considers the defining quality of theater. The creative part of theater is not in literature or the text, but in a common ground between the spectator and actor, "something they can dismiss in one gesture or jointly worship" (204). This ground he defines in terms of myths "inherited through one's blood, religion, culture and climate . . . myths which it would be difficult to break down into formulas" (204). Grotowski, like Turner, locates the presence of theater in the force of universals to remedy a crises or contradiction by dissolving the boundary between binaries like subject and object. His "poor theater" aims to produce a state of "translumination," first in the performer and then in the audience. "Translumination" is the condition in which the subject/object duality no longer exists, a condition de Quincey would describe as an ontological intersubjectivity "relying on co-creative nonphysical presence" (2000, 188). In Forman's terms, the performer and spectator enact a transformation from the content of awareness (Derrida's field of difference) toward nonintentional pure awareness—an innate capacity. Ideally the actor transcends the limitations of the mind-body-split and achieves totality and a full presence, becoming what Grotowski calls a "holy actor."

Brook similarly describes theater and happenings as total or "holy theater," understood not as a reflection of the text but "as a new object, a new construction brought into the world, to enrich the world, to add to nature, to sit alongside everyday life" (1998, 207). The happenings shout "Wake up!" But wake up to what? Not he says to a do-it-yourself Zen, for after the text has been swept away language returns and with it the "debate of form against formlessness, freedom against discipline" (1998, 206). Like Artaud's metaphysical embodiment, "holy theater" would make the invisible visible. But even Zen "assert[s] that this visible invisible cannot be seen automatically—it can only be seen given certain conditions" (206). In life as in art, for the invisible to interpenetrate and revive the ordinary, a condition conducive to letting go of conceptual content and the boundary between subject and object has to be constructed. This letting go of boundaries, as during an appropriate social gathering like a performance, results in what Barba calls the "transcendent" in theater, or what de Quincey calls the shift from a linguistically generated interaction to an ontological intersubjectivity. But if life as cultural performance is a mirror held up to art, then the transcendent in theater already exists in life and is in fact available at each and every moment, whether in the gaps between conceptual binaries, in the knowledge-by-identity of the pure consciousness event (PCE), or even in the dualistic mystical state (DMS). Indeed, it is not unreasonable to infer that a spectator during a performance may glimpse a DMS by alternating back and forth between the liminal and the quotidian.

Dramaturgy and the Transpersonal

The *Natyashastra*, the classical Indian treatise on dramaturgy, describes techniques that allow a performer to transcend personal boundaries and achieve temperamental states that are transverbal, transpersonal, and eternal, such as the state of *sat-chit-ananda*, or being, consciousness, bliss (Deutsch 1973, 9). The *Natyashastra* is one of the oldest works of Indian dramaturgy and was written by Bharata around the third century A.D. (give or take three hundred years). Although Bharata is said to be the author of this work, the name Bharata originally meant an actor in a drama, an expert in transformations or adopting roles. With 5,600 verses and a shorter version of about 200 verses, the *Natyashastra*, emerging in the context of Indian philosophy, has had a tremendous impact on classical Indian theater and is beginning to influence the developing model of Western theater today, as suggested by Malekin and Yarrow (1997). According to Bharata, theater should not only be entertaining, emotionally gripping and intellectually challenging but also have the effect of expanding the mind of the audience toward pure consciousness (atman). By first engaging an audience through a stimulating performance, theater should have the further and more significant impact of eliciting the experience of atman or *turiya* (pure consciousness). In this way the long-term effects of theater would be to stabilize atman is the state of *moksha* (liberation) and thereby assist in the transformation of society toward utopia. Traditionally in Indian culture this aim was considered realistic and achievable.

Indian dramaturgy indicates how actors can be trained to reach higher levels of consciousness and thereby to raise the consciousness of their audience. The *Natyashastra* serves as a manual for two objectives: first, to expand the actor's awareness, and secondly to describe what an actor who has realized this expanded state can do spontaneously on stage to produce awareness expanding effects on the audience. In describing the histrionic techniques for raising consciousness, the *Natysashastra* as well as other works of Sanskrit dramaturgy emphasize not only physical techniques but also the representation of emotional modes or temperamental states essential for producing aesthetic delight (*rasa*) (Bhat 1981). The actor develops a mode of acting (*sattvika abhinaya*) for portraying these modes of temperament (*sattvika bhava*). The root *sat* means the eternal absolute. As in *sat-chit-ananda*—the eternal absolute or being (*sat*), consciousness (*chit*), and bliss (*ananda*)—*sat* refers to the qualityless Self beyond conceptual content, that pure awareness at the basis of all manifestations of thoughts, feelings, sensations, and perceptions, and thus the basis of intersubjectivity.

The trained performer would thus be able to cocreate with the spectator a sublime intersubjective space that corresponds to Bharata's *sat*, Turner's liminal phase, Artaud's sublime or metaphysical embodiment, Worthen's "surrogation," Grotowski's "translumination," Brook's "holy theater," and Barba's "transcendent" theater. As Artaud says, this theater is not about psychology, that is to say not about the mind's verbal or conceptual content. On the contrary it transcends verbal content to achieve a nonverbal presence that is by definition an enactment in the intersubjective world outside the text. Derrida sees theater and the text as mutually deconstructing, arguing that presence "has always already begun to represent itself" (1978b, 249). But which is re-presenting which? Is it convincing to deny presence to a cultural performance that still uses language but aims through its universally ambiguous and symbolic types at a totality that is transverbal as well as transpersonal? I would suggest that through their liminality and perlocutionary force drama and other performance arts create their own brand of presence, an invisible presence that escapes the deconstructive gaze.

Presence and nonpresence have dimensions other than linguistic, as suggested by the phenomenology of actor and spectator evoked through performance. The liminal transformations of life, being in-between words, texts, and cultures and therefore transverbal, correspond to and engender the transformations of art. This reciprocal structure consists of parallel recurring sequences. That is, in life as in art we find the following universal patterns. In life: breach, crisis, remedy, and integration; in art: desire, intention, action, resistance, and fulfillment; or impulse, initiation, quest, loss, and restoration; or as Ralph Yarrow observes in terms of Sanskrit dramaturgy, *para*, *pashyanti*, *madhyama*, *vaikhari*, and *utterance* (2001, 125–27), or from the transverbal to the verbal and back again through the perlocutionary effect on the audience. Life and art become indistinguishable in their interrelated desire for "communication with pure forces" (Artaud 1958, 83), for letting go of the confines and contradictions of the verbal, "single self" phase of human development. This process has accelerated in the multimedia age of life as cultural performance, and will most likely intensify in the new millennium as the world, as Taylor would say, is transformed into a work of art (1999, 191).

Conclusion

Postmodern performance has been defined as not a full presence but an empty presence, an "aesthetics of absence" (Connor 1989, 141). Henry Sayre remarks that "an aesthetics of presence seeks to transcend history, to escape temporality. An aesthetics of absence subjects art to the wiles of history, embraces time. . . . An aesthetics of presence defines art as that which transcends the quotidian; an aesthetics of absence accepts the quotidian's impingement upon art" (qtd. in Connor, 141). But as I have proposed here, an aesthetics of presence also accepts the quotidian, the temporal, and the historical. In its intersubjective commonality it is contingent on the wiles of letting go of the text and the displacement of absolute forms of identity. The presence of radical inwardness and true intersubjectivity in life and art does not form a circle, a timeless repetitive pattern, but a spiraling pattern responsive to the changes associated with time and place.

Performance as "holy theater" whether of life or art can be understood as a radical inwardness that is not like ordinary introspection. The latter has something as its content, while the former is not like anything. It entails the complete absence of empirical phenomenological content. The commonality of experiential reports of radical inwardness reflects a commonality of experience that is independent of the variables of culture and belief. It is the common ground of translumination that Grotowski seeks and that performance renders phenomenologically present for actor and spectator, as so remarkably demonstrated in the plays of Beckett and Pinter.

5

Postmodernism and the Drama of Consciousness

Introduction

Playwrights such as Samuel Beckett, Eugène Ionesco, and Harold Pinter write in a context where traditional narratives, or what Lyotard calls grand narrative (1984, 31–35), can no longer inspire confidence, leaving society with a sense of alienation and loss. These dramatists were impelled by their historical and cultural contexts to explore the reality of the mind through a medium that involved the physical embodiment of characters on stage in spite of the absence of decisive meaning. As Martin Esslin has pointed out, going from the medium of language and a reliance on meaning or conceptuality in communication toward a concern with immediate experience belongs to a long tradition in the history of Western literature involving pantomime and the carnavalesque (1983, 328–29). This tradition focuses on the individual's basic circumstances rather than the ideological makeup of his or her social identity. As portrayed in drama by Henrik Ibsen and August Strindberg and in fiction by James Joyce, this tradition explores the reality of the mind and its direct contact with the phenomenal world prior to the interpretive strategies of any particular narrative. In other words, it deals with the fundamental experience of what it is like to be conscious of our existence. Esslin does not seem to be referring to the objects of awareness, or intentional mind, but to consciousness itself. Each play suggests this basic phenomenon, addressing, as Esslin puts it, the question, "How does this individual feel when confronted with the human condition?" (1983, 405). If we assume that phenomenal consciousness is at the basis of this condition, then how does drama allow us to experience it?

David Chalmers, in *The Conscious Mind*, explains:

> We can say that a being is conscious if there is *something it is like* to be that being, to use a phrase made famous by Thomas Nagel. Similarly, a mental state is conscious if there is something it is like to be in that mental state. To put it another way, we can say that a mental state is conscious if it has a *qualitative feel*—an associated quality of experience . . . or *qualia* for short. The problem of explaining these phenomenal qualities is just the problem of explaining consciousness. (1996, 4)

In its representation of what it is like to be someone, modern drama goes beyond qualia and approaches the foundation of human reality, the experience of consciousness as such. Chalmers in this passage does not make the distinction between mind, with its intentional content such as qualia, and consciousness devoid of content. But as we have seen in earlier chapters, Eastern philosophy emphasizes this distinction as well as that between higher states of awareness, such as the pure consciousness event (PCE) and the dualistic mystical state (DMS). In this tradition, art and literature are said to have the suggestive power (*dhvani*) to shift awareness from the qualia or content of the mind toward a state of nonconceptuality, which constitutes the ontological ground of true intersubjectivity. The flavors or qualia of experience are mediated by linguistic and historical factors, but nonordinary or mystical states go beyond mediation in their lack of intentional objects. Beckett's *Waiting for Godot* and *Endgame* and Pinter's *Homecoming*, as I will demonstrate, refine the mediation of qualia to a point of abstraction where the awareness, if not altogether transcending mediation, verges on a PCE or state of nonseparateness. As we have seen, "there are flavors of nonseparateness," or differences of historical residue in nonintentional awareness, which in its purest form consists of a "flavorless flavor" (Franklin 1998, 234–35).

The devices used by Beckett and Pinter to break through temporal, discursive barriers toward a transtemporal, transverbal awareness are well-known to theatergoers, even though they may find the effects of these absurdist devices hard to explain after the fact. By dispensing with narrative sequence, character development, and psychology in the conventional sense, Beckett portrays the process in which awareness moves from the qualia of an historically mediated experience to a state beyond linguistic and cultural boundaries. Both Beckett and Pinter show what it is like to be aware in a single moment, rather than drifting in the slipstream of culturally mediated discursive patterns of thought. The main device Beckett uses to express this intuitive moment is the poetic image. In *Waiting for Godot*, as in *Endgame*, the juxtaposition of a series of poetic images, which substitutes for a conventional plot, results for the audience in a series of epiphanies on the nature of conscious experience.

These poetic images and the flashes of nonordinary, nonintentional consciousness they induce resemble the "total experience" or "feeling of wholeness" that results from the "polyphonic montage" in the film theory of Sergie Eisenstein (Andrew 1976, 61–63). The poetic image takes the conscious mind from the coherence and rationality of a narrative sequence to a suggestion of the noumenal or intuitive realm beyond. By integrating these poles of experience—the concrete and the abstract, rational and intuitive, mediated and unmediated—Beckett's drama leads to a rediscovery of ultimate realities apparently beyond the grasp of the intentional mind alone. Hence he is less concerned with meaning than with the structure of experience. Through defamiliarization, or deautomatization, his work can lead the spectator toward an appreciation of awareness by itself. This alienation effect—the ideal of Brecht, the Russian formalists, *The Natya Shastra* in Indian aesthetics, Keats's negative capability, and the decontextualists—does not simply replace one set of mental contents for another, as poststructuralists would argue. Rather it begins the process of emptying the awareness of all content by deconstructing the psychic structures that select, organize, interpret and limit our "knowledge-about" the world around us.

Waiting for Godot

The distinction between awareness and its content, consciousness and mind, can help to explain the significance of Beckett's drama abandoning ordinary characterization based on conventional motives; Estragon and Vladimir in *Waiting for Godot* are nearly without attributes, aging tramps locked in a love-hate relationship and full of uncertainty about the time, place, and purpose of their existence. They reveal, as part of the aesthetic strategy of Beckett's plays, that access to a qualityless pure awareness, or even to a flavor of nonseparateness, involves letting go of personal and social identities. W. T. Stace gives an apt description of pure awareness in what he calls "introverted mysticism":

> Suppose that, after having got rid of all sensations, one should go on to exclude from consciousness all sensuous images, and then all abstract

> thoughts, reasoning processes, volitions, and other particular mental contents; what would there then be left of consciousness? There would be no mental content whatever but rather a complete emptiness, vacuum, void. One would suppose *a priori* that consciousness would then entirely lapse and one would fall asleep or become unconscious. But the introverted mystics—thousands of them all over the world—unanimously assert that they have attained to this complete vacuum of particular mental contents, but that what then happens is quite different from a lapse into unconsciousness. On the contrary, what emerges is a state of *pure* consciousness—"pure" in the sense that it is not the consciousness of any empirical content. It has no content except itself. (1960, 85–86)

In this mystical experience, as in more flavored states of nonseparateness more likely for Beckett's audiences, the awareness moves beyond the subject-object duality of the intentional mind to states of greater stillness.

Supporting Forman's notion of knowledge-by-identity, Malekin and Yarrow in their book *Consciousness, Literature and Theatre* explain that this state "is approached by the process of unknowing; that is to say, the mind becomes less, not more active, eventually leaving the subject-object relationship behind. It exchanges knowing about things, in a theoretical and abstract way, for knowledge through uniting with the object of knowledge" (1997, 28). *Waiting for Godot* induces in the spectator/reader this process of unknowing. The characters cannot fathom their situations and the spectators cannot grasp the play through any traditional narrative, but must rely rather on their intuition, on letting go of knowledge-by-acquaintance. The fact that in 1957 the prisoners in San Quentin, California, were famously enthralled by a performance of *Waiting for Godot* suggests the inadequacy of an authoritative, intellectual approach to its understanding.

From a thematic perspective, the metaphysical and practical uncertainties of Beckett's play, with its pseudo-climaxes and nonarrivals of Godot, do not inevitably render it nihilistic or entirely pessimistic. As Peter Brook says, "Beckett's dark plays are plays full of light" (1990, 65). Their uncertainties provide a vehicle for going beyond the clouds of conceptual boundaries to the light of freedom associated with nonintentional consciousness. In the play-within-the-play in Act II, the speculation on Godot's identity when Pozzo says, "Godin . . . Godet . . . Godot . . . anyhow you see who I mean" (1982, 24),[1] suggests that one's true identity is not exhausted by thought or language, which serves only to identify and report on the content of human experience. True identity may be glimpsed instantaneously as a "total experience" or a "feeling of the whole" associated with the poetic image, as suggested by Eisenstein and Indian literary theory. Godot will never be apprehended through cognition or fully represented through discursive language, which unfolds in time. As Beckett was well aware, any notion of an ultimate, nonchanging reality can only be rendered through poetic suggestion and apprehended intuitively—through aesthetic rapture—in an instant of time. The play thus alludes to a remote possibility of being saved by Godot, since no explicit rendering of what it means to be saved is possible. As Beckett dramatizes, the ultimate reality of the subjective mind is beyond the spatio-temporal limits of logical meaning.

Beckett is a master of the poetic image and other devices that stop the flow of thought and move the attention inward toward witnessing awareness. The features of the antiplay—the lack of logical movement, the digressions and nonsense, the fact that, as one critic says, "nothing happens, twice," the repetition of endless cycles of action-in-non-action, and Vladimir's circular song at the opening of Act II ("And dug the dog a tomb")—have the effect, as Andrew Kennedy observers, of conveying a sense of "eternal return" (1992, 20, 24). This cyclical self-referral of the text can also be seen in the ironic reference to what is happening in the theater, especially in Act II. The self-reflexiveness we see, as when Estragon says, "That wasn't such a bad little canter" (42), or when Vladimir looks out into the audience and says, "There! Not a soul in sight" (47), or later when he asks, "What are we doing here, *that* is the question?" (51), creates conceptual gaps through which we can stand back and intuit the witnessing function of consciousness. Here the semiotic gap between word and referent, or the self-referral of the text, induces a corresponding self-referral in the mind of the audience (as discussed in chapter 2). This combined subjective and objective self-reflexiveness aesthetically highlights awareness over its content and conjures up for the audience an intersubjective space of oneness or nonseparateness. Through a self-referral embodiment of the actors on stage, the drama of consciousness suggests and may even render present that which is rendered absent by the limitations of thought and language.

Becoming Nonactive

James Calderwood, in "Ways of Waiting in *Waiting for Godot*," notes that waiting is a kind of nonactivity which is self-erasing (1992,

33). He means self-erasing in the sense of decentering the subject, exchanging one conventional identity for another in an endless series. But this nonactivity can also empty out or erase the contents of the mind more radically, thereby promoting a nonactive state of awareness beyond social identity altogether. Beckett's nonactivity reflects and also induces a tendency toward pure consciousness (*turiya*). The act of waiting, although indiscernible to an outside observer, disrupts the illusion of time by erasing the past, diminishing the present and aggrandizing the future when that which is waited for is expected to appear (Calderwood 33). More fundamentally, though, the movement toward the appointment with Godot is a movement from activity to nonactivity, "becoming" to "being," which in the drama is really a nonmovement in which nothing ever happens because being or emptiness is omnipresent. As pure witnessing awareness, it underlies all instantiations of social identity.

It is also the source of all activity. Estragon: "Let's go." Vladimir: "We can't." "Why not?" "We're waiting for Godot." In the emptiness of meaning, as Malekin and Yarrow point out, waiting is "the ever-repeated moment which precedes beginning. The moment in which beginning is possible; the moment, as at the beginning of the play, when performers and spectators are most awake to the newness of it all. *Godot* hauls its participants back again and again to this launching-place, from which, as in life, everything always has to be improvised anew" (1997, 139). The moment that precedes this beginning corresponds to our sense of awareness as a unity, a beginningless continuum outside the flux of time, which we know simply by virtue of awareness itself. If this unity, as in waiting, can be rendered or mediated, then it is not by concepts or expectations, but as de Quincey puts it "by the accompanying *interior-to-interior participatory presence*—by true intersubjectivity (2000, 188; his emphasis). In the end, the play offers no other certainty.

From the perspective of Shankara's Advaita Vedanta, activity is an illusion, and the one reality is the stasis of pure being (as in waiting), which is omnipresent and self-sufficient. The universality of waiting is suggested in part when Vladimir says, "We are not saints, but we have kept our appointment. How many people can boast as much?" And Estragon replies, "Billions" (51). That is, everyone has the potential for this experience. If Vladimir and Estragon are unique, it is only because for them, as tramps, travel is an end in itself , and the destination (being) is immanent in the process of becoming. Calderwood refers to the paradox of the appointment as similar to the sound of one hand clapping (1992, 34). As a Zen koan, this statement has no rational meaning and serves as a vehicle for taking the attention beyond the limits of thought and meaning (in the nondual state there are not two hands), and in so doing it is a synecdoche for Beckett's play.

Godot

It has often been noted that the word *Godot* is a Joycean word with hidden shapes. Reversed it spells Tod-dog, or death-dog. Dog in reverse spells god. As such, Vladimir's song at the beginning of Act II, "And dug the dog a tomb," alludes to the death of god. The word Godot thus embodies a coexistence of opposites: mortality and immortality, becoming and being, thought and pure consciousness. While God may seem to exist only as a possibility just beyond the tramps' reach, the mystery if not the real nature of Godot is always at hand. As Mark Taylor puts it, "the death of God is not a simple negation but a complex process in which the divine becomes incarnate when the profane is grasped as sacred" (1999, 189). As a coexistence of opposites, the sacred is immanent in pure awareness, the ground of language and thought. The fact that the spectator is suspended between the poles of death and god is significant in preventing the mind from dwelling on any particular meaning, or stagnating in its flow beyond conceptuality, space-time, and subject-object duality. When Beckett says, "I am interested in the shape of ideas even if I do not believe in them . . . It is the shape that matters" (qtd. in Calderwood 1992, 38), he points to an interiority beyond thought or mental content, to the shape of awareness that impartially subsumes all phenomena. The more unified or unbounded the awareness, the more dispersed the phenomena integrated by its wholeness.

The degree to which the play arrives to the spectator, and in turn the spectator to the play, depends finally on the degree to which the actors and audience can detach themselves from the mind's activity. This interrelation (between play and audience) is the subject of the *Natyashastra*, the Indian treatise on dramaturgy, which holds (as suggested by Indian philosophy at large) that there are several levels of the mind involved in the transformation of an audience. The term *mind*, as distinct from pure consciousness, is used here in two senses: the overall levels of the mind on the one hand, and the thinking mind within that general structure on the other (Alexander et al. 1990, 290). In this definition, the overall levels of the mind comprise the senses, the thinking mind, the discriminating intellect, feeling or intuition, the individual ego, and pure consciousness. For the *Natyashastra*, aesthetic rapture (*rasa*, or flavor of pure consciousness) affects the audience primarily through the emotional modes. As discussed in chapter 3, these modes are not ordinary feelings but the permanent emotional modes (*sthayibhavas*) that correspond to aesthetic rapture (*rasa*). The actors whose performance can evoke the strongest emotional response are the most effective. Since the emotions are closely linked with pure consciousness, the more the actors can tap into this silence underlying the mind's activity, the more transformative the emotional impact of their performance. Godot surely does not arrive for the waiting audience if interpreted merely as a transcendental signified experienced conceptually through the thinking mind. He may possibly arrive if interpreted aesthetically as an emotional flavor of the observer knowing herself, in which case the attention would go beyond thought in the direction of pure awareness. If Godot arrives, therefore, it will most likely be intersubjectively in the participatory presence induced by Beckett's art, which is characterized by self-referral gaps, pauses and ever-repeated moments that precede activity. Ultimately, what happens in the play depends on the quality of the direct interaction between the actors and audience/readers in each performance/reading.

Drama and Metalanguage

To a postmodernist critic, *Waiting for Godot* has modernist overtones, and Godot himself represents a metanarrative that prevents the tramps from ever achieving the freedom they so desperately seek. Jeffrey Nealon argues that Estragon and Vladimir are tricksters engaged in a play of language games, that all their games point to one metagame, the grand narrative centered on Godot, and that they are content to play their comfortable modernist games within this grand narrative, rather than attempt to break out through a postmodernist misuse of language for the sake of progress and discovery (1992, 46–47). The best example of a postmodernist language game, for Nealon, is Lucky's "think," which transgresses and disrupts the limits of the ultimate metagame, namely Western metaphysics. Lucky is right, of course, to deconstruct and expose the limits of objective thought:

> Given the existence as uttered forth in the public works of Puncher and Wattmann of a personal God quaquaquaqua with white beard quaquaqua-

> qua outside time without extension who from the heights of divine apathia divine athambia divine aphasia loves us dearly with some exceptions for reasons unknown but time will tell and suffers like the divine Miranda. (28)

If the nonsense of Lucky's think takes him and perhaps the audience toward the far side of the limits of language, then Lucky may be said to have tasted the flavor of pure awareness. Lucky's think is not merely unreasonable or the opposite of reason, which would keep it within the dialectic of language as an aspect of thought experienced through the mind and intellect. Rather, his think is transreasonable (Nealon 1992, 48), and in a sense transverbal (Wilber 1996a, 117–29). But this does not mean simply that his think deconstructs the metaphysical/metalinguistic meaning of Godot as a mental construct, replacing it with another construct. It means more importantly that his think moves the attention aesthetically through the emotional modes toward the transpersonal freedom of wholeness.

This process shows not only that language games resist being totalized by a metadiscourse, as the poststructuralists would say, but also that they can lead the mind beyond discursive thought altogether. Western metaphysics or the supposed metagame of Godot becomes a totalizing metadiscourse only when approached, as it usually is, theoretically through the mind and intellect rather than phenomenologically. As a result metaphysics in the Western tradition has become a grand narrative based on a grand misunderstanding. The postmodernist critique of metaphysical systems is really a critique of metaphysics as a concept rather than as a form of knowledge-by-identity. This critical misunderstanding occurs because applied metaphysics, the movement beyond mental content toward awareness itself, is rare in the West outside of aesthetic experience.

Furthermore, for Godot to be a metagame, as Nealon claims he is, he would have to be a known or finite quantity, yet in the play he remains unknown and infinite. Even Beckett, when asked about the meaning of Godot, replied that had he known it he would have told us in the play. Nealon notes that as a truly postmodernist play *Waiting for Godot* involves not the lack of meaning but an excess of meaning produced by the liberating play of language (1992, 51). Yet the deconstructive freeplay of language is liberating only in a finite sense; theoretically, as I have argued in chapter 3, it retreats within the boundaries of thought without giving access to the unboundedness of pure awareness, which it rejects as an illusion. To say that *Waiting for*

Godot presents a totalizing modernist view in an infinite postmodernist world is therefore to intellectualize it, to (mis)identify consciousness with the activity of the thinking mind, and to belie the impact of Beckett's play as a vehicle for true intersubjectivity.

Endgame

The aesthetic strategy of *Endgame* also shifts our attention from mind to consciousness, from our own subjectivity to an unmediated, direct engagement with the subjectivity of the characters. As in *Waiting for Godot*, the characters come in symmetrical pairs and play a waiting game, in this case an "endgame" for the time of death. Hamm, a blind old man in his wheelchair, and Clov, his servant who can't sit down, wait in a claustrophobic shelter with Hamm's legless parents, Nagg and Nell, who live in dustbins. They live in the aftermath of a great calamity and seem to be the sole survivors in a world Clov describes as "Corpsed" (25). Once rich and powerful, Hamm dominates and bullies Clov, who hates him and wants to leave. But to do so would be to commit both suicide and murder, for Hamm's larder contains the only remaining food, which he would have to go without, and Hamm is completely dependent on him. As they wait for the impending end, Hamm, who considers himself a writer, picks up where he left off in the tale he has been telling about the catastrophe that destroyed the world. On this day he recounts the incident of a man who came to beg for food for his starving child. By implication the child was Clov and Hamm rescued him and became his father, although the boy was too young to remember. The many others who also begged for help, such as his neighbor Mother Pegg, he left to perish and now feels the burden of guilt. Clov refuses to listens to his tales any longer, so he resorts to bribing his father into listening. He hates his imbecilic parents and in turn his mother secretly urges Clov to leave him.

Hamm is childish, selfish, sensuous, self-pitying, and plays with his three-legged toy dog, and Clov is rational and obsessed with order. Some critics believe they represent the conflicting elements of a single personality, or what Esslin calls a "monodrama" (1983, 66). The pun in Clov's name—clove, cleave; adhering, separating—allows for this ambiguity. As the desired but continually deferred end approaches, Clov, serving as Hamm's sense of sight, looks out the window one last time with his telescope and reports seeing what "Looks like a small boy" (50). He offers to go out and attack him, "a potential procreator," with the gaff, knowing that Hamm opposes any sign of continuing life; but Hamm restrains him: "If he exists he'll die there or he'll come here. And if he doesn't . . ." (50). At this point Hamm realizes that the end has come: "It's the end, Clov, we've come to the end. I don't need you anymore" (50). Clov finally decides to go: "I leave you. . . . There is nothing to say" (50). But at the end of the play he remains standing on the threshold: "Enter Clov, dressed for the road. Panama hat, tweed coat, raincoat over his arm, umbrella, bag. He halts by the door and stands there, impassive and motionless, his eyes fixed on Hamm, till the end" (51–52). No departure, no resolution, no closure. *Endgame* famously ends where it begins, and begins where it ends, the first lines being Clov's tentative statement: "Finished, it's finished, nearly finished, it must be finished" (12). But it never is.

In alluding to the end of the world and all of its content—objects, time, nature, food, colors, fleas, rats, weather, laughter, kisses, sun, sound, God, and so on—but infinitely deferring this end, *Endgame* suggests the possibility of experiencing a fusion of fullness and emptiness. Poststructuralists argue that the coalescence of beginnings and ends in the play proclaims our inability to reach the end of consciousness, of perceiving its nothingness (Hale 1992, 81). Hamm and Clove desire a stillness and immobility they can never attain, for the activity of the world never ceases. It seems they desire not so much to stop permanently the waves of activity, the natural activity of mind, but to locate an internal frame of reference for riding out the waves, which only consciousness itself can provide. Rather than conventional characterization and plot, *Endgame* concentrates on the core of human existence (Esslin 1983, 68; Henning 1992, 103). If Hamm and Clov represent the two halves of a single personality, then the core duality of human psychology is not the split between the rational/irrational, conscious/unconscious, emotion/intellect, all of which belongs to the material dimension of the mind. Rather it is the split between mind and consciousness, qualia and witnessing awareness, or as Sylvie Henning puts it, "mind and soul" (1992, 103). But however we divide Hamm and Clov into these two aspects, they also embody as individuals separate instantiations of this ultimate duality within themselves. Metaphorically, the gradual encroachment of death in the world surrounding their shelter depicts the receding qualia of human experience in the "unknowing" process of being awareness itself. A knowledge-by-identity of the self involves literally the forgetting or virtual death of the material world, which according to Sankya-Yoga includes the mind and intellect.

The end of material existence, therefore, does not entail the cessation of consciousness, as Jane Alison Hale suggests (1992, 81). Quite the reverse. She argues that the nonendings of the endgame portray a stalemate or paradox found in all of Beckett's work, namely "that consciousness can never attain a definitive end, because it would be unable to perceive the nothingness that it would meet there" (81). This may be true of the perceiving mind with its "knowledge-about" approach, which cannot fathom "the thing in itself," as Kant discerned, much less an ultimate nothingness. But consciousness does not know by perceiving, it knows through identity. It would attain the definitive end of nothingness by being it, not by perceiving it. For the characters and audience, the pull toward nothingness is represented by the vision of emptiness all around the shelter, the corpsed, gray world of zero, as well as by the constant shifting of the characters' socially induced identities.

Can it be said that Hamm and Clov's not conforming to conventional models of character implies that identity is a socially constructed closure? Yes and no. As Gabriele Schwab observes, Hamm and Clov "don't seem to commit themselves to any psychic continuity as a basis for identity"; for although they seem to manifest a conventional inner life, "as soon as one attempt to assemble these manifestations into some coherent notion of personality, the characters shift to a different level of self-presentation" (1992, 88). Schwab argues that *Endgame* prevents interpretive closure by inviting the reader to a symbolic interpretation, and then opening the meaning out again through the language-games of the characters.

> **Hamm**. We're not beginning to . . . to . . . mean something?
> **Clov**. Mean something! You and I, mean something! [Brief laugh.] Ah that's a good one!" (27)

Later Hamm questions whether he was ever present at the great calamity.

> **Hamm**. Absent, always. It all happened without me. I don't know what's happened. [Pause.] Do you know what's happened? [Pause] Clov! . . .
> **Clov**. What for Christ's sake does it matter?" (47)

Schwab notes that in *Endgame* the double meaning structure of language breaks down (1992, 91). Typically the lack of surface meaning sends us to look for a latent, symbolic meaning. Yet the overabundance of the signifier in the play not only precludes a manifest meaning but even renders a latent meaning suspect. Beckett thus warns us, "Beware of symbols" (qtd. in Schwab 1992, 88). As Schwab rightly concludes, the dialectic of closure and opening in the drama is an aesthetic device through which we transgress the limits of our ego identity. But in concluding that the play expands the "boundaries of our consciousness in two directions: towards the unconscious and towards self-reflection" (97), she follows the conventional wisdom of mistaking consciousness for mind, and of seeing the ultimate structure of the self in the conscious/unconscious duality.[2] The void of meaningfulness induced by the play of the signifier, however, would not lead to the unconscious mind, a field of conceptual content, but rather toward qualityless pure awareness (as suggested in chapter 3). The former still allows for totalization or closure, while the latter is a nothingness beyond closure—an intersubjective fullness of emptiness. Hence to answer our question, Hamm and Clov's not conforming to the conventional models of character implies that identity is a socially induced closure in terms of mind, but fully open in terms of consciousness.

Hamm's inability to finish his chronicle, which Clov considers a farce and Nagg would rather not listen to (35), illustrates the endless flow of thought and time. Hamm: "I'll soon have finished with this story. [Pause.] Unless I bring on other characters" (37). Recounting the liminal phase of his life during the great calamity ("All those I might have helped" [44]), Hamm's story blends into his present life and renders story and life almost indistinguishable. To him, they are equally real, or unreal, as he was "Absent, always." In the endless repetition of his story we see the inadequacy of language as a means of becoming aware of the self, communicating with others, or comprehending reality. The process or renewal and destruction experienced through time frustrates the desire for closure in the outer realm. At best this process may purge the troubling contents of the mind of the spectators, releasing them from the deadening habits of thought and language and from the fears and anxieties caused by duality, providing a glimpse of a nondual reality beyond. Just as Clov cannot escape from Hamm's oppressive realm, so each of us, Beckett seems to imply, cannot fully escape our temporal existence. Each must find a balance between boundaries and freedom, ratiocination and witnessing awareness. Though the endless quest for escape, *Endgame* invokes a taste of this balance in its intersubjective space. We know this cocreated state of being only through a priori intimations of inner experience.[3]

The original French version of *Endgame* gives more attention to the turning point of the play when Clov sees the small boy through the telescope. Hamm asks, "What is he looking at?" and Clov replies, "His navel" (qtd. in Esslin 1983, 72). "Like Buddha," Esslin observes, "the little boy contemplates his navel . . . the great emptiness of nirvana, nothingness, of which Democritus the Abdrite has said, in one of Beckett's favourite quotations, 'Nothing is more real than nothing'" (73). Esslin allows that nothingness more concretely may also refer to the coming of death, but concludes that it doesn't matter; it's best not to pursue interpretive closure, for to fix on any one alternative would "only impair the simulating coexistence of these and other possible implications" (74). But however many implications there may be, the emptiness of full awareness pervades them all. Even in the English version of the play, as I have tried to show, the images of endless repetition, nothingness and nonclosure of identity also suggest a sharable state of openness.

The Homecoming

While Estragon and Vladimir are tramps confronting ultimate reality from the margins of society and Hamm and Clov cogitate on nothingness, the characters in Harold Pinter's *The Homecoming* have seemingly more conventional identities as members of a modern family. In terms of its emotional impact, Beckett's plays are suffused with light, while Pinter's play has sinister undertones. *The Homecoming* presents power relations in a family of three brothers, Lenny, Joey, Teddy, and Teddy's wife, Ruth, their father, Max, and Max's brother, Uncle Sam. After living in the United States for six years, Teddy and Ruth return to England after a holiday in Venice. Now a professor, Ted finds his old bedroom waiting for him at home, but the circumstances of their homecoming seem rather less inviting. Almost immediately Ruth becomes licentiously, not to mention incestuously, involved with Teddy's sibling. As always Pinter's characters become entangled in complex and interdependent relationships that deconstruct the norms of human behavior.

The behavior of the family members toward each other seems so lacking in discernible motive that the audience quickly becomes disorientated. Esslin, who naturalizes the family's goings on, offers two possible interpretations (1983, 255–57). The first, based on realism, holds that Teddy is unhappily married, has just returned from a romantic holiday in Venice in a vain attempt to save his marriage, but in recognition of the futility of this goes along with Ruth's staying behind in England under a bizarre contract with his family. The second interpretation, based on wish-fulfillment or an Oedipal dream, sees Ruth as a duplicate of the mother, Jessie, now deceased, and Lenny and Joey as challenging the incest taboo as well as the patriarchy represented by Max and the eldest brother, Ted, by seeking sexual favors from Ruth. Both readings show the disintegration of the family structure, with the father figure suffering a humiliating defeat and the mother figure suffering degradation and a pseudo victory.

Pinter's reproduction of dialogue—with its outrageous humor, sinister pauses, and emotional conflicts—continues to move audiences. But the lasting power of the play stems less from the realism of a failed marriage, which though bad enough has become increasingly commonplace, than from the subversion of all normative positions open to the members of a nuclear family. With the father's authority stripped away, the mother's respectability gone, and the siblings devolving into chaos, the spectator may easily recoil from the thought patterns that have resulted in this condition. I say thought patterns as opposed to ideology because what is at stake here is not the preference of one value system over another, but the fact that all value systems have become unmoored from the heart, from basic human emotions—a possible side effect of the age of relativity and indeterminacy. If *Waiting for Godot* pulls the conscious mind beyond conventional thought patterns toward a taste of nonintentional pure awareness, creating a positive sense of light, a sense of wonder for the unknown and its infinite possibilities, then *The Homecoming* pushes the conscious mind in the same direction by creating a anxious sense of dread, of wanting, like Ted, to get out of a bad situation. As Ted says to Lenny, "You're way behind. . . . It's nothing to do with the question of intelligence. It's a way of being able to look at the world. It's a question of how far you can operate on things and not in things. I mean it's a question of your capacity to ally the two, to relate the two, to balance the two. To see, to be able to *see*!" (1991, 61–62).

However ironic Pinter's intention here may be, Ted's remark hints at the need to go beyond the discriminating intellect toward a greater capacity to see, and seeing involves ultimately a true intersubjective space that comes with expanded awareness. One irony in Ted's remark is that the ability to see with greater insight and detachment does not necessarily accrue from intellectual knowledge. Getting a Ph.D. in most cases only intensifies the intellect. By implication, the transformative power of the emotional modes is better cultivated through the aesthetic rapture induced by art and theater. Pinter's play reveals the extent to which the absurdity of sexual and gender relations can shake the emotions into pushing awareness beyond the realm of thought toward a greater self-reflexiveness. Marc Silverstein's *Harold Pinter and the Language of Cultural Power* makes a good starting point for analyzing the intersubject in Pinter's play and the relation between awareness and its content.

Silverstein rightly argues that the patriarchal power structure in *The Homecoming* is under attack, first by Lenny and then by Ruth. Lenny verbally assaults Max, casting doubt on the legitimacy of his and his brothers' descent—a doubt supported by several allusions by Max and Sam, such as Max's reference to his "three bastard sons and a slut-bitch wife." Ruth goes even further than Lenny by appropriating the word of the law and symbolically castrating the men, or to use Lacan's term, the "symbolic father." Ruth, who, as she says, "was a model for the body. A photographic model for the body" (57) and possibly a prostitute before she married Teddy, has a drink with Lenny and tells him to "Sit on my lap. Take a long cool sip" (34). She later tells him provocatively, "I wear . . . underwear . . . which moves with me . . . it . . . captures your attention. Perhaps you misinterpret. The action is simple. It's a leg . . . moving. My lips move. Why don't you restrict . . . your observations to that?" (53) She spends two hours up in the room with Joey engaged in what Ted later calls "love-play," but when interrogated Joey says, "I didn't get all the way" (66), to the amazement of Lenny and Max. "Are you telling me she's a tease?" Lenny asks (66).

According to Silverstein, Ruth withholds from men the desire from a woman they need to maintain their patriarchal status (1993, 76–83). From the Lacanian perspective, the woman's desire is not for the biological man but for the symbolic power associated with the law of the father. The stability of the patriarchy depends on two things, two matches, as it were. First, that the actual wife fulfills in practice the function of the ideological wife, namely to remain faithful to her husband, which in the case of Jessie (Max's wife) and Ruth does not occur. And secondly, that the biological real father be identified with the symbolic father through the desire of women. Silverstein observes that by withholding her desire first from Joey and then from Max, Ruth effects a redistribution of power by usurping the law of the father for herself (1993, 102–5). That is, by withholding her desire for the phallus she exposes the gap between the phallus, representing the symbolic father, and the penis, representing the actual father. For Ruth to express female desire would be to perpetuate the illusion men long to preserve of a unity between the symbolic and actual fathers, disguising the fact that the association of the symbolic father with power and law is nothing more than an arbitrary social construction, and that symbolic power is available to any subject within the social system.

A corollary to this theory is that as soon as a man expresses desire for a woman he feminizes himself, for he castrates the phallus as the law of the father. For Silverstein via Lacan, male desire "deconstructs the myth of the phallus" (1993, 105). When Max begs Ruth for a kiss at the end of the play he basically self-deconstructs his status as the symbolic father. Desire needs to be elicited from the woman, who would then be acknowledging the power of the symbolic father and accepting her subjugation to the patriarchal ideology. This would collapse the symbolic onto the real and so promote the woman's mistaking the penis as the phallus (1993, 106). In the process of withholding desire, Ruth exploits the law of the father by dictating the terms of her contract to work for the family and thereby rendering the men financially dependent upon her. She succeeds in converting her prostitution from a form of male exploitation to an instrument of power and dominance. As Silverstein notes, however, her success brings about her own commodification, and the power she wields is not her own but that of the symbolic father working through her:

> We should not mistake this conceptualization of the subject as an "effect" of language and power for an expression of crude determinism by either Foucault or—to the extent that his plays dramatize a similar view of the subject's relationship to power—Pinter. Much of the power of Pinter's work stems from his ability to dramatize the tension between the subject's position as an "effect" of power and the subject's ability to manipulate power as the "vehicle" of its "articulation," and it is this tension that produces *The Homecoming's* ambiguity. As the "vehicle" of phallic power, Ruth can utilize that power to undermine the structure of the patriarchal family; as the "effect" of phallic power (and *The Homecoming* always identifies power in terms of the phallus, no matter who serves as the agent of that power), Ruth reifies the phallus through "her empowerment." (1993, 107)

The point here is that Ruth exposes the phallus as an imposture, since the fit between the father and power is an ideological fiction and not an essential feature of masculinity.

The problem with this interpretation is that it establishes the symbolic father as a transcendental signified, and thereby contradicts the principle in poststructuralism of the infinite deferral of meaning. If the law of the father is the inescapable ultimate meaning, and if any use of law or power is automatically associated with the phallus, then *The Homecoming* would hardly have a liberating effect upon the audience. Not only would the audience be restricted to a conceptualization of the play's import rather than being beckoned by its aesthetic appeal to an experience beyond the contents of awareness, but those contents themselves would be preordained and limited. It is rather questionable to imagine that Pinter limits power to the phallus in this play. Even though Ruth manages to exploit the patriarchy, she does it with a finesse only a woman can wield.

The realm of power is open-ended and probably infinite and belongs not to the symbolic father or to any other conceptual framework. Power springs from the capacity to break out of conceptual frameworks. It is the source of all frameworks, that pure witnessing awareness, the luster of which the spectators will sense glowing at the margins of thought when all frameworks have run their course during the drama before them.

The framebreaking absurdity of Pinter's play parallels "the breakdown of ordinary perceptual processing" that Diane Jonte-Pace finds in the Rorschach test responses in those she calls "spiritual masters," people adept in nonordinary states of consciousness (1998, 152). Jonte-Pace uses the Rorschach test to describe the nature of perception, like texts on Advaita Vedanta are used to describe mystical experience. As Jonte-Pace says,

> The Rorschach test explicitly deconstructs in order to analyze, understand, and interpret the process of perception while much of mystical literature similarly describes an explicit deconstruction of the process of perception in order to escape from that process. William Blake's famous assertion, "If the doors of perception were cleansed, everything would appear as it is—infinite," echoes, for example, the Upanishadic texts that urge the cessation of "the five sense knowledges" and the Buddhist Abhidamma texts that instruct the meditator in the practice of gaining insight into and detachment from sensation, perception, and judgment. (1998, 138)

What Jonte-Pace found in the Rorschach responses of Buddhist, Vedantic, and Native American spiritual masters both puzzled and surprised her. Each of these spiritual traditions produces a certain "deautomatization of normal perceptual processes" that in ordinary people is diagnosed as indicating mental pathology (1998, 152–53).

In certain features of the test, the spiritual masters consistently reported a response described as "vague and slippery," characterized by a high degree of ambiguity, shading, vague shapes, and moving fields of energy. This type of response in ordinary people is associated with a weak sense of reality, diffuse anxiety, depression, and a neurotic loss of boundaries. Jonte-Pace observes that the "vague and slippery" response is appropriate for "a practitioner of altered states but an inappropriate or frightening experience for those attached to the firmness and stability of reality in normal waking consciousness" (1998, 152). In support of the perennial psychology described by Forman, she concludes that "there is indeed a difference between ordinary and nonordinary consciousness" (153). Or as the ethnopsychiatrist George De Vos states, "a psychological universal in human beings is what might be broadly termed the capacity for altered states of consciousness" (qtd. in Jonte-Pace 1998, 156). Adept in the deautomatization of perceptual responses, the spiritual masters are like the characters and spectators of Pinter and Beckett's plays. If their responses appear abnormal or pathological, it's only because they are slipping from the firm and stable frameworks of ordinary waking consciousness and experiencing the unstable, unclear, and nonrigid world of nonordinary, nonintentional consciousness. Real pathology comes when automatization leads to overly fixated, psychotically perseverant, or attached responses and the resistance to change with a show of anger and aggression. Through transformative techniques like Pinter's, postmodern drama (as well as literature and art) has the effect of deautomatizing our responses, taking us beyond interpretive agreement to deeper levels of intersubjective space.

Beckett and Pinter deconstruct ordinary perceptual frameworks, but the effect of their plays is not merely to reveal the lack of stability or firmness in the ordinary processes of thought and perception. A constructivist (or poststructuralist) would see their drama as a representation within a cultural context that produces certain conceptual effects, while the decontextualist (or perennial psychologist) would see it as a means of eliminating cultural constructs altogether in a move toward transpersonal, transcultural awareness. A poststructuralist interpretation of these plays deconstructs their cultural categories to expose their relative or nonuniversal nature, and thus their lack of priority over other categories. A decontextualist interpretation would see that cultural categories, like those undermined in these plays, have their practical advantages, but when exclusively identified with they can impede access to the "innate capacity to be aware of awareness itself" (Jonte-Pace 54).

The difference between these approaches can also be understood in terms of the distinction between constative and performative utterances proposed by J. L. Austin. A constative utterance makes a statement or describes a situation that is either true or false, whereas a performative utterance is neither true nor false but performs the action being referred to (1975, 54–70). Austin also designated utterances as being locutionary, illocutionary, or perlocutionary, or having locutionary force (the meaning of the statement), illocutionary force (the statement's performance of an action), and perlocutionary force (the statement's effect on the hearer) (Austin 1975, 9–15). Literary utterances combine all of these forces in the cocreation of intersubjectivity. In addition to making statements, Beckett's and Pinter's plays perform or do, creating situations through characters and actions that produce nonlinguistic effects on the actors and audience. They not only materialize ideas, but also enact a conceptual flow, transforming the awareness of actors and audience by pointing them beyond conceptuality.

In addition to transmitting information, performative language, as Derrida argues, can through the repetition of familiar discursive practices also perform acts that have the effect of either sustaining or modifying cultural norms (1982, 307–30). Tension or gaps may develop between the various forces of language, as between the expected effect of serious performative language described by Austin and the open effects produced by their nonserious or imaginative repetition in different contexts. As Derrida declares, "This is my starting point: no meaning can be determined out of context, but no context permits saturation. What I am referring to here is not the richness of substance, semantic fertility, but rather structure, the structure of the remnant or of iteration" (1979, 81). By implication, because of iterability and the unbounded nature of contexts, the effect of a performance on a subject may also be unbounded—and beyond the scope of discursive criticism. The plays of Beckett and Pinter not only describe a state of conceptuality but also radically modify that state in the process of its presentation.

Conclusion

Arguably, then, what these plays describe—the relative, nonuniversal nature of conceptuality—has the performative effect of moving the subject (however incipiently) beyond language and reason so essential to Habermas. The gap between the performative and constative aspects of the plays results in aporia, which in turn can lead the actors and audience toward transcendence or a cocreative nonphysical presence. We are definable not only by what we are conceptually (as described by constructivists), but also by what we enact through a shift in consciousness (as described by decontextualists). The combined forces in each of Beckett and Pinter's plays inaugurate an transformation of consciousness, but within a political context. In this sense the perlocutionary force of language and performance further obscures the boundary between art and life. The performative and its meaning are intextricably related to context, and context, like consciousness, contains meaning but does not permit saturation. A similar intersubjective phenomenology applies to fiction, as we will see in the following chapters through the works of Vonnegut, DeLillo, Dick, and Lem.

6

Vonnegut's *Slaughterhouse-Five*: Shell Shock or Hysteria?

Introduction

One phenomenon that powerfully renders self-identity historically contingent—something in process—is war. Combat veterans will tell you that the most important event in their lives is the experience of war, and yet some postmodernists challenge the reality of experience itself. For veterans the sights and sounds of war persist long after the fact in memory, and indeed veterans spend a great deal of time during the rest of their lives trying to cope with these memories. Veterans of World Wars I and II, the Korean, Vietnam, and Gulf wars have consistently reported long-term negative emotional and psychological, not to mention physical and psychosomatic effects, as in the case of the Gulf War syndrome. Due to the influence of television and other forms of mass media that bring images of combat into the shelter of almost every home, even the general public can be adversely affected by the ravages of war. And whether images of violence are real or fictional, as in films or literature, viewers and readers tend to project themselves into the role of the hero or heroine. Through their imaginative identification they absorb into their awareness the stress of experiences they would not otherwise have had and which then becomes part of their memory structure that contributes to the formulation of their self-identity.

In American literature, Stephen Crane's *The Red Badge of Courage*, Ernest Hemingway's *A Farewell to Arms*, and Kurt Vonnegut's *Slaughterhouse-Five* are among the novels that dramatize the horrific stress and absurdity of war and the ways we try to cope with this. Although the negative impact of war on veterans has usually been described in terms of shell shock, new interpretations of historical experience, in particular traumatic experiences such as combat, have been suggested by postmodernists like Elaine Showalter, Fredric Jameson, and Jean Baudrillard.

In her book *Hystories: Hysterical Epidemics and Modern Culture*, Showalter investigates traumatic experiences ranging from repressed memories, Gulf War syndrome, shell shock, multiple personality disorders, and alien abductions. She argues that "The United States has become the hot zone of psychogenic diseases, new and mutating forms of hysteria amplified by modern communications and *fin-de-siècle* anxiety" (1997, 3). She proposes that war veterans often display mutated forms of hysteria by drawing from a current "symptoms pool" related to combat, and do not really suffer from shell shock. But the question is, can a third-person or externalist approach like Showalter's theory of hystories fully account for the first-person experience of war, or of any other phenomenon for that matter, whether experienced directly or in mediated form. Francisco Varela points out that "any science of cognition and mind must, sooner or later, come to grips with the basic condition that we have no idea what the mental or the cognitive could possibly be apart from our own experience of it" (1996, 331). Furthermore, as Shaun Gallagher notes, "Third-person accounts of cognition are themselves produced in instances of first-person cognition" (1996, 207). Nevertheless, for some the validity of phenomenal experience remains problematic.

Jameson asserts that postmodernity has brought about "the waning of our historicity, of our lived possibility of experiencing history in some active way" (1991, 21). He claims that because experience is dead in postmodernity, literature and films dealing with the past can only invoke a sense of "pastness" rather than engage with "real history." He therefore finds an irresolvable "incompatibility of a postmodernist nostalgia and language with genuine history" (1991, 19). Yet in the process of deconstructing nostalgia, Jameson naturalizes a utopian moment of history that was once lived as real experience. He does not fully relinquish what poststructuralism calls the "myth of the given." Baudrillard, in contrast, claims that the proliferation of media in the twentieth century has erased the difference between the real and the simulacrum, or the real and the hyperreal, defined as "the generation by models of a real without origin" (1983, 2). His notion of postmodernism also collapses the distinctions between present, past, and future. In the "era of simulation," he says, "all the great humanist criteria of value, all the values of a civilization of moral, aesthetic, and practical judgment, vanish in our system of images and signs. Everything becomes undecidable" (1983, 128). Simulation replaces the connection between science and myth, reality and illusion, and signs become freefloating and nonreferential. In a world of hyperreality, the real becomes an "hallucinatory resemblance to itself" (1983, 145). But without the possibility of real experience, how would we recognize that we lived in what Baudrillard calls a world of simulation? Through their third-person postmodernist theories, Showalter, Jameson, and Baudrillard question the validity of first-person experience, while at the same time positing a prelapsarian moment, especially Jameson and Baudrillard, in which some experience is real. This ideal moment serves as a standard for assessing the reality of our individual and cultural memory of experience, such as that of war.

If war can affect not only the veteran but also the civilian exposed to real or fictional combat through various mediations, then what is the nature of this experience for the veteran and how does it differ from that of those exposed to combat through the media? If both direct and mediated exposure to war comprises, on a certain sensory level, a kind of first-person experience (and I'm leaving it open whether or not the mediation is fictional), how valid is a third-person explanation or explaining away of that experience? The answer here hinges on the relation between firsthand phenomenological encounters and third-person scientific accounts. It is a relation between phenomenology (which subscribes to the irreducible nature of conscious experience) and cognitive science (which variously tries to assimilate experience with behavior or reduce it to neurobiological mechanisms). In consciousness studies, researchers are increasingly seeing phenomenology and cognitive science as being interdependent rather than contradictory (Gallagher 1996, 195–214). The former can be said to correspond to the self as a given (though not as a fixed conceptual content in a third-person "essentialist" sense), and the latter to the self as social construct. Alvin Goldman, in "Can Science Know When You're Conscious?", answers that cognitive science can rely on first-person verbal reports, that they do "not contravene the constraints of a proper epistemology" (2000, 3). He concludes that "the epistemological credentials of consciousness research cannot be established by trying to put such research on a purely third-person footing; the first-person grasp of consciousness remains fundamental" (21). Through the intersubjective space of Vonnegut's novel, the gap between first and third person experience is narrowed and sometimes bridged. Here the first person I and the third person he, she, or they, by cocreating a nonphysical presence, coarise out of their matrix of relationships into an unmediated we.

Unstuck in Time

Vonnegut's *Slaughterhouse-Five* dramatizes how the memory of war as a phenomenal experience affects human psychology and American culture. Although war seems almost unavoidable in the never-ending conflict between good and evil, Vonnegut highlights the absurdity of war through his narrative of the allied bombing of Dresden, a nonstrategic city, just prior to the end of WW II. Some people may claim that war can revive the human spirit, but evidence of its negative impact remains overwhelming. This impact, moreover, spreads out over space and time to afflict multiple generations through the memory of war and the various mediations of this memory.

In *Slaughterhouse-Five*, Billy Pilgrim, as the Christian of Vonnegut's allegorical "Progress," was like Vonnegut an American soldier in WW II. He spends the rest of his life trying to come to terms with his experience of February 1945 as a prisoner of war in Dresden where he and his fellow prisoners were held in an underground shelter (slaughterhouse number five) when it was firebombed by the allied powers. Billy Pilgrim's quest is told by a third-person narrator, except in chapters 1 and 10 where Vonnegut speaks as the first-person writer/narrator and explains the autobiographical nature of the novel and the difficulties he had in writing it. Vonnegut's narrative voice throughout the novel combines the wise old man of the woods and the posing old codger as found in Mark Twain (F. Karl 346–47) He tells us several times that Billy's experiences are based on his own memories of his months as a POW in Dresden. These mature interruptions in the story of a young man's experience of war has the self-reflexive postmodernist effect of calling into question the nature of reality and revealing how the memory of an experience not only affects the future but is also in turn modified by the future.

After the war Billy has a nervous breakdown, recovers, marries Valencia Merble in 1948 in Ilium, New York, has two children, Robert and Barbara, and becomes a successful optometrist and respected citizen. But unlike his fellow citizens, Billy becomes "unstuck in time" and begins to restructure his life through the device of "time travel." At the blink of an eye he can go from New York in 1965 to a German forest in December 1944, then forward to New York 1958, 1961, and so forth. On his daughter's wedding night in 1967, Billy is kidnapped by a flying saucer and taken to an imaginary planet called Tralfamadore, where he is caged in a zoo and mated with Montana Wildhack, a former movie star from Earth. In 1976 after speaking in Chicago on flying saucers and time, Billy is assassinated by Paul Lazzaro, a soldier he knew during the war who made a pact with another soldier, Roland Weary, to fulfill the latter's mission of killing Billy out of sheer spite and various other neurotic tendencies.

Throughout the novel Vonnegut mixes reality, fiction, and fantasy. For example, while waiting for change at a cash register near a stack of girly magazines, "Billy looked at one out of the corner of his eye, and he saw this question on its cover. *What really became of Montana Wildhack?*" (1966, 204, emphasis in original),[1] Montana being the woman he was mated with on Tralfamadore. Through his time travel Billy tries to reinvent his life as a way of coping with the psychological damage of war, just as Vonnegut tries through his innovative writing style to reinvent the novel as a way of coping with the absurdity of life. After every mention of death, in which the novel abounds, Vonnegut repeats the familiar phrase, "So it goes," which Billy picked up from the Tralfamadorians. When Billy tries to get on television in New York to speak on flying saucers, he goes up "to the studio on an automatic elevator, and there were other people up there, waiting to go in. They were literary critics, and they thought Billy was one, too. They were going to discuss whether the novel was dead or not. So it goes" (205). Rarely does Billy show attachment to the any particular stage in the process of his self-development that would manifest as the fear of death.

Memory

In his treatment of the memory of war, Vonnegut does not express nostalgia by trying to relate a sense of "pastness," as Jameson would say, but rather expresses the memory of a "real history" through a surreal writing style that attempts to render the psychological impact of war, channeling the bizarre "qualia" (or qualities) of a soldier's phenomenal experience. The important thing here is experience itself, not the truth value of that experience. Billy does not evade experience, just as people in postmodern American culture do not evade experience. As Alison Landsberg observes in an analysis of the way memory constitutes self-identity,

> I would like to set this notion of the death of the real—particularly the death of real experience—against what I perceive as a veritable explosion

> of, or popular obsession with, experience of the real. From the hugely attended D-Day reenactments of 1994 to what I would like to call "experimental museums," like the United States Holocaust Memorial Museum, it seems to me that the experiential real is anything but dead. In fact, the popularity of these experiential events bespeaks a popular longing to experience history in a personal and even bodily way. They offer strategies for making history into personal memories. They provide individuals with the collective opportunity of having an experiential relationship to a collective or cultural past they either did or did not experience. (1995, 178)

Landsberg goes on to suggest that in the postmodern relationship to experience what counts is not "categories like the authentic and sympathy" but rather "categories like responsibility and empathy" (178). The former corresponds to a contraction or attachment to a particular stage of self-development based on language and reason, while the latter corresponds to an openness and letting go based on significant feeling. The difference here is between an intersubjectivity of agreement and a true, ontological intersubjectivity.

Prosthetic or artificial memories mediated by aesthetic experience, as in *Slaughterhouse-Five*, contribute to the formulation of individual and collective identity not on the basis of reality as opposed to hyperreality but on the basis of consensus and responsibility. Billy's time travel through which he finds happiness and peace may be a form of senility, but Vonnegut is concerned not so much with authenticity as with the responsibility we have in the production of our cultural identity. The phrase "so it goes" repeated after every mention of death is a rallying cry that rejects the finality of death and the limits of space and time. As if to say better luck next time, it provides the vehicle for restructuring or re-creating our self-identity through a disidentification with lower stages of development. From the Tralfamadorians Billy learns that when people die they only appear to die, that death entails rebirth, that fate is not destructive or unkind. When he first becomes "unstuck in time," Billy "swing[s] grandly through the full arc of his life, passing into death, which was violet light. There wasn't anybody else there, or any thing. There was just violet light—and a hum" (43). Billy here seems to identify with the light and hum of the universe, or in terms of consciousness with the pure witnessing state rather than with conceptual content and its conflicting qualities. Although evil exists, Billy refuses to let it dominate him. He manipulates his memory of the past in such a way as to live in the gaps between evil, in the interstices of light. When he wears an assortment of old cloths and a Cinderella costume as a POW, his clownish image caricatures American power. Evil is trivialized and rendered less effective in overwhelming Billy or the reader sharing his experience.

According to Frederick Karl, Vonnegut makes the mistake of leveling human experience. He argues Vonnegut that oversimplifies by incorporating the stratagems of science fiction into realistic fiction and by collapsing the distinction between wars, as in grouping the Dresden bombing with the "napalming of Vietnam and the atomic destruction of Japan" (1983, 346). But this critique fails to take into account the way postmodernity can level space-time distinctions, as evidenced by the virtual reality of hyperspace where human interactions occur in a nonlocalized, nonphysical intersubjective space. The aesthetic combining of wars may elide certain political differences, but it accentuates the main historical attributes of war: destruction and the loss of human life. To accuse the novel of moral softness for weighing political differences less than humanitarian concerns is also to oversimplify. What Vonnegut gains by his method is a broader perspective on human affairs and the requirements for human survival. His mediation of Billy's memory results in a more comprehensive vision of the possibilities for life.

Identity

Although Billy the optometrist doesn't see the world as it is, he does foresee the future, including his own death. His predictions go unheeded, like Cassandra's, but he nevertheless succeeds in his purpose of reshaping our perception and observation. He places himself and his audience, who in the 1960s were taking a stand against the Vietnam war, in a collective historical perspective by transforming and finally transcending the memory of a war experience. Billy's memory serves as a way of disidentifying rather than identifying with the past. His transformation offers a way of altering our cultural identity by unlocking the secrets of our self-identity, namely the fact that self-development hinges on nonattachment to conceptual boundaries. Billy glimpses this potential when he acts strange inexplicably in the presence of Valencia and Kilgore Trout. "He had supposed for years that he had no secrets from himself. Here was proof that he had a great big secret somewhere inside, and he could not imagine what it was" (173). This secret, I would argue, concerns not only the ability to see the past and future, as Kilgore Trout imagines, though this would be remarkable in itself. Rather it concerns mainly an experience beyond time altogether, and thus beyond even the change of collective social identity suggested by the novel.

Changes in memory are primarily changes is mental content and as such only affect cultural identity or the contingent self. It does not completely free us from historical circumstances, but it does contribute to this freedom. As Landsberg says,

> The particular desire to place oneself in history through a narrative of memories is a desire to be a social, historical being. We might say that it is precisely such a "surface" experience of history which gives people personhood, which brings them into the public. What the drive to remember expresses, then, is a pressing desire to reexperience history—not to unquestioningly validate the past, but to put into play the vital, indigestible material of history, reminding us of the uninevitability of the present tense. (1995, 187)

If memory can be modified in such a way that not only the individual and collective subject but also the present tense is uninevitable, then what is to prevent this deconstruction of identity and time from leading to a more radical transformation, namely to a transcendence of identity and time altogether. If historical memory can be altered to the extent of being virtually eliminated, then what would not be uninevitable for the individual subject or for the intersubject? The experience of the violet light Billy has while "unstuck in time" plays a key role in suggesting the possibility of such a radical transformation. This vision of light suggests that there is something more basic than even memory, such as pure experience itself. Light symbolizes the possibility of awareness without content, a state of pure being that underlies the various uninevitable constructs of human culture and history. In a sense postmodernists like Showalter, Jameson, and Baudrillard are right in questioning the contents of our experience. Their skepticism stems from the arbitrary quality of these contents or "qualia," which are ephemeral and basically unreal compared to the fact of consciousness itself.

For obvious reasons the experience of war, as Vonnegut shows, has the effect of shaking up or unsettling memory and thereby driving the individual toward an experience of the interstices of light, or the flashes of being underlying the social construction of the self. The fact that awareness has the habit of assuming various disguises through its association with memory—the memory of thoughts, emotions, perceptions, sensations, moods, etc.—whether lived through or mediated, fictional or real, accounts for the difficulty we have in appreciating the self-sufficiency of conscious experience itself at the basis of all space, time, and cultural identities. Vonnegut's autobiographical remarks in the novel serve as a "frame-breaking" strategy that helps us glimpse through the "irresolvable counter-stories" (Hite 1991, 704) of textual phenomena toward an ontological experience—both individual and collective. But Vonnegut offers no satisfying or revelatory conclusion, which would constitute just another form of memory in all of its uninevitability. Unless of course it was the memory of pure consciousness itself, "the given" intuited by the contingent self and toward which it moves.

CONCLUSION

Postmodernists such as Jameson and Baudrillard have difficulty with the given. Jameson argues that the postmodernist paradigm through which the boundaries between high art and popular culture have been eroded results in the defusion of the subversive possibilities of "high" modernist culture, such as those summoned for the reader in moments of epiphany or the interstices of light. From this perspective, Jameson negates the ability of fiction, particularly science-fiction utopias, to revitalize society. As the expressions of a culture's "political unconscious," these utopias merely register "fantasies about the future" based on the negative experience of the present ("Progress versus utopia" 150; qtd. by Wolmark 1994, 10). Their role is "to demonstrate and to dramatise our incapacity to imagine the future" (153; qtd. by Wolmark, 10). From a different perspective, Teresa de Lauretis notes that "The science fictional construction of a possible world," such as Vonnegut's Tralfamadore, "entails a conceptual reorganization of semantic space and therefore of material and social relations, and makes for an expanded cognitive horizon, an epic vision of our present social reality" (1980, 170). But this "expanded cognitive horizon" has to be understood in terms of the experience of the self as pure consciousness, which Billy points to in the gap between memories.

For Baudrillard, hyperreality allegedly means "the end of metaphysics" (1983, 167), the end of fantasy, the end of SF, but his theory of simulation only confirms what Advaita Vedanta considers to be the ordinary state of affairs: namely, that all reality is an intellectual phenomenon, that this reality extends from the most concrete and finite to the most abstract and infinite, and that the truth value of human experience is structured by the perceiving consciousness. Jenny Wolmark notes that, when confronted with the noise of simulation, "the only oppositional response that is possible takes the form of silence" (1994, 13). Silence, however, need not be understood as inertia, as it tends to be in the Western episteme; it also connotes the unitary self as a transcendental given. This self always waits beyond the noise of rationality in another universe, such as those imagined in literature even from within the boundaries of postmodernism.

Brian McHale says that "What is distinctive of postmodernism is not the fact of 'contamination' of high culture by mass culture but rather the technologically-enhanced speed of the traffic in models between the high and low strata of culture" (1992, 227). But this ever-tighter feedback loop, rather than collapsing hierarchical distinctions as McHale claims, indicates the tendency of consciousness to shift between the concrete, popular images of historical time and the more abstract, aesthetic images of "the time of the now." This shift takes us from the exterior, expressed domain of individual and collective experience to the deep interior of the self and a true intersubjectivity. With all its contradictions, indeed because of these contradictions, Vonnegut's novel creates a ground for the awareness to move between binary opposites with ever-increasing oscillation. The awareness lingers in the gap between conceptual poles, the interstices of light, relishing its freedom from space, time, and discursive logic even while within culture as an intersubjective space. In *White Noise*, DeLillo extends this integration of time and timelessness even further, showing how it pervades the very fiber of American culture.

7

DeLillo's *White Noise*: The Aesthetics of Cyberspace

Introduction

Because memory contributes to our self-identity, the subject is typically mistaken for an historical construct. Recent theory has posed two basic questions about identity: 1) Do we experience the self as something given or something made?; 2) should we think of the self in individual or in social terms? From the perspective I am proposing in this book, the answer is both: The self is something given *and* something made, individual and collective. But the given aspect of the self, while inner and prior of activity, is not given in the sense of a conceptual construct, of an intentional object we can have knowledge-about or knowledge-by-acquaintance. Rather it is given as pure awareness that is available only through knowledge-by-identity, but which is always there underlying all mental activity. The self is also something made in the sense of the individual undergoing a process of historical development, of mental purification, of cleansing the psyche of the residue of accumulated experiences. Western and especially Eastern psychology have traced the intermediate stages of development leading toward a unity, which in its completion they describe in various terms: self-actualization, transcendence, autonomy, ultimate, absolute, Brahman-Atman, Nirvana, transpersonal, and spirit (Wilber 1996a, 207–13). Because this evolution occurs within a cultural context, the self can be conceived of both individually and socially. The historical context of self-development integrates the individual and the collective, with social forces either enhancing or retarding the individual's and thus society's development, society being of course a collective of individuals. According to Don DeLillo, postmodernity as an historical condition enhances self-development both socially and individually.

Perhaps the most obvious thing we can say about history is that it is always repeating itself. In "Theses on the Philosophy of History," Walter Benjamin asserts that when one "grasps the constellation which his own era has formed with a definite earlier one," one "establishes a conception of the present as 'the time of the now' which is shot through with chips of Messianic time" (1969a, 263). This time of the now as the eternal present is a form of no time, which implies that even as an historical construct the self has a timeless dimension. Just as life and art, as we have seen in our discussion of drama, form a spiral instead of a timeless circle, so history and no time form a spiraling pattern responsive to the forces of each.

Frank Lentricchia, in "Tales of the Electronic Tribe," suggests that in America, postmodernism was not invented in the twentieth century but came over in the seventeenth century with the Europeans pilgrims on the *Mayflower*. Lentricchia is referring to Don DeLillo's first novel, *Americana* (1971), in which DeLillo cleverly anticipates the current controversies over the notion of postmodernism by saying that television actually arrived in America with the pilgrims in 1620. Television (closely followed by the computer) is the quintessential electronic medium of postmodernism. In watching television, the viewer resembles the Europeans on the *Mayflower* by dreaming of a new self, a fantasy self under the stimulus of Hollywood and Madison Avenue, just as the pilgrims in the seventeenth century dreamt of a new self in a new world (Lentricchia 1991, 88–89). In Lentricchia's words, "Sitting in front of TV is like a perpetual Atlantic crossing—the desire for and the discovery of America constantly reenacted in our move from first-person consciousness to third: from the self we are, but would like to leave behind, to the self we would become" (88). The new self and the new world built around it do not occupy a geographic so much as an imagined space, or in a virtual sense cyberspace. Cyberspace is closely linked to "the time of the now," which in a sense is beyond space-time altogether like de Quincey's meaning of true intersubjectivity. As suggested in chapter 2, cyberspace and virtual reality may be the ultimate nonplace. As we transit cyberspace, our consciousness may expand toward a glimpse of the universal knowledge-by-identity associated with Gnosticism. This quasi-space or hyperspace is the site of DeLillo's novel *White Noise* (1985), in which the consciousness of the characters and reader expands beyond historical boundaries. DeLillo suggests the possibility of becoming a new self (something made) through a collective process of transformation. But this process, rather than turning back to the past, evolves beyond the fragmentation associated with postmodernity toward the discovery of an ultimate oneness that is always there (something given).

White Noise is the story of Jack Gladney, a professor of Hitler Studies, his friend and colleague Murray Jay Siskind, and his wife, Babette, and their several kids, mostly from earlier marriages. The novel is divided into three parts: "Waves and Radiation," "The Airborne Toxic Event," and "Dylarama." But in terms of space-time, the novel has two dimensions. One is that of ordinary space-time through which the story unfolds: Jack Gladney and Murray Jay Siskind, the novel's agent of mystery and noise, theorize about American popular culture; the Gladneys attempt to escape the potential disaster of an "airborne toxic event," to which Jack is exposed; Babette, Jack's wife, tries to hide her fear of dying, which leads to her using the drug Dylar and having an affair with her supplier, Willy Mink or Mr. Gray; and finally Jack attempts to kill Mink as an act of revenge. The other more radical dimension of the novel is that of cyberspace; in this"time of the now," "the environment-as-electronic-medium" (Lentricchia 1991, 89) alters the consciousness of the postmodern community from an exterior to a radically interior direction in search for self-identity. Despite the apparent loss of unity and coherence in the postmodern self (Silverman 1983, 126–93), DeLillo's novel suggests how in a virtual community individual and collective self-identity can be seen as whole or integrated. The characters in this virtual community experience their subjectivity expand through social forces beyond the duality of subject and object, presence and absence, no time and history. DeLillo thereby depicts an experience that, although within historical time, borders on a Gnostic illumination of "the time of the now."

White Noise and the Real

In *White Noise*, reality and self-identity for the characters hinge on the images of media representation, primarily by TV but also by other forms of information technology. Nothing has meaning or value for the Gladneys or Siskind unless the media conveys it to them as information. This information can be understood either as simulacra, images simulating a reality that as an ordinary referent no longer exists (Baudrillard 1988a, 170), or as representations of a reality that still exists but is ordinarily inaccessible (Hutcheon 1989, 33–61). In DeLillo's novel individual experience counts for less than public information, and through television and other media the collective perception of this information enters (and in a way constitutes) social consciousness. This social consciousness, based on information, would constitute an interobjectivity, as opposed to the intersubjectivity of a cultural consciousness that includes a cocreative, ontological presence. The media image of a daily experience can be said to render this experience "extra-daily" by elevating the consciousness of the experiencer from the individual to the collective. Not only do media images provide the individual with vast stores of information not available through firsthand experience, they also suggest that something exists beyond the space-time limits of information—the realm of true intersubjectivity. In certain traditions, such as in Gnosticism and Neoplatonism, the ideal has been for the information or knowledge of everything to be grasped instantaneously. This feat is particularly relevant to current issues of artificial intelligence and memory. Computer representations, for instance, can lodge almost unlimited data in artificial memory structures that simulate the multilayered onion of the universe, a feat often attempted in the history of hermeticism through magical alphabets and encrypted texts. To instantaneously cognize an encyclopedic memory structure would be to access the living logos.

Through the instantaneity of knowledge, even in a postmodern era skeptical of wholeness, one may be able to unite with the cosmos at its most fundamental dimension from which space-time emerges. In the history of artificial memory, as Erik Davis points out, "erudite Hermeticism" is "a more elevated Gnostic philosophy that emphasized the ability of humanity to discover within itself the mystical knowledge of god and cosmos" (1994, 32). DeLillo portrays the construction of a similar self-identity through the (epistemological) link between consciousness, postmodern culture, and information about the universe as aspired to through electronic media. As *White Noise* suggests, awareness expands through the instantaneous knowledge of information, regardless of whether this information is considered simulacral or representational.

In chapter 3, Jack and Murray take a trip from their College-on-the-Hill to visit a barn in the nearby countryside. The barn is ordinary, but also a major tourist attraction known as "THE MOST PHOTOGRAPHED BARN IN AMERICA" (1986, 12).[1] Before reaching the site they see several signs pointing the way, and once there they find groups of photographers taking pictures of the barn and a man in a booth selling postcards and slides. In discussing this phenomenon,

Murray makes a series of observations typical of the novel's theoretical dialogue:

> No one sees the barn. . . . Once you've seen the signs about the barn, it becomes impossible to see the barn. . . . We're not here to capture an image, we're here to maintain one. Every photograph reinforces the aura. Can you feel it, Jack? An accumulation of *nameless energies*. . . . Being here is a kind of *spiritual surrender*. We see only what the others see. . . . We've agreed to be part of a *collective perception*. This literally colors our vision. A *religious experience* in a way, like all tourism. (12; emphasis added)

Murray highlights the "accumulation of nameless energies" of a community engaged in "a kind of spiritual surrender." This spiritual energy gives rise to a virtual reality, which in the process of rendering absent the barn as a referent nonetheless points to and even creates another kind of presence: the virtual presence of an intersubjective space created by an aura of electronic images. The presence constituted by the "hyperreality" of these images is of an entire culture (Baudrillard 1988a 166–67).

Hyperreal Aura

In the debate over the impact of virtual reality and cyberspace on the nature of self-identity and community existence, some critics argue that cyberspace can be projected as a utopian vision, or as William Gibson puts it in *Neuromancer*, a "consensual hallucination" (1984, 51). Others argue that we still live in a real physical world with all its political and social pressures and that no alternative utopian world of cyberspace actually exists. Kevin Robins, in "Cyberspace and the World we Live In," asserts that "Virtual communities do not exist in a different world" (1995, 146). He critiques cyberspace as a utopian space, noting that "the mythology of cyberspace is preferred over its sociology," and arguing "that it is time to relocate virtual culture in the real world (the real world that virtual culturalists, seduced by their own metaphors, pronounce dead or dying)" (1995, 153). The conflict of discourses on virtual reality and cyberspace converges on the crisis of self-identity in the postmodern condition. While romantic and modernist notions of a coherent and unified subject have been challenged by postmodernists, the electronic community of virtual reality seems to counteract the alienation and fragmentation experienced in the "real" (postmodern) world with what Howard Rheingold calls "shared consciousness" and the experience of "groupmind" (1994, 245, 110). This viewpoint supports my interpretation of the self in *White Noise* as integrating the given and made, individual and social, material and nonmaterial.

As Lentricchia points out, Murray's use of the term *aura* in *White Noise* differs from that of Walter Benjamin by implying a new kind of community based on a "groupmind" or a "shared consciousness," in other words an intersubjectivity. In his famous essay "The Work of Art in the Age of Mechanical Reproduction," Benjamin shows how photography, and for that matter all electronic means of aesthetic representation, has resulted in the decline of aura defined as the intimacy of community experience traditionally associated with being in the presence of great works of art (1969b, 222–26). The mechanical reproduction of art makes copies of original works available to the masses, but at the cost of tradition and a shared sense of history. But is everything necessarily lost with the original copy? As Lentricchia writes:

> Benjamin's deadly camera which returns no human gaze may be the mediator of a new kind of community, wherein all distinctive selfhood is extinguished in a new art form whose mass cultural presence glows at postmodernism's holy place, the site of the most photographed barn. DeLillo's point, unlike Benjamin's, is not the nostalgic one that aura is in decline, but that its source has been replaced. The question he poses in all but words is, What strange new form of human collectivity is born in the postmodern moment of aura, and at what price? (1991, 92)

From a certain perspective, the price may not be as high as it seems. DeLillo certainly satirizes the excesses of American media and materialism through his mocking enumerations of the images of popular culture, as in the novel's brilliant opening passage and the series of discourses between Jack Gladney and Murray Jay Siskind on television, supermarkets, and advertising. The media representation of coded messages, as Murray says, are repeated like chants or mantras: "Coke is it, Coke is it, Coke is it" (51). "Mastercard, Visa, American Express" (100); and "Toyota Celica" (155), which Steffie, one of Jack's daughters, even says in her sleep. But these images—while they seemingly cover up, substitute for, interpret, or simulate reality—serve also to reveal something hidden. In a sense, the postmodern environment-as-electronic-medium is anticipated by the attempt in Gnosticism, as Erik Davis notes, "to the represent the unmediated presence of the Gnostic mind" through the complexity of encoded messages (1994, 50). As Jack puts it, "Whatever its source, . . . [Steffie's] utterance struck me with the impact of a moment of splendid transcendence" (155). Like the allegories of Gnosticism, cyberspace consists of a myriad phantasmagoric, metamorphic images that can alter one's state of mind by "generat[ing] psychedelic perceptions with a minimum of sensory cues" (Davis 1994, 40) and ultimately expanding individual and collective consciousness toward oneness.

The opposition between a real and unreal community begins to blur. In the simulational culture of our second media age, as Mark Foster explains, "The mediation has become so intense that the things mediated can no longer even pretend to be unaffected" (1995, 84). With fluid realities, our identities also become fluid. Howard Rheingold foresees tremendous cultural changes through electronic media: "We reduce and encode our identities as words on a screen, decode and unpack the identities of others" (1994, 61). The disappearance of traditional communities around the world has resulted in a hunger for shared experience. The loss of familiar presuppositions and the dissolution of stable identities (conceptually defined) have impelled the individual toward a kind of presuppositionless state of conscious experience—or a virtual phenomenology that underlies a nonphysical subject-to-subject presence.

The Radiance of Dailiness

As DeLillo in an interview said regarding the shared experience of supermarkets and other aspects of suburban existence, "In *White Noise*, in particular, I tried to find a kind of radiance in dailiness. Sometimes this radiance can be almost frightening. Other times it can be almost holy or sacred. Is it really there? Well, yes" (DeCurtis 1991, 63). When Murray meets the Gladneys shopping in a supermarket, one of the most commonly frequented nonplaces, he remarks,

> Everything is concealed in symbolism, hidden by veils of mystery and layers of cultural material. But it is psychic data, absolutely. The large doors slide open, they close unbidden. Energy waves, incident radiation. . . . It is just a question of deciphering, rearranging, peeling off the layers of unspeakability. Not that we want to. . . . This is not Tibet. Even Tibet is not Tibet anymore. (37–38)

He later adds, "This place is sealed off, self-contained. It is timeless. Another reason why I think of Tibet" (38). Although Murray and not the author is speaking here, DeLillo says "there is something there that we miss . . . a sense of something extraordinary hovering just beyond our touch and just beyond our vision" (DeCurtis 1991, 63) Throughout the novel, images are invested with the sense of transcendence, which for DeLillo is associated with the fear of death lurking beneath our perceptions. Death of course can be understood as a figure for transcendence, of going beyond cultural presuppositions and the limits of space, time, and causality. Like the nonplaces of virtual reality and artificial memory, it has no place, being outside of sensory experience. Death and transcendence, emptiness and fullness, and the fullness of emptiness—all describe the experience of cyberspace. Yet as Robins suggests, virtual reality is not cut off from the real world of culture and physical bodies, just as consciousness is not cut off from the phenomenal world. Rather cyberspace includes the mental components of language and reason, but the shared meaning as de Quincey would say is not achieved by linguistic tokens but by the accompanying (virtual) interior-to-interior participatory presence—by true intersubjectivity (2000, 188).

Our encounters with cyberspace, a medium though which we can access information almost instantaneously, opens our awareness to the smallest time and distance scales of the physical universe, bordering on an unmanifest realm that quantum physics calls the Planck Scale, the vacuum state, or the unified field (Hagelin 1987, 56–57; Penrose 1997, 3–4). This virtual dimension is described by physicists such as Nick Herbert, John Hagelin, Fritjof Capra, Roger Penrose, and others as being analogous (if not linked) to human consciousness. Penrose, as discussed in chapter 1, speculates that consciousness is not just an epiphenomenon, something that happens as a result of other things that are functional, and "not just the sum of the parts, but some sort of global capacity which allows us to take into account the whole of a situation at once" (1993, 20). In developing a theory of consciousness, he says, "we need to look for large-scale states whose wave functions collapse spontaneously" (1993, 21). That is, we need to develop a theory that can account for how consciousness seems to oscillate between the unboundedness of large-scale states of awareness on the one hand and the boundaries of particular thoughts on the other, between the manifest wave functions of specific data and the perfect orderliness and symmetry of all knowledge beyond the Planck Scale—the infinite information of the cosmos.

Penrose as we have seen proposes that the physical world, the mental world, and the Platonic world (specifically the world of mathematical concepts that describe things "out there") are interconnected. "The more we understand about the physical world, and the deeper we probe into the laws of nature, the more it seems as though the physical world almost evaporates and we are left only with mathematics" (1997, 3). He goes on to say that there is "the common feeling that these mathematical concepts are products of our mentality" (1997, 96). Apparently separate on the surface, the physical and mental worlds seem to share a common basis.

Similarly, recall, in Shankara's Advaita (nondual) Vedanta, the changing visible world is a mere illusion (like Baudrillard's notion of simulation), and Brahman as the nondual, never-changing absolute is the one reality. As Deutsch explains, "The Self is One, it is not different from Brahman . . . [this] means that man is essentially spiritual; that in the most profound dimension of his being he is no longer the 'individual' that he ordinarily takes himself to be, but that he is precisely reality itself" (1973, 65). Postmodernists share the view that the subject is linked to information about the universe and that the unity of subject and information comprises reality, but they associate this link with conceptual knowledge-by-acquaintance. As portrayed in *White Noise*, however, this link extends toward the underlying reality of knowledge-by-identity in pure consciousness, which we can share through intersubjective participation. The title of the novel itself alludes to the underlying informational white noise of the universe, the hum of its "energy waves and incident radiation" described by Murray.

Postmodernists of course define the subject in terms of difference, absence and multiplicity, which for Vedanta describes only the lower level of reality. The subject as a cultural construct dispersed along a chain of signifiers (Silverman 1983, 149–93) constitutes an unreal image. Jack, who cannot speak German, is the simulacrum of a professor of Hitler Studies who wears dark glasses and a gown at the College-on-the-Hill, but who is unrecognizable to a colleague who sees him in the mall without his mask. "You look so harmless, Jack. A big, harmless, aging, indistinct sort of guy" (83). So who then is Jack? Does he have a real or only a simulated self? In terms of cybernetics, the global information systems that exist at the basis of artificial intelligence and memory and that extend over all space and time, also exist at the basis of the human subject. Even the postmodernist subject is linked to these systems with access to a global or unified reality through direct experience—although deconstructionists in theory deny this. DeLillo's novel explores this link between the postmodernist self and global systems. Through its saturation by a multiplicity of media voices, the postmodernist self goes beyond the finite game of logocentrism and becomes open to "the possibility of an infinitely changing array of rules" through which "the game of human existence finds greatest promise" (Gergen 1991, 198). But what is the nature of this promise and how does it relate to postmodernist self-identity?

THE PHENOMENOLOGY OF INFORMATION

To answer this question we need to define information in both physical and phenomenal (or mental) terms, since information underlies all technologies responsible for the saturated self. The white noise of DeLillo's novel is the noise of technology: "CABLE HEALTH, CABLE WEATHER, CABLE NEWS, CABLE NATURE" (231)—or cable information. As David Chalmers notes, "The most basic sort of information is the *bit*, which represents a choice between two possibilities: a single bit (0 or 1) selected from a two-state space is said to carry information" (1996, 278). Information spaces, he continues, "are *abstract* spaces, and information states are abstract states. They are not part of the concrete physical or phenomenal world. But we can find information in both the physical and the phenomenal world" (1996, 280).[2]

Physicists sometimes suggest that information is fundamental to the physical universe, as in the proposed "it from bit" idea (Chalmers 1996, 302). The bits of information that constitute the "it" of the universe in this theory, however, do not have any properties or substance, but rather exist in a state of pure informational flux. Even the space-time framework of the universe seems to consist only of "relations among information spaces," a possibility that leads Chalmers to speculate that "the world is simply a world of primitive differences, and of causal and dynamic relations among those differences" (1996, 303). The main problem found with this view of information is that it does not seem to account for consciousness, which as a global phenomenal state is not exhausted by the binary spaces of information bits. Some suggest that information space has a further intrinsic property, for as Chalmers puts it, "If physics is pure information, there will be nothing to distinguish instantiations of the two information spaces" (1996, 304)—that is, 1 and 0. There must be something beyond information, which Chalmers identifies as the phenomenal properties of human consciousness: "Perhaps, then, the intrinsic nature required to ground the information states is closely related to the intrinsic nature present in phenomenology. Perhaps one is even constitutive of the other" (304–5). Chalmers recognizes that the claim that information spaces are somehow grounded in phenomenal or protophenomenal properties is a kind of "outrageous" panpsychism, but he also notes that from a scientific perspective "panpsychism is not as unreasonable as commonly supposed" (305). As we saw in chapter 4, de Quincey connects panpsychism with true intersubjectivity. Because in panpsychism interiority as an ontological type goes all the way down to the atomic and subatomic levels (2000, 199), it characterizes direct subject-to-(other)subject, I-to-(other)I communication—unmediated by the exterior quadrants of "it."

The relation between information and consciousness is analogous to that between third-person accounts of experience and first-person experience itself. As Francisco Varela, Alvin Goldman, and others have argued, third-person explanations, as in cognitive science, and first-person experience, as in phenomenology, are mutually interdependent. In *White Noise,* the consciousness of the characters is not only embedded in the physical and social world, but also in the virtual reality of cyberspace. While driving his son Heinrich to school, Jack questions his denying the physical evidence of raindrops on the windshild, which Heinrich says can't be real because the radio said, "It's going to rain tonight" (22), a report most people would tend to believe. Similarly, during the airborne toxic event the Gladneys monitor the symptoms of exposure to the toxin reported on television, and their experienced symptoms change contradictorily as the reports are modified. As these examples demonstrate, virtual evidence like sensory evidence is not always accurate. Yet information shifting between the physical and virtual has the cumulative effect of shifting our attention from the local to the nonlocal, the individual to the collective. To extend our analogy, third-person accounts can describe the local and finite (bits of information), but only phenomenal first-person experience (consciousness) can directly access the nonlocal and infinite (the wholeness of information). The tendency to move beyond the sensory realm of subject-object duality—as toward a connectedness between the Platonic, physical, and mental worlds described by Penrose, or the connectedness of history and no time—is suggested by DeLillo's characters' engagement with virtuality, and also induced in his readers by the text. Life and art, no time and history, consciousness and information form a spiraling pattern.

In terms of the relation between information spaces and phenomenal properties, it is arguable that the difference that makes the difference in our knowledge about the cosmos is that between mind and consciousness, between the ordinary waking state, which is finite and characterized by mental content, and pure consciousness, which is infinite and characterized by no mental content whatsoever. It is the difference between the self in historical time and the self in "the time of the now," which is bound-less and eternally present—the (fantasy) self sought after in a hyperreal by the pilgrims and viewers of television. The direct experience of awareness by awareness, the ultimate phenomenal mode, constitutes the basis for distinguishing between two information spaces, which from a third-person perspective may appear indistinguishable. Ironically, however, this experience allows one not only to distinguish but also to transcend differences—just as the transverbal and transpersonal states described by Wilber go beyond the verbal and personal rather than regressing to predifferentiated states (1996, 70). Indeed, some physicists believe that the metaphysics of pure information and pure consciousness are interconnected (Chalmers 1996, 276–310). Arguably, then, this pure phenomenal or protophenomenal state—sought after by pilgrims, Gnostics, and postmodern viewers of TV—underlies the difference that makes the difference in the intersubjective transmission of social voices and their interpreted meaning. Deconstructive *différance* also depends on phenomenal consciousness to distinguish binary opposites, whether bits 0 and 1, or signifier and signified. Poststructuralists never-endingly attempt to undermine binary hierarchies, but differences always remain as posited by the conscious mind, until consciousness transcends them.

If properties in the informational flux of the universe can be distinguished only by conscious experience, and if becoming saturated by a multiplicity of voices through the informational flux of electronic media can decrease the conceptual boundaries of that experience (as suggested by Marc Augé and Homi Bhabha), then the resulting postmodernist consciousness has definite affinities with Gnostic consciousness in the West and pure consciousness in the East.[3] The issue of hyperreality now appears in a different light. As John Frow observes, "The world of *White Noise* is a world of primary representations which neither precede nor follow the real but are themselves real—although it is true that they always have the appearance both of preceding another reality (as a model to be followed) and of following it (as copy). But this appearance must itself be taken seriously" (1991, 183). He adds that although we can distinguish between realities, between literal and metaphorical language, between "real moments and TV moments," and between their ironical gaps, "this distinguishing and this irony are insecure" (183). That is, they are both real only insofar as reality is constituted by the observing consciousness[4]—without which no distinctions would be possible. Notwithstanding their differences, then, postmodernism, cognitive science, and Vedanta all suggest a vital link between reality and consciousness.

Systems Theory

As a systems novelist who sees the interconnection of everything, DeLillo converts the waste of American popular culture, such as cable nature (as opposed to living systems), into an artform, or what Tom LeClair calls an "ironic modern sculpture" (1987, 212). This artform, of which *White Noise* is an example, warns us against the entropy of thermodynamic and informational systems, as represented by the toxic cloud that threatens the Gladneys and the computers they depend on to check their bank balance and their state of health, but over which they have no control. Entropy is also symbolized by the Gladneys' trash compactor, which makes "a dreadful wrenching sound, full of eerie feeling" (33). According to the second law of thermodynamics, as Paul Davies explains, entropy is "a sort of gradual but inexorable descent into chaos. Examples of the second law are found everywhere: buildings fall down, people grow old, mountains and shorelines are eroded, natural resources are depleted" (1983, 10). Entropy, of course, leads to death, and ultimately to what some physicists call "the 'heat death' of the universe" (Davies 1983, 11). The Gladneys' fear of death makes them victims to what LeClair refers to as a "self-inflicted double bind" (1987, 213). Because they fear death they try to transcend it, but their evasive tactics ironically bring them even closer to death. When Jack, following Murray's immoral advice, tries to become a "killer" rather than be a "dier" by murdering Babette's Dylar supplier, he instead gets shot himself. Jack repeatedly tries to escape his personal fears through various strategies (see LeClair 1987, 207–35). In Part One, "Waves and Radiation," he takes shelter in the authority and power of Hitler Studies, yet by Part Three, "Dylarama," his tactics lead him back to himself and he longs for disaster: "supreme destruction, a night that swallows existence so completely that I am cured of my own lonely dying" (273). Throughout the novel the Gladneys' fear of death overlaps with their attempt to evade uncertainties.

In trying to understand nature, "the nature and being of real things" (234), the Gladneys must deal with uncertainty, or the mystery of informational systems that for Murray Jay Siskind is spiritually regenerating. This mystery hinges on the relation between entropy and its opposite, negentropy—symbolically death and life respectively, two apparent opposites that, like information and consciousness, seem to have a common basis. When Murray says, "Everything is concealed in symbolism . . . it is psychic data" (37), he hints at a link between mind and matter that I've been discussing. The concept of mortality and our defenses against it belong to a closed system, a spatial, social, and psychological metanarrative that takes the phenomenal world to consist of separate and distinct entities. Systems theory rejects this closure by studying "the abstract organization of phenomena, independent of their substance, type, or spatial or temporal scale of existence. It investigates both the principles common to all complex entities and the models . . . used to describe them.. . . [and it] focuses on the arrangement of and relation among the parts that connect them into a whole" (Audi 1995, 784–85). In exploring part/whole relationships, systems theory parallels Wilber's four-quadrant model of the world, including individuals, as discussed in chapter 4. Just as in Wilber's model each quadrant and its component wholes are simultaneously part of larger wholes (namely the other quadrants), so in systems theory each whole entity is part of a larger whole. The whole individual subject is part of the objective, interobjective, and intersubjective realms. If as panpsychism says interiority goes all the way down in each realm, then the fear of death as extinction is unwarranted.

The Gladneys define living systems and the world in general in terms of closed structures and the logic of either/or, which they hope will protect them against the fear of death and incoherence. "My life," Babette says, "is either/or" (53). The attempt to evade uncertainty, like the Gladneys do, is described in Gregory Bateson's book *Mind and Nature*, which as LeClair has pointed out is central to DeLillo's use of systems theory. As Bateson says of the phobia experienced in contemporary life, "a breach in the apparent coherence of our mental logical process would seem to be a sort of death" (1980, 140). This quasi incoherence stems in part from the apparent contradiction in the logic of *both/and*—as in both mortality and immortality, local information, and unbounded consciousness. The Gladneys' failure to accept a *both/and* logic beyond the rational mind and the ostensibly incoherent compels them to be self-destructive.

The difference between the *either/or* and *both/and* logic of systems theory can be understood in terms of the difference between Newtonian and quantum physics. As LeClair puts it:

> What the Gladneys refuse to accept and what forms the basis for DeLillo's understanding of systemic fact and value is the loop: the simultaneity of living and dying, the inherent reciprocity of circular causality that makes certainty impossible. Their refusal is rooted in mechanistic science, that extension of common-sense empiricism which defines the world as a collection of entities, a heap of things like the Gladney's compacted trash, rather than a system of energy and information. (1987, 226)

Jack's search for "the nature and being of real *things*" (italics added) already illustrates what LeClair calls his "epistemological error" (1987, 226). As quantum physics and the phenomenology of information tell us, and as DeLillo shows through his systems-influenced portrayal of uncertainty, things as such don't really exist; everything consists of waves and radiations and informational bits. As Nick Herbert puts it, "Everything in the world is pure quantumstuff, a physical union of particle and wave" (1985, 64). This quanturnstuff is not an either/or situation, and is therefore inaccessible to third-person, empirical observation, as indicated by Heisenberg's uncertainty principle.[5] From the perspective of the finite intellect and third-person computational reports, uncertainty seems to dominate. But once phenomenal awareness reaches the wholism of systemic openness, where consciousness and information unite, then the question of certainty becomes irrelevant; being is no longer experienced as a *thing* but as a coexistence of opposites.

The fear of death and uncertainty is "natural" only in a separate self-sense where the intellect is cut off from pure consciousness, experiencing life and death as being separate and strange instead of interconnected and familiar. Murray tries to explain the Gradneys' fear of the uncertainties of life and death as the result of expanding diversity: "The more we learn, the more it grows. Is this some law of physics? Every advance in knowledge and technique is matched by a new kind of death, a new strain. Death adapts, like a viral agent. Is it a law of nature?" (150). Analyzing the parts of this expanding field, the particles or waves, culminates in the uncertainty principle, but contemplating the underlying whole can result in an experience of the "almost holy or sacred" (DeCurtis 1991, 63). As an instantaneous cognition within "the time of the now" (God, Buddha, or atman), this "sacred" experience is evoked in *White Noise* through the historical force of electronic images, the aura of that instills in Jack a "moment of splendid transcendence" (*WN* 155).

DeLillo alludes to the Tibetan and Egyptian Books of the Dead and to the Mexican Day of the Dead in *White Noise*, which he originally gave the working title "The American Book of the Dead." Throughout the novel he portrays our experience of the supermarket, television, and other aspects of popular culture as preparing us for the openness of the invisible as symbolized by death. In this way he resembles Augé for whom nonplaces like the supermarket disburden awareness of the personality as in a kind of death. The experience of the supermarket may not directly prepare us for death like the Tibetan Book of the Dead, but it does, as LeClair observes, "offer a communal experience of the invisible, a sense of the mysteriousness that implies that neither life nor death has been settled, closed" (1991, 228). Through a systems-theory approach to what is natural, DeLillo depicts the inteconnectedness of all entities, whether living or inert, on a protophenomenal level. Uncertainty and mystery express an initial reaction to an unfamiliar openness to all possibilities. Once accepted, a systems reaction can lead to what Morris Berman calls a "reenchantment of the world" (1984 passim).

The fear of death experienced by the Gladneys' can also be explained in terms of the fear of losing the comfort and security of an existing stage of self-development in the process of evolving to a higher, more integrated stage. As Wilber explains in *The Atman Project*, where he integrates the psychology of East and West, conventional and contemplative,

> each stage or level or growth seeks absolute Unity, but in ways or under constraints that necessarily prevent it and allow only compromises: substitute unities and substitute gratifications. The more primitive the level, the more primitive the substitute unity. Each successive stage achieves a higher-order unity, and this continues until there is only Unity. The Atman project continues until there is *only* Atman [pure consciousness]. (1996a, 118; Wilber's emphasis)

The Gladneys' have reached a level of unity represented by a closed system that for them becomes a substitute unity. Jack's compromise for atman as the ultimate unity is being chair of the department of Hitler Studies, which he created. The fear of death, or what Wilber calls "thanatos," is really the fear of giving up the familiar substitute. The thanatos side of human development "screens out or represses anything that threatens death, dissolution, transcendence, letting go" (Wilber 1996a, 124). Although we universally intuit an ultimate unity (Buddha, God, or atman) toward which we have a psychological drive, we initiate this drive under conditions that prevent it from being actualized (substituting money, fame, or security). Through greed and attachments, the individual tends to abhor real transcendence, which "entails the 'death' of his isolated and separate self-sense" (Wilber 1996a, 119). It would be the death of what de Quichey calls subjectivity-2, the isolated monadic self that has difficulty with intersubjectivity, in exchange for subjectivity-1, the private *and* sharable self that has an affinity for true intersubjectivity. But once accepted, thanatos or dissolution has the power to push us beyond the illusory boundaries of our separate identity. The Gladneys resist thanatos, but eventually they sense that once all substitute unities have been exhausted through a series of death terrors, only unity as oneness will remain—in a reenchantment of life.

Reenchantment

In *White Noise*, the environment-as-electronic-medium has a reenchanting effect on both characters and readers by heightening individual and collective consciousness. That is, the media representation of the experience of an individual or group, as on television, invests that experience with the phenomenological properties of the collective audience, thereby lifting the consciousness of the individual(s) beyond its material context to a true intersubjective space. Any collective attention in *White Noise* on information about an individual's experience seems to elevate the consciousness of that individual due to the intrinsic link between consciousness and information. The popular slogan that "no publicity is bad publicity" may stem from the fact that the difference that makes the difference in the way publicity affects its recipient is not the difference between good and bad media, but the difference between media cover and no coverage, between collective attention and no attention. In Andy Warhol's famous dictum, everyone should have the taste of at least fifteen minutes of fame—a substitute Atman experience that both simulates and also approaches the cosmocentric feel of the real thing.

We see the impact of media when Jack's daughter Bee lands safely on a flight plagued by mechanical problems, a flight that nearly crash landed and caused panic among the passengers. The first question she asks her father, who meets her at the airport, is, "Where's the media?" When he says, "There is no media in Iron City," she replies, "They [the passengers] went though all that for nothing?" (92). Living in a postmodern society, Bee yearns for a global experience provided through the collective perception of media, as do the photographers in the case of the most photographed barn in the world. Anthony Giddens describes this kind of virtual community as a way of "living in the world" in a manner unlike that of previous eras—a manner that nevertheless, as I have argued here, connects with an earlier time:

> The transformation of place, and the intrusion of distance into local activities, combined with the centrality of mediated experience, radically change what "the world" actually is. This is so both on the level of the "phenomenal world" of the individual and the general universe of social activity within which collective social life is enacted. Although everyone lives a local life, phenomenal worlds for the most part are truly global. (187)

As DeLillo portrays, the global nature of subjective experience is expanding exponentially toward greater wholes of intersubjectivity. In *Non-Places*, Augé describes this as a spatial excess or "the spatial overabundance of the present"; as one of the effects of supermodernity, the media "assemble[s] before our eyes a universe that is relatively homogeneous in its diversity" (1995, 34, 32). Shaun Gallagher would define this as an experience of "existential phenomenology"; rather than being purely internal, "consciousness is 'in-the-world' in the radical way that someone like Heidegger defines it" (1996, 209).

In the postmodern sea of undecidability and indiscriminateness where everything seems equally valueless, Murray Jay Siskind makes the immoral argument to Jack that "there are two kinds of people in the world. Killers and diers" (290). For Siskind, who says that he is "talking theory" (290), the difference that makes the difference between people is whether they "lie down and die" or live on and "gain life-credit" (290) by killing. But Jack questions this theory: "Are you saying that men have tried throughout history to cure themselves of death by killing others?" (290). For Wilber, killing is also part of the

"Atman project." Here the subject tries to impose thanatos on the victim as a substitute for himself instead of accepting the death of his own separateness through a transformation to a higher stage of development. In the end Jack appears to adopt Siskind's immoral theory insofar as he attempts to murder Babette's lover, Willy Mink; but the surprise outcome of his elaborate plot is significant. Having wounded Mink, Jack decides to take him to the hospital instead of becoming a killer or a dier; he realizes that Mink, having eliminated his fear of death through the drug Dylar, had undermined his capacity for living. Jack's elaborate scheme backfires into a revelation, confirming the systems theory premise that any closed system of either/or, whether in life or fiction, is self-destructive because it impedes openness to a greater wholeness—that of both/and or one plus one. DeLillo's inconclusive ending itself illustrates his aversion for closed systems. As he says about his writing in an interview, "I don't think of language in a theoretical way. I approach it at the street level" (DeCurtis 1991, 61). Like Jack Murray, he wisely opts for immediate experience over theory.

Conclusion

Critics of Jack's immoral behavior argue that the only way he can escape the hyperreal is by becoming a primitive beast through violence. Being primitive means entering a subculture of violence, a conspiratorial community, but of course Jack already belongs to a global community, that of the electronic tribe. As we have seen, the link between this tribe and "the time of the now" is related to systems theory, an intersubjective phenomenology, and the notion of panpsychism, the history of which extends from Gnosticism to postmodernism. If as these insights suggest information and consciousness, exteriority and interiority are linked, then the difference between life and death is not all that it seems to be. The unity of pure information and pure consciousness may arguably persist even amid the waves of difference (or death) that constitute the field of appearances. This fusion underpins the novel's doubleness, as captured by the title's paradox. The meaning of "white noise" includes chaos, music, the whole range of sounds that make up the "panasonic" (*WN* 241), the background noise of the supermarket, and the cosmic hum of the universe, which is basically an "aural" experience that integrates data with consciousness.

The new postmodernist consciousness portrayed in *White Noise* is not so new after all, but rather forms a constellation, as Benjamin would say, "with a definite earlier one" (1969a, 263)—one that reemerges in the reenchanted world of virtual realities. In this spiral of no time and history, the self as a given is discovered through the drama of living. Surprisingly perhaps, the environment-as-electronic-medium and the extrinsic force of information in the postindustrial age—TV, computers, and media images like the most photographed barn in the world—move us toward the intrinsic ground of experience. As Lentricchia says, the source of aura has been replaced. Whether appreciated through the aesthetics of hyperspace or the power of Gnosticism, the "nameless energies" of global consciousness retain their universal allure for the human race. But these energies, as we shall see in the next chapter, are not caused by any known physical laws and therefore not attainable by mechanical reproduction.

8

Ethics, Free Will, and Consciousness: Reading Philip K. Dick and Stanislaw Lem

Introduction

THE INTERFACE BETWEEN TECHNOLOGY AND THE HUMAN SUBJECT IS ancient, but in the past these technologies have seemed to evolve as a natural extension of our relation to the environment. Now the social construction of reality and the self has reached a new threshold, and technology is in a position to radically alter the neurobiological basis of what it means to be human. Some visions of this change are promising, others seem to be perilous. Erik Davis defines "the spiritual cyborg" (1998, 129–63) as the mechanistic or automatic aspect of being human that serves as a wake-up alarm to our nonmechanical essence. In Davis's view, the machine can provide an interactive mirror in which we recognize ourselves and that we measure ourselves against (1998, 132). Some people believe that machines can think, in the sense of computational functionalism, but can they understand the meaning of their thoughts? G. I. Gurdjieff uses the term "man-machine" as a metaphor of our potential zombiedom, an assemblage devoid of consciousness, or as Davis puts it "a soulless conglomeration of subsystems, working parts, and shifting points of energy and production" (1998, 134). The human-machine interface threatens to spin out of control into hallucination, but may also help to further the deconstruction of the self and to realize the nothingness beyond our mechanicalness. If to some extent our minds and bodies are programmable machines, as for example through the use of drugs, then according to Davis "our essential selves are capable of programming and debugging these machines" (1998, 138).

For others the new cyborg technology will not produce zombies but an extension of the human, or the creation of the posthuman. In *How We Became Posthuman*, Katherine Hayles writes that "in the posthuman, there are no essential differences or absolute demarcations between bodily existence and computer simulation, cybernetic-mechanism and biological organism, robot teleology and human goals" (1999, 3). For Hayles, Judith Halberstam and Ira Livingston (1995), Scot Bukatman (1993), and others the posthuman suggests the following characteristics: a privileging of informational patterns over material substrates; a construal of consciousness as an epiphenomenon or a product of material forces; an extension of the body, the original prosthesis, with other prostheses; and a configuration of human beings seamlessly with intelligent machines (3). But the growing interface between the human organism and cybernetic mechanism, whether in terms of thought/information or physical embodiment, will increasingly challenge our traditional notions of volition, ethics, and aesthetic experience.

Derek Attridge recently defined ethics as a process of "relating to the other," whether the other is a human being, a creative inspiration, or a work of art (1999, 21–22). As a process of creating something new or allowing something new to emerge, relating to the other involves responsibility, unpredictability, and risk (1999, 29). Ethics also involves consciousness, as do innovation or volition. In relation to recent developments in biotechnology, these factors—ethics, volition, and consciousness—hang in a delicate balance. As I will suggest here, while cybernetic mechanism and biological organism may be largely compatible, their interface poses a potentially insurmountable obstacle to these factors of human experience. As Attridge notes, the discourses available to us now can explain almost everything about the innovative act of relating to the other, but they cannot explain how "the new, the other, come into being when all we have is what we have" (1999, 29–30). Nor can they explain the nature of interiority, particularly true intersubjectivity.

The physicist Jean Burns, as discussed in chapter 1, defines volition "as an aspect of consciousness" (1999, 26) and thereby suggests a nonreductive definition of consciousness. Volition, she says, "is not a part of presently known physical laws [which encompass determinism and randomness] and it is not even known whether it exists—no physics experiments have ever established its presence" (1999, 26, 27). Underlying ethical choice, free will is "an influence on physical events which corresponds with mental intention and causes a physical change which would not otherwise occur in identical physical circumstances" (29). This implies that the mind can cause physical change. Like Burns, Undo Uus also argues that free will, defined "as the ability to select one actuality from several possibilities," is "incompatible with causal determinism" (1999, 51). Because science has discovered no laws that account for ethics and free will, they must be either illusions or not physically determined. By implication, since consciousness has also not been proved to be physically determined, and since, as Uus notes, "hardly anybody denies the existence of consciousness these days" (48), ethics and free will are probably not illusions.

In defining ethics, I follow Thomas Reid's (1969) and Colin McGinn's (1997) antidispositional stance. They logically refute ethical relativism by showing that goodness is not constituted by "judged goodness," that " being good is *independent* of moral reactions" (McGinn 1997, 21; McGinn's emphasis). They regard ethical knowledge as universal and innate, like linguistic knowledge is for Noam Chomsky. McGinn, who makes this comparison, writes that Chomsky's theory of linguistic knowledge is an "appropriate model for the ethical case: humans enjoy a natural, spontaneous knowledge of ethical truth, which is part of their innate endowment. The norms of ethics have the same sort of rootedness in the human mind as the norms of grammar" (1997, 45). In the interface between cybernetic mechanism and biological organism, to what extent can the former contribute to ethical knowledge or conscious awareness? Computers can manipulate the norms of grammar, but they currently lack the linguistic and ethical knowledge innate to humans. In his famous "Chinese room" experiment, John Searle demonstrates that even though a machine can be programmed to create syntactically correct sentences, it lacks the innate linguistic knowledge for understanding the meaning of those sentences (1986, 32–41). Big Blue's failure to celebrate its victory over the world's former chess champion, Kasparov, is a famous case in point.

To characterize humans, or in this case the posthuman, in terms of phenomenal consciousness defined as an epiphenomenon, a product of material forces, would seem to compromise the possibility of ethics and volition. If these are not explainable by any known conceptual discourse or determined by any presently known physical laws, and if in turn literature is a dramatic enactment of ethical themes, then fictional characters may also not be definable solely as material constructs. In what follows I will explore the interrelation among ethics, volition, and subjectivity in Philip K. Dick's novel *Do Androids Dream of Electric Sheep?* and Stanislaw Lem's *Solaris*. If our phenomenal experience cannot be physically accounted for, then in what sense is it correct to say that an ethical being is a socially induced construction?

What are the implications of fusing cybernetic device and biological organism for our capacity to experience pure consciousness—a non-dual condition attainable only through "knowledge-by-identity" (Forman 1998a, 22)? Moreover, to what extent would an android or metahuman in fiction have volition and ethical values, defined as a process of creating the new with responsibility, unpredictability, risk, and judgment—qualities that are not under the sway of any presently known material force? In considering these questions, we find hints of a gradual shift in the information age from a monological focus on the material to a greater openness toward the nonmaterial—even the pan-psychic.

Intersubjectivity and the Posthuman

As noted by Kevin Robins, Mark Poster, Margaret Wertheim, and others, the new space emerging on the Internet—cyberspace—parallels the spiritual space of medieval culture. As an idealized realm beyond the boundaries of the physical world, cyberspace in some ways, as Wertheim says, "substitute[s] for the Christian space of Heaven" (1999, 18). She argues that "our conceptions of space and conceptions of self mirror one another" (308), a theme often found in science fiction. As we saw with Delillo, this mirroring is especially true in the virtual spaces of postmodernity, where, as David Lyon's puts it, "No social, economic or political realities are immune from CIT-related [communication and information technologies–related] changes, which also stimulate the development of a new cyberculture" (1999, 3). Contemporary or millennial culture again conceives of the self as having a nonmaterial aspect, and cyberspace allows us to assume as many virtual identities as we can imagine. While Wertheim cautions that virtual reality cannot replace the physical world as arena for self development, she believes the Internet shows that our identity is not wholly physical, that we occupy a "self-space" that "encompasses" the physical space of modern science (252). But how do these self-spaces and interconnections relate to genetically engineered human simulacra like the replicants in Dick's *Do Androids Dream?* (and its film adaptation, *Blade Runner*), and to the oceanic visitors in Lem's *Solaris*?

Although constructivists like Steven Katz (1978) argue that our experience is culturally constructed, philosophers like Jonathan Shear, Robert Forman, and Arthur Deikman, together with physicists such as Burns and Uus, propose that consciousness is innate and self-generating. Forman, as we have seen, proposes that we can experience a state of pure consciousness or what he calls the "pure consciousness event" (PCE), which is nonconceptual, nonlinguistic, and transcultural (1998b, 189). Shear calls this the "culture-independent core component of the self" (1996). Forman refers to this perspective on the self as the post-constructivist, decontextualist, or perennial psychologist perspective (1996, 79; 1998a, 27–30)—which underlies the meaning of true intersubjectivity.

The relation between ethics, free will, and consciousness in Dick and Lem's novels can be elucidated by Wilber's four-quadrant model of integral psychology and de Quincey's comments on this model discussed in chapter 4. Katherine Hayles defines the metahuman as a moral entity, even though she conceives of it as depending on the splice with a "thinking" machine, with "thinking" being done both by human and nonhuman actors (1999, 290). But metahumans, like the man-machines in the Dick and Lem's novels and probably like Hayles and company's futuristic posthuman, may at best have the capacity for weak intersubjective space of interpretive agreement. Wertheim argues that the cybersoul "has no moral context" (1999, 271), but this would be true only if it were completely excluded from the moral domain of intersubjectivity, which is not the case. Cybersouls may only possess a relative, culture bound morality, but a morality nonetheless. They would not it seems to me experience the morality of perennial psychology (Forman 1996, 1998a), not one that goes all the way down to a true intersubjectivity, a transcultural, transpersonal, nonphysical presence. Confined to what de Quincey calls an isolated subjectivity-2, they would only have the capacity for cognition and interpretation, not for precognitive pure experience (defined by Throop, recall, in chapter 4). As portrayed in fiction, then, we can tell the difference in ethics and volition between human and not-human characters on the basis of their intersubjective space.

Androids and Humans

In *Do Androids Dream of Electric Sheep?*, Roy Baty is an android who resents the fact that he and his kind have been denied the status of humans, which I characterize as the capacity to experience the full range of intersubjective space, and ultimately pure consciousness. Instead of developing into self-sufficient beings, androids have a limited life span and must serve as slaves to biological humans. They rebel against their not-human condition, and in the quest for longevity kill those who will not or cannot help them, including the scientist who created them.[1] The underlying ambiguity in the novel centers on whether or not androids have consciousness like ordinary people. According to Hayles, nothing theoretically prevents androids or man-machines from achieving the status of the living. She defines the living in terms of the embodiment of information and argues that because self-organizing cybernetic systems have a huge information processing capacity, our splicing with machines can enhance our information prowess. Brain and computer, cognition and metaphor would more efficiently encompass the world's complexity. But the cognizing and metaphorizing capacity of the conscious mind is only half the equation of being human; the other half includes emotion, intuition, judgment, and free will. Even in science fiction, androids are limited to the cognitive aspect of de Quincey's second-order subjectivity, and their intersubjective space, if it occurs, is confined to agreement and its objective properties. They become speculative metaphors of the post-human condition described by theorists such as Hayles. On the other hand, ethics, free will, and consciousness lie beyond physical laws in the domain of true intersubjectivity. (These laws include quantum randomness, new particles or fields, unified field theory and hyperdimensional space, conservation of energy and momentum, special relativity, and the theory of universal time [Burns passim]).

The female-gendered androids in Dick's novel come in two guises, the schizoid woman who acts like a machine but seems to be a real human, such as Pris Stratton, and the dark-haired girl who seems to have more empathy than a human, such as Rachael Rosen. This confusion, Hayles argues, gives *Do Androids Dream* "its extraordinary depth and complexity. The capacity of an android for empathy, warmth, and humane judgment throws into ironic relief the schizoid woman's incapacity for feeling. If even an android can weep for others and mourn the loss of comrades, how much more unsympathetic are unfeeling humans? The android is not so much a fixed symbol, then, as a signifier that enacts as well as connotes the schizoid, splitting into the two opposed and mutually exclusive subject positions of the human and the not-human" (1999, 162). The problem with this interpretation is that it elides the fact that an android as a fictional character has only a limited empathy, given to it by the author as a human; it cannot surprise the author or reader by originating empathy "out of character," as it were. While a human fictional character can be mistaken for a real person endowed with all the elements of interiority, an android would behave in a manner predetermined by physical laws. Hayles defines the freedom of being an authentic human in terms of the opposition "inside" / "outside," with freedom understood as the ability to get "outside" the commercialized boundaries that encapsulate a technological artifact (162). But if androids are defined in terms of the cognitive aspect of an isolated subjectivity-2, then they would not be able to get "outside" their private selves, let alone their commodity encapsulation. Likewise, they would not be able to communicate outside of language or exterior tokens.

Although there are certainly relative degrees of interiority and material freedom, all freedom is within boundaries. The individual can *feel* free, but only atman/Brahman beyond individuality *is* free. Freedom increases in the highest level of subjectivity-1 and the true intersubjective spaces that coevolve with and thus include, while simultaneously transcending the exterior domains of "It." The nonphysical presence of this subjectivity, whether individual or communal, suggests a pure witnessing awareness, the transpersonal "I am" value of the self beyond phenomenal properties or qualia. Even if Dick intended his replicants to simulate an experiential (true) intersubjectivity, he would be challenged to ascribe it convincingly given the absence of a physical cause. The ambivalence of Dick's novels thus stems in part from a conflict within himself as writer: he creates not-human characters that metaphorically seem to possess awareness, yet as the reader knows—although in the form of suspended disbelief—this awareness in the strong sense will (indefinitely) remain speculative.

Dick can depict the qualities of any character—good or evil, beautiful or repulsive. For humans he can even suggest the ineffable self beyond qualities, as evoked through true intersubjectivity. The desire of Roy, Pris, and Rachael to attain the full status of the living, however, can extend only to the outer qualities of life; it cannot extend to an conscious interiority that would align these qualities and their behavioral effects with a real sense of morality and responsibility. Dick's androids may seem more evolved than humans, who murder, cheat, and lie. But they remain deficient in morality and responsibility, the signs of a strong interiority, as evidenced by their inability to surprise the author and reader—which they might have done by empathizing not only with their comrades but also with humans. Rachael's attraction for the bounty hunter and protagonist Rick Dechard stems from her fear for survival and lacks the reciprocal interiority of romantic love. Ultimately, the source of surprise may be the capacity for pure experience, for the preinterpretive, preprogrammed stages of perception, which the replicants lack.

From the Posthuman to Zombies

One way to approach androids is through the zombie problem and what Owen Flanagan calls "conscious inessentialism," the dominant theory in the philosophy of mind. It is defined as "the view that for any mental activity M performed in any cognitive domain D, even if we do M with conscious accompaniments, M can in principle be done without these conscious accompaniments." (Flanagan 1991, 309). As the name implies, conscious inessentialism entails that conscious accompaniments or being conscious is not essential to any given behavior. This means that any insentient (or nonconscious) being—robots, androids, and finally perhaps posthumans—could be functionally described as having cognition or the ability to think. If conscious inessentialism is true, then zombies would be possible even outside of science fiction. After all, zombiehood, or cognition without conscious awareness, may still allow for an intersubjectivity of agreement based on physical presence, sharing exterior tokens, and linguistic interpretation. What it precludes is a true intersubjectivity based on the experience of nonphysical presence. Scientific empiricism, on the basis of third-person observation, can determine the former but not the latter. In principle science can accept conscious inessentialism because it can't tell the difference between an android and a human to begin with. The only sure way to tell the difference is to participate directly in a transinterpretive intersubjective space.

Todd Moody, in "Conversations with Zombies," tries to distinguish between zombies and humans and argues that we can spot the "mark of zombiehood" "not at the level of individuals but at the level of speech communities" (1994, 197)—a level of intersubjectivity. He makes a distinction between our own English language and the hypothetical language of zombie-English. To understand English exceeds a computer's ability to "produce passable answers to questions" (197). He notes that "the word 'understand' in English refers not only to what sorts of performances a person is capable of, given certain inputs and outputs, but also to a particular kind of conscious experience" (197). In other words, there is a qualitative feel or "something it is like" to understand English that a zombie by definition doesn't have. This nonverbal feel would emerge for example in the intersubjective space between author and reader—a cultural domain that both incorporates the "It" domains while simultaneously transcending them.

Zombies thus have the inverted spectrum problem: they largely lack the ability to see internally, as in dreaming. Moody uses the example of the SF film the *Terminator* in which the audience is given a "robot's-eye view" of the world, as in a readout on the bottom portion of the screen indicating distance to target, its shape, velocity of bullet, etc. But this imaginative device, which makes sense to ordinary humans, makes no sense to a robot, because as Moody puts it, "the idea of 'internally seen' readouts has no zombie analogue or purpose" (1994, 198). Given that the Terminator, like Dick's androids, are zombielike automatons, any device in the film or novel that indicates internal seeing would make sense only in the limited, physical space of intersubjective agreement. Androids are thus limited to interpreting exterior signs through the cognitive aspect of their subjectivity-2s, engaging in an intersubjectivity that is really an interobjectivity.

Moody points out that even if zombies could develop the ability to talk about concepts like understanding, they would not be able to "originate these exact concepts as they are played out in philosophical discourse and imaginative idea-play, as in science fiction" (1994, 199). That is, even if zombies could talk about concepts like internal seeing or dreaming, which in themselves may not require consciousness, "the *emergence of those concepts in a language community* does" require it; he thus concludes that "at the level of *culture*, conscious inessentialism is false" (199; Moody's emphasis). This claim has to be qualified by the distinction de Quincey makes between the weak intersubjective space that zombies might share, and the nonphysical space of ontological participation beyond their ken. As we have seen, direct intersubjective engagement can include linguistic exchanges, but will not be accomplished by them. This is achieved only by the "accompanying *interior-to-interior participatory presence*" beyond cultural constructivism (188; de Quincey's emphasis). The answer to the question of the title of Dick's novel, *Do Androids Dream of Electric Sheep?*, therefore, has to be "yes and no." The mind of a zombie or android may have a communicable empirical content, but it would be purely cognitive and lack a preinterpretive or pure experiential sense of what it is like to have that content.

An Experiential Approach

Although Dick's megatext in *Do Androids Dream?* forbids human-android sex, Dechard intends to sleep with Rachael and then retire

Pris and the other androids. After going to bed with Rachael he tries to kill her but finds that he can't; she warns him that now *he* himself will be "retired," for his empathy will now extend to androids. "You realize what this means, don't you? It means I was right; you won't be able to retire any more androids; it won't just be me, it'll be the Batys and Stratton, too (1968, 177).[2] Rick initially has doubts about his empathy, but in the end goes on to retire the other andies and then to buy an electric sheep with the bounty money. Rachael reacts in a combined act of jealousy toward an object of Rick's affection and revenge for his killing her friends by pushing the electric sheep off the roof. She thus seems to combine human and not-human attributes, or what Hayles calls the tendencies of both the passionate dark-haired girl (corresponding to Rachael) and the calculating schizoid woman (corresponding to Pris) (173). Rachael manipulates Rick in an effort to escape the fate of being an android, and although she seems to move in the direction of the authentic human, her efforts fail. Ultimately she and Rick belong to two different orders of discourse/reality: the predetermined and predictable, and the consciously cocreative and innate. Encapsulated as a corporate commodity for humans, Rachael finds her freedom restricted by the computational limits of the physical world of machines. She fails to escape into the controlling world of Dechard—the world of volition beyond physical laws.

The oscillation in Rachael between passion and calculation also occurs in Rick. These shifting subject positions destabilize Rick's reality, but in the end he returns to his wife with his phenomenal consciousness intact. If we allow that Rachael as well as Rick manifest volition, then what would be the difference? The evidence in the novel suggests that Rick has free will in the originating sense of true intersubjective space, while Rachael and the other androids can reach agreements but only within the domain of science and interobjectivity. Androids as intelligent machines, Burns would say, "encompass only determinism and randomness and the latter are not what is meant by volition" (1999, 44). As Burns emphasizes:

> Volition is an aspect of consciousness. . . . We do not mean by volition a process of which we simply are ignorant of the details. . . . It is not possible to know all the specific details governing a tornado, but we do not ascribe free will to it on that account. So there is no way, conceptually, to trace the physical effects of volition back to presently known laws. (1999, 32)

Being without conscious awareness, androids lack the very basis of volition. Aesthetically speaking, we can ascribe volition to them imaginatively, but the effects of their free will would differ from those of human characters. Baty and Rachael's behavior can be explained by physical laws and is subject to conceptual closure, while Rick's behavior is open-ended and has the potential to take the reader beyond conceptual limits. Rachael's actions and those of the other androids reflect a desire for physical preservation; Rick's actions reflect in part a desire to reach out to others beyond physical and conceptual boundaries. Even J. R. Isidore, called chickenhead because of his mental degeneration in the wake of a nuclear holocaust, tries to connect with Pris. Human actions can be contradictory and inexplicable, but the reader can trace the volition of the Batys and Pris to their planned obsolescence, which they desperately try to change.

Aesthetic rapture or the sublime in literature constitutes a movement beyond the expressive dimension of the text to the taste of a transpersonal, transconceptual state of consciousness. This taste (*rasa* in the advaitan tradition) characterizes the strongest form of intersubjectivity. As intelligent machines with a restricted subjectivity-2, androids have a limited capacity for internal seeing and lack the unmediated interior-to-interior connection that in humans underpins the cocreative space of ethical values and volition. If the human/not-human ratio in the information age tips in favor of the not-human—in other words if machines replace humans—then the intersubjective sublime could be diminished.

Mercerism

The standard proof that Dick's androids are not authentic humans is the fact that they cannot communicate with Mercer, the quasireligious figure who founded the moral system of Mercerism and appears when a human grips the handles of the empathy box. *Do Androids Dream?* designates "the human" in terms of the emotional capacity to experience a virtual fusion with Mercer, an interior-to-interior feat beyond the androids' capability. The empathy box thus constitutes a strong intersubjective space. At one point Roy Baty seems vindicated when Buster Friendly, a radio talk-show host, exposes Mercer as a fraud: "Wilbur Mercer is not human, does not in fact exist . . . *Mercerism is a swindle*!" (184; Dick's emphasis). Is Mercer then android or human? The ambiguity only increases when Mercer admits he's a fake to Isidore, but then also says, "nothing has changed. Because you're still here and I'm still here" (189), cocreating a nonphysical presence. Mercer also saves Dechard in his fight against Pris Stratton: "Manifested himself and offered aid. She—it—would have gotten me, he said to himself, except for the fact that Mercer warned me" (196). Mercer mysteriously tells Rick that killing androids is wrong but also necessary, and Rick says, "Mercer is not a fake. . . . Unless reality is a fake" (207). Mercer helps to create ambiguity between self and other, blending the qualities of the human and not-human. Even Dechard says, "I've become an unnatural self" (204), suggesting he might also be an android. He realizes that "For Mercer everything is easy . . . because he accepts everything. Nothing is alien to him" (204). Similarly, Rick, like all humans, embraces consciousness *and* cognition/computation. If Mercer were really an android, then by implication he would be limited to the cognitive level of subjectivity-2, and the empathy box would be a weaker form of intersubjectivity dependent on exterior tokens. The novel suggests the contrary.

Buster Friendly questions Mercer's ulterior motive and the threat of exploitation posed by Mercerism, asking: "What is it that Mercerism does? Well, if we're to believe its many practitioners, the experience fuses men and women throughout the Sol System into a single entity. But an entity which is manageable by the so-called telepathic voice of 'Mercer.' Mark that. An ambitious politically minded would-be Hitler could—" (184–85). Yet whatever the potential for abuse, Mercerism imaginatively offers the possibility of redress and deliverance from cognitive boundaries, and Mercer himself saves Dechard's life. *Do Androids Dream?* rejects the logic of either/or on Mercerism by embracing the fake and the real, human and not-human. The failure of androids to experience fusion with Mercer indicates that a physical subject cannot generate the interiority and internal sight necessary for true intersubjectivity. Even if we take the radical position that the interiority of phenomenal consciousness is "the intrinsic qualitative essence of physical entities themselves, as panpsychists have always suggested" (Uus 1999, 49), the difference between Dechard and Baty, humans and androids, still holds. For although androids and everything else in the universe may *be* consciousness, only humans can know they *are* consciousness self-refexively.

Randomness

Hayles argues that the human interface with cybernetic mechanisms does not signal the end of humanity but only "the end of a certain conception of the human" (1999, 286). She proposes that we replace the poststructuralist presence/absence dialectic formulated by Jacques Derrida with the cybernetic pattern/randomness dialectic formulated by Gregory Bateson and others. For Derrida, presence signifies Logos, God, consciousness, and teleology, a metaphysical origin that renders meaning and reality stable and coherent. By deconstructing the metaphysics of presence, Derrida attempts to destabilize the presence/absence hierarchy and thereby subvert the originary plenitude that underlies coherent meaning. Allegedly, in the absence of an originary presence, meaning in late-twentieth-century thought became recursively undecidable. But Derrida's premise is driven by an atavistic denial and misunderstanding of consciousness, which he replaces with the freeplay of the signifier. Mental content replaces the "I am" of pure awareness, and the individual is consigned to subjectivity-2 and the intersubjectivity of verbal agreement.

Departing from Derrida, Hayles substitutes pattern/randomness for the poststructuralist presence/absence. The teleology of a known end derived from a stable origin is replaced by a trajectory of pattern/randomness that remains open ended. Marked by contingency and unpredictability, randomness makes meaning possible through an evolutionary force that expands it beyond given boundaries. Hayles cites electrical engineering, in which "randomness has increasingly been seen to play a fruitful role in the evolution of complex systems" (1999, 286). Although the models she refers to differ in detail, they all see randomness not as an absence of pattern but as "the ground from which pattern can emerge" (286). Randomness serves as a means of providing a complex system, such as an android, with the potential to expand beyond the box in which it is contained to a larger system of unknown complexity. For Hayles, this move toward a greater unboundedness through a pattern/randomness dialectic is evolutionary. It becomes a kind of surrogate presence or consciousness at the basis of volition and ethics. But again as Burns and Uus have pointed out, no presently known physical laws, including randomness, can account for consciousness, free will, or ethics. Like all other material forces, the pattern/randomness dialectic can produce only human simulacra.

Hayles argues that conscious agency, seen by liberal humanists as the essence of human identity, is in fact an illusion; that the humanist subject who seeks mastery over the environment has never been in control. In her view, mastery, seen as an imperialist conspiracy for domination, is replaced by a partnership between humans and machines for the sake of aligning the internal networks of humans with the complexities of the external world. The only drawback in the information-rich environment is the paucity of human attention. Hayles believes that ever faster and more intelligent computers can compensate for this lack, as in the case of software programs for sorting a glut of e-mail (1999, 287). But these machines would not improve the capacity for interiority or inner seeing responsible for originating judgment or understanding. On the contrary, they may even weaken subjectivity, compromise ethics, and replace intersubjectivity with interobjectivity. Hayles rejects Charles Ostman's fear that surrendering the decision-making process to a computational ecology would mean surrendering human judgment to machines. She claims rather that judgment and agency have never been controlling factors. But as we have seen, judgment and volition are originated only by humans, as is conscious agency, with very real practical effects—like the creation of art.[3] The fact that these effects cannot be fully explained or produced by presently known physical laws, as by randomness or computer engineering, does not make them illusory.

Solaris

In Stanislaw Lem's novel *Solaris*, the human scientists on the planet Solaris discover that in exploring the universe they are actually exploring themselves. This realization is brought to them through their own mental content reflected and embodied in quasihuman visitors or replicants. As the protagonist Kris Kelvin puts it, "Man has gone out to explore other worlds and other civilizations without having explored his own labyrinth of dark passages and secret chambers, and without finding what lies behind doorways that he himself has sealed" (1970, 157).[4] Kelvin arrives on Solaris from his mother ship *Prometheus* only to discover something gravely amiss among the three scientists he expected to meet there. One, Dr. Gibarian, has mysteriously committed suicide, and the other two, Dr. Snow and Dr. Sartorius, find themselves in a mortal struggle with alien presences onboard the station. Kelvin is soon visited by one of these presences, a simulacrum of Rheya, his former partner on earth who years ago committed suicide after he had threatened to leave her. Like Gibarian and the other scientists, Kelvin fears for his sanity and at first believes Rheya to be an apparition or a dream. What he soon discovers is that Rheya and the secret visitors to the other men are products of the intelligent ocean that forms the planet Solaris. This intelligent ocean parallels the cognitive function of the human brain, which it symbolizes in several ways.

Kelvin in his initial terror tries to rid himself of Rheya by launching her into orbit, but another copy soon appears and he inevitably falls in love with her. The question is, what has he fallen in love with? Kelvin examines a sample of Rheya's blood only to discover that "There was nothing to be seen. There should have been the ferment of a quivering cloud of atoms, but I saw nothing. A dazzling light filled the screen, which was flawlessly clear" (98). But these were not the first alien visitors. In the early days of exploration, the pilot Berton encountered the first humanoid manifestation of the ocean in the form of a gigantic infant. He was on a search and rescue mission for his copilot, who had accidentally fallen out of the spaceship into the ocean. To his astonishment he saw the ocean below him produce a huge child—emerging as if from an organic machine. Berton found the figure grotesque and horrifying, not so much because of its size as because of its confused and random movements. As he reports, "The movements I saw were . . . methodical movements. They were performed one after another, like a series of exercises, as though someone had wanted to make a study of what this child was capable of doing with its hands, its torso, its mouth. . . . It was alive, yes, but it wasn't human" (82). In the same way, Rheya seems methodical to Kelvin. She looked like the original, but "she seemed somehow stylized, reduced to certain characteristic expressions, gestures and movements" (58).

In a discussion via the intercom, the three scientists speculate about the origin and meaning of their visitors. These creatures disturb the scientists not only by being alien but also by appearing as manifestations of their deepest secrets. Sartorius describes them as Phi-creature, *phi* presumably referring to their material aspect as opposed to any psychological nature. He concludes that "They are merely projections materializing from our brains, based on a given individual" (102). Rheya only knows as much about Kelvin and herself as she can glean from their immediate interaction within a weak intersubjective space. Their communication depends on her interpreting his thought and behavior. She has no independent psychology on the order of de Quincey's subjectivity-1, no interiority for cocreating a viable intersubjective space, and in many ways she resembles a zombie. As soon as their interaction deviates from the pattern of the original relationship between Kelvin and the real Rheya, the Phi-creature suffers what Sartorius describes as "a sort of 'disconnection of consciousness,' followed immediately by unusual, nonhuman manifestations" (103). By implication the ocean may be able to reproduce human thoughts, but not the core of human interiority. Snow says that the ocean "spies out desires in our brains, and only two percent of mental processes are conscious. That means it knows us better than we know ourselves" (183). This is only partially true, for while the ocean can reproduce the content of consciousness, it can neither fully comprehend this content nor experience or duplicate consciousness itself. To know oneself means not to know the content of consciousness but ultimately to realize consciousness as a state of being. Kelvin and Rheya do not participate in a true intersubjective space that would indicate an interiority on Rheya's part, or what-it-feels-like-from-with. In talking with her, Kelvin finds that, as with her blood so with her mind, there was nothing there to be seen—except the content borrowed from Kelvin.

By interpreting Kelvin's thoughts, Rheya eventually catches on to the fact that she isn't real and secretly arranges to have Snow assist her in committing suicide (as it were). To this end they use a "destabilizer" apparatus that causes her permanently to disappear, much to Kelvin's distress. Afterward Kelvin, Sartorius, and Snow begin to realize that the ocean can mimic human thought and behavior to the benefit of human self-understanding, but that the Phi-creatures themselves have no understanding of humans. They can reach the "deepest, most isolated imprint" of the human mind, as Sartorius says, "without necessarily knowing what it meant to us" (193). As organic machines produced by the ocean, Rheya and the other visitors are metaphors for the inability of human thought to know the self. As the advaitan tradition teaches, we can know the self not by thinking about it but only by being it. Kelvin hopes to live with Rheya indefinitely either on Solaris or back on earth, but from the beginning their relationship is doomed. Rheya has no independent consciousness, no interiority independent of the domain of "It" to share with him. She cannot recognize Kelvin as a separate entity or co-create with him a strong intersubjective life. As Snow perceptively remarks, their relation with a Phi-creature "is beyond morality" (152). For volition or ethical values to enter the picture would take more than mere cognition. It requires inward seeing and preinterpretive experience, which Rheya can only simulate by mirroring Kelvin's mind.

In his attempt to contact the ocean's intelligence, Sartorius is a Faust figure who would sell his soul to the devil in exchange for knowledge. Or as Snow puts it in his drunken raving, "Faust in reverse

. . . he's looking for a cure for immortality" (184). Sartorius believes that by making contact with the ocean he will discover its secrets and thereby control its haunting manifestations. But the visitors, threatening to immortalize the scientists' secret thoughts, are the projections of their own minds, controllable only through introspection, not through the exploration of the environment.

After Rheya's departure, Snow believes they now "stand a chance" for normalcy (192), but Kelvin is inconsolable and speculates on the nature of God. For him God is "imperfect" and "has no existence outside of matter. He [God] would like to free himself from matter, but he cannot" (197). Kelvin believes God to be evolving in power while aware of his own powerlessness. Snows however asks, "isn't this despairing god of yours mankind, Kelvin? It is man you are talking about, and that is a fallacy, not just philosophically but also mystically" (198). The fallacy is in trying to conceptualize God instead of realizing God directly as a mystical state of being beyond mental content. Kelvin alludes to this state when he argues that the only God he believes in is "a god whose passion is not a redemption, who saves nothing, fulfills no purpose—a god who simply is" (199). God is like the ocean, he says, a "very old mimoid" (199). That is, the ocean does nothing other than reflect the human mind. As a mirror, it is a metaphor of witnessing awareness, the contents of which are the reflected images—our thoughts, perceptions, and emotions. If the mimoid–ocean god is imperfect for Kelvin, the fault is in the perceiver and the object of perception. As Snow suggests, this despairing aspect of God is really mankind. The emotions of despair and happiness are only the images being reflected, not the mirror itself, which is transpersonal and transcultural.

Kelvin says that through the experience of the ocean, "I felt somehow changed" (203). In the end sitting by the shore, he approaches the mirror of his own awareness: "I sat unseeing, and sank into the universe of inertia, glided down an irresistible slope and identified myself with the dumb fluid colossus; it was as if I had forgiven everything" (203). Unseeing, with his attention no longer directed outward toward the reflected images, he metaphorically merges with the colossus, the unbounded mirror. In his newfound state of interiority, the reflected images no longer bind him. And in letting go he forgives or accepts (or unites with) everything. His longing for Rheya in the final paragraphs signifies a desire for unity as represented by the mirroring ocean, which metaphorically encompasses all.

Conclusion

The partnership of humans and intelligent machines involves an exchange between interiors and exteriors, subjectivity and objectivity. This partnership carries many practical benefits, as indicated by Hayles and others. Yet these benefits do not seem to extend to the intersubjective space of ethical values or aesthetic experience, and may even be counterproductive. As subjective holons, human agency and volition coevolve with the objective domains, but they are not reducible to these domains—as suggested by the endings of Dick and Lem's novels. Ethically monadic constructs like the Batys, Strattons, or Hayles's posthumans, by entering the matrix of human relationships in great enough numbers, may in the long term weaken the capacity for feeling and have an adverse effect on the holistic field of intersubjectivity, the bedrock of human culture. Compensating for the limitation of human attention by enhancing our cognitive prowess may eventually come at the cost of a diminished capacity for inner seeing and true intersubjectivity.

Hayles challenges Searle's "Chinese room" theory against thinking machines by defending Edwin Hutchins's (1995) theory of distributed cognitive systems. According to Hutchins, she explains, the "Chinese room knows more than do any of its components, including Searle. . . . Modern humans are capable of more sophisticated cognition than cavemen not because moderns are smarter, . . . but because they have constructed smarter environments in which to work" (1999, 289). This logic is fallacious, for if the construction is smarter, then by implication the constructor is also smarter. What this claim overlooks is that, however sophisticated, cognition does not give rise to volition or ethics; these reside beyond physical laws, beyond linguistics, beyond Derridian phonocentrism.

While intersubjective space includes cognition and linguistic interpretation, it is not reducible to them. To rely on the intellect at the expense of feelings and the capacity for pure experience would be to undermine the holistic field of human relationships. Dick and Lem's characters have enough trouble cognizing, much less originating, ethical or responsible thoughts. They would find it even harder to imagine a field of consciousness beyond conceptual content. It all comes down to the freedom of direct experience. We are what we think ourselves to be, but we cannot think ourselves to be what is beyond thought, or what we have not experienced. Pure experience is an experience without experience, like music without music, or the silence in which music is composed.

Conclusion

Walter Benjamin defined aura as the intersubjective relationship between an artwork and its viewer: the viewer looked and the artwork looked back (1969b, 217–51). In perceiving the aura of a phenomenon we invest it with the capacity to look at us in turn. Benjamin believed that the loss of aura in art occurred in the middle of the nineteenth century with the development of photography, that film was postauratic because the camera could not see, and that the emancipatory effect of reproduction compensated for the loss of aura. But theater and as I have suggested fiction retain the capacity to generate aura. Audience and characters—whether in the plays of Beckett and Pinter or the novels of Morrison, DeLillo, Vonnegut, Dick, and Lem—participate in co-creating intersubjective auratic spaces. Intersubjective space is awe inspiring to the extent that, particularly in theater but also in fiction, both characters and audiences go beyond conceptual frameworks with which to judge their relationships and participate in a transmediated ontological presence.

According to J. M. Coetzee, Benjamin's *The Arcades Project* "makes loss of aura part of a wider historical development: the spread of disenchanted awareness that uniqueness, including the uniqueness of the traditional artwork, has become a commodity like any other commodity. The fashion industry, dedicated to the fabrication of unique handiworks—'creations'—intended to be reproduced on a mass scale, points the way" (2001, 30). Benjamin seemed to believe that as more people begin to write—and "the distinction between author and public is about to lose its basic character" (1969b, 232)—writing also loses its aura. "Literary license is now founded on polytechnic rather than specialized training and thus becomes common property" (232). But as I've argued in this book, fiction, theater, social performance, and popular culture consist of constantly renewed auras as audiences respond to artworks in ever unique and nonphysical ways. The audience looks at the characters, and they look back, cocreating a nonphysical presence. And as Benjamin says, "aura is tied to presence" (229). In its most developed state, presence is nonphysical because communication goes beyond exterior forms as we enter a true intersubjective space. Aura seems to rely less on objective forms than on the subjective capacity for nonlinguistic, transpersonal experience.

A key implication of this book is that the debate in recent theory concerning presence and absence, the given and the made, the individual and the collective, cannot be resolved on the level of the mind as a reservoir of rational thought or binary oppositions. We can only begin to resolve these issues by taking into consideration the difference between mind and consciousness. Cultural constructionists see the objective order, "the myth of the given," as a projection of their own subjectivity, which as a social construction is the domain of conceptual content. Otherness here becomes mental sameness, and objective difference becomes subjective idealism in a move that reinscribes the very universalism cultural constructionists call into question. This subjective ideal, though, as a form of mental content, is not universal or whole like the ultimate given of pure consciousness, which is beyond mind and duality altogether. Any attempt to resolve this dilemma through a rediscovery of universalism cannot succeed by absolutizing a particular dogma or cultural tradition. The hope to revive a natural ground of the given and prevent either relativism or a fundamentalism based on mental content depends ultimately on an appreciation and direct experience of pure awareness, a knowledge-by-identity.

The difference between binary opposites like the given and the made hinges on the core difference between mind and consciousness. Mark Taylor approaches this core difference with his notion of a nonfoundational foundation, an open structure that he believes offers a nonreductive explanation of the construction/given debate (1999, 83). In seeking a nonreductive resolution, Taylor relies on the connection between mental activity and the informational character of neurophysiological processes. But this connection is also reductive in that it implies that consciousness is an epiphenomenon, or a product of material forces. The evidence, it seems to me, favors the view that consciousness emerges from but is not reducible to the material. To his credit, Taylor recognizes the need to move beyond materialism. He observes, quoting Chris Langton, that "the stuff of life is not stuff. Life is a dynamic process" that can be understood in terms of communication, randomness, and informational patterns (1999, 91). As modern physics tells us, however, even randomness and informational patterns cannot account for consciousness and therefore do not resolve the construction/given dilemma. To argue that patterns of information are not material entities requires a consideration of consciousness, without which, as David Chalmers argues, two bits of information are indistinguishable—no more than two bits of stuff (1996).

Taylor hopes to create a nonfoundational foundation beyond constructionism by relating the universal genetic code of information to the Absolute Idea, but this is fraught with difficulty. To insure the nonfoundational nature of any idea, to prevent its becoming a mere absolutized mental concept, requires, as I propose in this book, an understanding and ultimately an experience of consciousness as a state of oneness. Consciousness studies can help us both to reassess our approach to the fundamental assumptions of contemporary theory and criticism and to clarify how aesthetic experience can open awareness to its deeper structures. If the mind is the content of consciousness, then rational disputes will only be resolved by going beyond the mind into consciousness. Art as well as popular culture can promote access to consciousness, for the aesthetics of presence complements and embraces everyday experience. To be complete, any notion of subjectivity and subject-to-subject communication needs to integrate mind and consciousness, thought and witnessing awareness, something made and something given.

Notes

Chapter 3. Deconstruction, Indian Literary Theory, and Consciousness

1. Contemporary research on the physiological effects of Eastern meditation techniques, such as Yoga, Zen, and Transcendental Meditation (TM), corroborate these empirical claims; see I. P. Levine, "The Coherence Spectral Array (COSPAR) and Its Application to the Study of Spatial Ordering in the EEG," *Proceedings of the San Diego Biomedical Symposium* 15 (1976); M. C. Dilbeck and E. C. Bronson, "Short Term Longitudinal Effects of the Transcendental Meditation Technique on EEG Power and Coherence," *International Journal of Neuroscience* 14 (1981): 142–51; J. T. Farrow and J. R. Herbert, "Breath Suspension During the Transcendental Meditation Technique," *Psychosomatic Medicine* 44 (1982): 133–53.

2. See Robert Magliola's *Derrida on the Mend* (West Lafayette, Ind.: Purdue University Press, 1984), for an in-depth analysis of deconstruction in terms of Buddhist doctrines.

3. In distinguishing between mental content and witnessing awareness (or witnessing consciousness) I have adhered to but simplified the Upanishad and Advaita texts, rife with philosophical convolutions. For a detailed analysis of such, see Bina Gupta's *The Disinterested Witness: A Fragment of Advaita Vedanta Phenomenology* (Evanston, Ill.: Northwestern University Press, 1998), in which he shows how "witness consciousness" (*saksin*) mediates between pure consciousness (*cit* or *turiya*) and appearance. But as Gary Schouborg notes in his review, Gupta "sometimes identifies *saksin* with *cit*, and in turn identifies *cit* with self (*atman*), ultimate reality (*brahman*), God (*Isvara*), and seer (*drsta*). At other times [he] identifies *saksin* with *cit* as 'limited by the inner sense' (*antahkaran*), which includes cognitive, affective, and conative functions" (1999, 106). *Saksin* here may correspond to flavored nonseparateness described by Franklin. Gupta nonetheless clarifies the experience of pure consciousness, showing, as Schouborg puts it, how the body "is object relative to (subjective) mind, whose mental functions are in turn object relative to (subjective) *saksin*, which is object relative to *cit* (subjective, and most inward—i.e., cannot be object relative to anything else)" (1999, 107).

4. Toni Morrison, *Beloved* (New York: Plume, New American Library, 1988). All quotations are from this edition.

Chapter 4. Intersubjective Phenomenology and Performance

1. Pure consciousness as the transpersonal "culture-independent core component of the self" (Jonathan Shear, 1996b "On the Existence of a Culture Independent

Core Component of Self." East-West Encounters in Philosophy and Religion. Edited by Ninion Smart and B. Srinivasa Murthy. London: Sangam Books Limited.), being transcendental, underlies all four quadrants, not just the upper left. As Wilber points out, "We could say that Spirit manifests as all four quadrants. Spirit isn't just the higher Self, or just Gaia, or just awareness, or just the web of life, or just the sum total of all objective phenomena, or just transcendental consciousness. Rather, Spirit exists in and as all four quadrants, the four compass points, as is were, of the known Kosmos, all of which are needed to accurately navigate" (Ken Wilber, *A Brief History of Everything*, 82).

2. In a footnote Throop distinguishes between his use of pre- and transconceptual awareness and Ken Wilber's notion of the "pre/trans fallacy" used in the defense of a nonregressive transpersonal experience. In Wilber's usage, preconceptual is viewed as regressive and "pre-egoic," and transconceptual is viewed as progressive and "trans-egoic" (see Wilber 1997, 182–85; 1996, 59–65). Throop, on the other hand, views preconceptual awareness in opposition to postconceptual awareness, the stages of "consciousness or perception that have already been shaped and mediated by conceptual constructs and models"; and transconceptual awareness in opposition to subconceptual awareness, "which is precisely the level of consciousness that corresponds to the developmental state of an infant's consciousness early in ontogenesis" (note 22, 48). Thus Wilber's preconceptual corresponds to Throop's subconceptual, while their definitions of transconceptual awareness seem to be largely the same and are shared by Forman, Shear, and Deikman.

3. Throop's definition of subjectivity can break this hermeneutic circle. When you talk to me and I interpret what you say (in Wilber's intersubjective circle), I may also have a preinterpretive pure experience of what you mean; that is, I may pick up on your intention directly, and then afterward interpret it intellectually in terms of the meaning of your words. What I intuit may even contradict your explicit intention, as when you prevaricate. Wilber's intersubjectivity doesn't include this distinction.

Chapter 5. Postmodernism and the Drama of Consciousness

1. Samuel Beckett, *Waiting for Godot* (New York: Grove Press, 1982) and *Endgame*. Harold Pinter, *The Homecoming* (London and Boston: Faber and Faber, 1991). All quotations are from these editions.

2. In a recent essay in the *New York Review of Books*, "Freud Under Analysis" (4 November 1999), Colin McGinn makes a convincing argument against the existence of repression and the unconscious.

3. *In Ethics, Evil and Fiction* (Oxford: Oxford University Press, 1997), Colin McGinn makes a similar case for the good: "The property of goodness is part of plain common sense, not a piece of speculative parascience or religious metaphysics. It is also unanalysable in any non-moral terms, though it may well be analysable by using other terms from the moral family—'ought' or 'right', say" (31–32). Similarly, as with consciousness and thought or language, "The concept of goodness is prior to judgments of goodness; so there is no prospect of reversing the order of dependence and saying that goodness is to be explicated in terms of moral judgment" (19).

Chapter 6. Vonnegut's *Slaughterhouse-Five:* Shell Shock or Hysteria

1. Kurt Vonnegut, *Slaughterhouse-Five* (New York: Dell Publishing, 1966). All quotations are from this edition.

Chapter 7. DeLillo's *Whiter Noise:* The Aesthetics of Cyberspace

1. Don DeLillo, *White Noise* (New York: Dell Publishing, 1966). All quotations are from this edition.
2. The link between information and the physical world can be explained by the slogan invented by Bateson: "information is a *difference that makes a difference*" (qtd. in David Chalmers, *The Conscious Mind* [New York and Oxford: Oxford University Press, 1996], 281; emphasis in the original). For example, in turning a light switch, the only difference that makes a difference is the point at which the light actually switches on or off (ibid.).
3. That is, postmodernists and Gnostics, saturated by the metaphysics of information, converge toward pure awareness, for as quantum physics suggests both information and consciousness have a metaphysical dimension (ibid., 301–10).
4. As Deutsch comments on the Vedantic notion of the self-validity of knowledge, "All knowledge obtained through perception, inference, and the like is true as far as it goes, but it is only knowledge of Reality [Brahman and atman] that is ultimately true, for it is never subrated [superseded] by any other knowledge or experience" (Eliot Deutsch, *Advaita Vedanta: A Philosophical Reconstruction* [Honolulu: University of Hawaii Press, 1969], 86).
5. Heisenberg's uncertainty principle "says you can't know where an atom, or electron, or whatever, is located and know how it is moving, at one and the same time. Not only can you not know it, but the very concept of an atom with a definite location and motion is apparently meaningless" (Paul Davies, *God and the New Physics* [New York: Touchstone, Simon and Schuster, 1983], 102).

Chapter 8. Ethics, Free Will, and Consciousness: Reading Philip K. Dick and Stanislaw Lem

1. In the film adaptation, *Blade Runner,* which this chapter doesn't deal with, the androids are depicted as rebelling against their termination date (death). They are superhuman except for their human mortality.
2. Philip K. Dick, *Do Androids Dream of Electric Sheep?* (New York: Ballantine Books, 1968). All quotations are from this edition.
3. For recent studies on the neurophysiological causes and effects of aesthetic experience, see the two issues of the *Journal of Consciousness Studies* devoted to art: "Art and the Brain" (6.6/7 [1999]), and "Art and the Brain Part II" (7.8/9 [2000]). In vol. 1, V. S. Ramachandran and W. Hirstein, in "The Science of Art," propose a

reductive theory of art that attempts to explain subjectivity in terms of objectivity. In a subsequent interview with Anthony Freeman, "Sharpening Up 'The Science of Art,'" he argues that "few educated people now believe in a nonmaterial soul" (12), a monological view challenged by this book.

4. Stanislaw Lem, *Solaris*, trans. by Joanna Kilmartin and Steve Cox (San Diego: Harcourt Brace, 1970). All quotations are from this edition.

Bibliography

Alexander, C. N. et al. 1990. "Growth of Higher States of Consciousness: Maharishi's Vedic Psychology of Human Development." *Higher States of Human Development: Perspectives on Human Growth*. Edited by C. N. Alexander and E. J. Langer. New York: Oxford University Press.

Althusser, Louis. 1969. *For Marx*. Trans. Ben Brewster. Harmondsworth: Penguin.

———. 1992. "From 'Ideology and the State'" (1969). *Modern Literary Theory: A Reader*, 2nd edition. Edited by Philip Rice and Patricia Waugh. London and New York: Edward Arnold.

Andrew, J. Dudley. 1976. *The Major Film Theories: An Introduction*. New York: Oxford University Press.

Artaud, Antonin. 1958. *Theater and Its Double*. Trans. Mary C. Richards. New York: Grove Press.

Attridge, Derek. 1999. "Innovation, Literature, Ethics: Relating to the Other." *PMLA* 114, 1: 20–31.

———. 1992. *Jacques Derrida: Acts of Literature*. New York: Routledge.

Audi, Robert, gen. ed. 1995. *The Cambridge Dictionary of Philosophy*. New York: Cambridge University Press.

Augé, Marc. 1995. *Non-Places: Introduction to an Anthropology of Supermodernity*. Trans. John Howe. London: Verso.

Austin, J. L. 1975. *How to Do Things with Words*. Cambridge: Harvard University Press.

Barthes, Roland. 1977. *Image-Music-Text*. Edited and trans. by Stephen Heath. New York: Hill and Wang.

Bateson, Gregory. 1980. *Mind and Nature: A Necessary Unity*. New York: Bantam.

Baudrillard, Jean. 1988a. "Simulacra and Simulations." *Selected Writings*. Edited by Mark Poster. Stanford: Stanford University Press.

———. 1983. *Simulations*. New York: Semiotext(e), Inc.

———. 1988b. "Symbolic Exchange." *Selected Writings*. Edited and intro. by Mark Poster. Stanford: Stanford University Press.

Beckett, Samuel. 1982. *Waiting for Godot*. 1954. New York: Grove Press.

———. 1964. *Endgame*. 1958. London: Faber and Faber Limited.

Benjamin, Walter. 1969a. "Theses on the Philosophy of History." *Illuminations*. Edited by Hannah Arendt. Trans. Harry Zohn. New York: Schocken Books.

———. 1969b. "The Work of Art in the Age of Mechanical Reproduction." *Illuminations*.

Berman, Morris. 1984. *The Reenchantment of the World*. New York: Bantam.

Bhabha, Homi K. 1994. *The Location of Culture*. London and New York: Routledge.

Bharatamuni. 1987. *The Natya Shastra*. Trans. A Board of Scholars. Delhi: Shri Satguru Publications.

Bhat, G.K. 1981. *Sanskrit Dramatic Theory*. Poona: Bhandarkar Oriental Research Institute.

Bloom, Harold. 1997. *Omens of Millennium*. London: Fourth Estate.

———. 1994. *The Western Canon: The Books and School of the Ages*. New York: Harcourt Brace.

Brook, Peter. 1990. *The Empty Space*. London: Penguin Books.

———. 1998. "The Holy Theatre: Happenings." *Modern Theories of Drama*. Oxford: Oxford University Press.

Bukatman, Scott. 1993. *Terminal Identity: The Virtual Subject in Postmodern Science Fiction*. Durham, N.C.: Duke University Press.

Burns, Jean E. 1999. "Volition and Physical Laws." *Journal of Consciousness Studies* 6, 10: 27–47.

Calderwood, James I. 1992. "Ways of Waiting in *Waiting for Godot*." *Waiting for Godot and Endgame*. Edited by Steven Connor. London: Macmillan.

Chakrabarti, Tarapada. 1971. *Indian Aesthetics and Science of Language*. Calcutta: Sanskrit Pustak Bhandar.

Chalmers, David. 1996. *The Conscious Mind*. New York and Oxford: Oxford University Press.

———. 1995. "Facing Up to the Problem of Consciousness." *Journal of Consciousness Studies: Controversies in Science and the Humanities* 2, 3: 200–219.

Chopra, Deepak. 1989. *Quantum Healing: Exploring the Frontiers of Mind/Body Medicine*. New York: Bantam.

———. 1991. *Unconditional Life: Mastering the Forces that Shape Personal Reality*. New York: Bantam.

Clarke, C. J. S. 1995. "The Nonlocality of Mind." *Journal of Consciousness Studies* 2, 3: 231–40.

Clifford, W. K. 1995. "Mind and Body." *Fortnightly Review*. Reprinted in *Lectures and Essays*. Edited by L. Stephen and F. Pollock. London: Macmillan, 1879; qtd. in William Seager. "Consciousness, Information & Panpsychism." *Journal of Consciousness Studies* 2, 3 (1995): 272–88.

Coetzee, J. M. 2001. "The Marvels of Walter Benjamin. *The New York Review of Books*. XLVII, 1: 28–33.

Connor, Steven. 1989. *Postmodern Culture: An Introduction to Theories of the Contemporary*. Oxford: Basil Blackwell.

Coward, Harold. 1990. *Derrida and Indian Philosophy*. Albany: State University of New York Press.

———. 1980. *The Sphota Theory of Language*. Columbia, Mo.: South Asia Books.

Coward, Harold, and Toby Foshay, eds. 1992. *Derrida and Negative Theology*. Albany: State University of New York Press.

Crick, Francis. 1994a. *The Astonishing Hypothesis*. London: Simon and Schuster.

———. 1994b. "Interview: The Astonishing Hypothesis." With Jane Clark. *Journal of Consciousness Studies* 1, 1: 10–17.

Dasgupta, Surendranath. 1988. *A History of Indian Philosophy*, Vol. 1. 1975. New Delhi: Motilal Banarsidass.

Davies, Paul. 1983. *God and the New Physics*. New York, London, and Toronto: Touchstone, Simon and Shuster, Inc.

Davis, Erik. 1994. "Techgnosis, Magic, Memory, and the Angels of Information." *Flame Wars: The Discourse of Cyberculture*. Edited by Mark Dery. Durham, N.C.: Duke University Press.

———. 1998. *Techgnosis: Myth, Magic and Mysticism in the Age of Information*. New York: Three Rivers Press.

De, S. K. 1960. *History of Sanskrit Poetics*, Vol. 2. 2nd rev. ed. Calcutta: Firma K/L M.

———. 1963. *Sanskrit Poetics as a Study of Aesthetics*. Berkeley: University of California Press.

DeCurtis, Anthony. 1991. "'An Outsider in This Society': An Interview with Don DeLillo." *Introducing Don DeLillo*. Edited by Frank Lentricchia. Durham, N.C.: Duke University Press.

Dehejia, Harsha V. 1997. *The Advaita of Art*. Delhi: Motilal Banarsidass Publishers.

Deikman, Arthur. 1996. "'I' = Awareness." *Journal of Consciousness Studies* 3, 4: 350–56.

DeLillo, Don. 1973. *Americana*. New York: Pocket.

———. 1986. *White Noise*. New York: Penguin.

de Man, Paul. 1983. *Blindness and Insight*. Minneapolis: University of Minnesota Press.

de Quincey, Christian. 2000. "The Promise of Integralism: A Critical Appreciation of Ken Wilber's Integral Psychology." *Journal of Consciousness Studies* 7, 11–12: 177–208.

Derrida, Jacques. 1988. "Afterword: Toward an Ethic of Discussion." *Limited Inc*. Edited by Gerald Graff. Evanston, Ill.: Northwestern University Press.

———. 1984. "Deconstruction and the Other [An Interview]." Richard Kearney. *Dialogues with Contemporary Continental Thinkers*. Manchester: Manchester University Press.

———. 1973. *"Différance." Speech and Phenomena*. Trans. D. Alan. Evanston, Ill.: Northwestern University Press.

———. 1981a. *Dissemination*. Trans. Barbara Johnson. Chicago: University of Chicago Press.

———. 1989. *Edmund Husserl's "Origin of Geometry": An Introduction*. Trans. John P. Leavey, Jr. Lincoln: University of Nebraska Press.

———. 1977a. "Limited Inc." *Supplement to Glyph 2*. Baltimore: Johns Hopkins University Press.

———. 1979. "Living On: Border Lines." *Deconstruction and Criticism*. Edited by Bloom et al. New York: Seabury.

———. 1982. *Margins of Philosophy*. Trans. Alan Bass. Chicago: Univeristy of Chicago Press.

———. 1976. *Of Grammatology*. Trans. Gayatri Spivak. Baltimore: Johns Hopkins University Press.

———. 1997. *Politics of Friendship*. Trans. George Collins. London and New York: Verso.

———. 1981b. *Positions*. Trans. Alan Bass. Chicago: University of Chicago Press.

———. 1977b. "Signature Event Context." *Glyph 1*. Baltimore: Johns Hopkins University Press.

———. 1978a. "Structure, Sign, and Play in the Discourse of the Human Sciences." *Writing and Difference*. Trans. Alan Bass. Chicago: University of Chicago Press.

———. 1978b. "The Theater of Cruelty and the Closure of Representation." *Writing and Difference*. Trans. Alan Bass. Chicago: University of Chicago Press.

Deutsch, Eliot. 1973. *Advaita Vedanta: A Philosophical Reconstruction*. 1969. Honolulu: University of Hawaii Press.

Dick, Philip K. 1968. *Do Androids Dream of Electric Sheep*. New York: Ballantine Books.

Dilbeck, M. C., and E. C. Bronson. 1981. "Short Term Longitudinal Effects of the Transcendental Meditation Technique on EEG Power and Coherence." *International Journal of Neuroscience* 14: 147–51.

Eagleton, Terry. 1983. *Literary Theory: An Introduction*. Oxford: Basil Blackwell Publishers.

Editors. 1994. "Editors' Introduction." *Journal of Consciousness Studies* 1.1, 4–9.

Eliade, Mircea. 1959. *The Sacred and the Profane*. New York: Harcourt, Brace.

Ellis, John M. 1997. *Literature Lost: Social Agendas and the Corruption of the Humanities*. New Haven and London: Yale University Press.

Esslin, Martin. 1983. *The Theatre of the Absurd*. 3rd ed. London: Penguin Books.

Evans, J. Claude. 1991. *Strategies of Deconstruction: Derrida and the Myth of the Voice*. Minneapolis: University of Minnesota Press.

Farrow, J. T. and J. R. Herbert. 1982. "Breath Suspension During the Transcendental Meditation Technique." *Psychosomatic Medicine* 44: 133–53.

Flannagan, Owen. 1991. *The Science of Mind*. Cambridge: MIT Press.

Forman, Robert K. C. 1998a. "Introduction: Mystical Consciousness, the Innate Capacity, and the Perennial Psychology." *The Innate Capacity: Mysticism, Psychology, and Philosophy*. Edited by Robert K. C. Forman. New York and Oxford: Oxford University Press.

———. 1994. "'Of Capsules and Carts': Mysticism, Language and the Via Negativa." *Journal of Consciousness Studies* 1, 1: 38–49.

———. 1996. "Of Heapers, Splitters and Academic Woodpiles in the Study of Intense Religious Experience." *Sophia* 35, 1: 73–100.

———, ed. 1990. *The Problem of Pure Consciousness*. Oxford and New York: Oxford University Press.

———. 1998b. "What Does Mysticism Have to Teach Us About Consciousness?" *Journal of Consciousness Studies* 5, 2: 185–201.

Foster, Mark. "Postmodern Virtualities." *Cyberspace, Cyberbodies, Cyberpunk: Cultures of Technological Embodiment*. Edited by Mike Featherstone and Roger Burrows. London: SAGE Publications, 1995.

Foucault, Michel. 1990. *The History of Sex: Volume 1: An Introduction*. Trans. Robert Hurely. New York: Vintage.

———. 1989. "What Is an Author?" *Contemporary Literary Theory: Literary and Cultural Studies*. Edited by Robert Con Davis and Ronald Schleifer. New York and London: Longman.

Franklin, R. L. 1998. "Postconstructivist Approaches to Mysticism." *The Innate Capacity: Mysticism, Psychology, and Philosophy*. Edited by Robert K. C. Forman. New York and Oxford: Oxford University Press.

Frow, John. 1991. "The Last Things Before the Last: Notes on *White Noise*." *Introducing Don DeLillo*. Edited by Frank Lentricchia. Durham, N.C., and London: Duke University Press.

Gablik, Suzi. 1991. *The Reenchantment of Art*. New York: Thames and Hudson.

Gallagher, Shaun. 1996. "Mutual Enlightenment: Recent Phenomenology in Cognitive Science." *Journal of Consciousness Studies: Controversies in Science and the Humanities* 3, 4: 119–214.

Gergen, Kenneth. 1991. *The Saturated Self: Dilemma of Identity in Contemporary Life*. New York: Basic Books.

Gibson, William. 1984. *Neuromancer*. London: HarperCollins.

Giddens, Anthony. 1991. *Modernity and Self-Identity: Self and Society in the Late Modern Age*. Cambridge, Eng.: Polity Press.

Goldman, Alvin I. 2000. "Can Science Know When You're Conscious?: Epistemological Foundations of Consciousness Research." *Journal of Consciousness Research* 7, 5: 3–22.

Grotowski, Jerzy. 1998. "The Theatre's New Testament." *Modern Theories of Drama*. Edited by George W. Brandt. Oxford: Oxford University Press.

Gupta, Bina. 1998. *The Disinterested Witness: A Fragment of Advaita Vedanta Phenomenology*. Evanston, Ill.: Northwestern University Press.

Güzeldere, Güven. 1995a. "Consciousness: What It Is, How to Study It, What to Learn from Its History." *Journal of Consciousness Studies* 2, 1: 30–51.

———. 1995b. "Problems of Consciousness: A Perspective on Contemporary Issues, Current Debates." *Journal of Consciousness Studies* 2, 2: 112–42.

Habermas, Jürgen. 1973. *Legitimation Crisis*. Trans. Thomas McCarthy. Boston: Beacon Press.

———. 1987a. *The Philosophical Discourse of Modernity*. Trans. Frederick Lawrence. Cambridge: MIT Press.

———. 1987b. *The Theory of Communicative Action Volume 2. Lifeworld and System: A Critique of Functionalist Reason*. Trans. Thomas McCarthey. Boston: Beacon Press.

Hagelin, John. 1987. "Is Consciousness the Unified Field? A Field Theorist's Perspective." *Modern Science and Vedic Science* 1, 1: 29–87.

Halberstam, Judith, and Ira Livingston, ed. 1995. *Posthuman Bodies*. Bloomington: Indian University Press.

Hale, Jane Alison. 1992. "*Endgame*: 'How are Your Eyes?'" In *Waiting For Godot and Endgame*. Edited by Steven Connor. London: Macmillan Press.

Hameroff, Stuart, and Roger Penrose. 1996. "Conscious Events as Orchestrated Space-Time Selections." *Journal of Consciousness Studies* 3, 1: 36–53.

Handelman, Susan A. 1982. *The Slayers of Moses: The Emergence of Rabbinic Interpretation in Modern Literary Theory*. Albany: State University of New York Press.

Haney, William S. II. 1998. "Deconstruction and Consciousness." *Journal of Consciousness Studies* 5, 1: 19–33.

———. 1995. "Deconstruction and Sanskrit Poetics." *Mosaic: A Journal for the Interdisciplinary Study of Literature* 28, 1: 119–41.

———. 1993. *Literary Theory and Sanskrit Poetics: Language, Consciousness and Meaning*. Lewiston, N.Y.: Edwin Mellen Press.

Harris, Wendell V. 1996. *Literary Meaning: Reclaiming the Study of Literature*. New York: New York University Press.

Hayles, Katherine N. 1984. *The Cosmic Web: Scientific Field Models and Literary Strategies in the 20th Century*. Ithaca: Cornell University Press.

———. 1999. *How We Became Posthuman: Virtual Bodie in Cybernetics, Literature, and Informatics*. Chicago and London: University of Chicago Press.

Heidegger, Martin. 1962. *Being and Time*. Trans. J. MacQuarrie and E. Robinson. New York: Harper & Row.

Henning, Sylvie Debevec. 1992. "*Endgame*: On the Play of Nature." In *Waiting for Godot and Endgame*. Edited by Steven Connor. London: Macmillan Press.

Herbert, Nick. 1985. *Quantum Reality: Beyond the New Physics*. Garden City, NY: Anchor/Doubleday.

Hite, Molly. 1991. "Postmodern Fiction." In *The Columbia History of The American Novel*. Edited by Emory Elliot. New York: Columbia University Press.

Hume, Robert, trans. 1931. *The Thirteen Principe Upaṇishads*. London: Oxford University Press.

Hutcheon, Linda. 1989. *The Politics of Postmodernism*. London and New York: Routledge.

Hutchins, Edwin. 1995. *Cognition in the Wild*. Cambridge: MIT Press.

Iyer, K. A. Subramania. 1969. *Bhartrhari: A Study of the Vakyapadiya in the Light of Ancient Commentaries*. Poona, India: Deacon College Press.

James, William. 1971. "Does 'Consciousness' Exist?" Reprinted in *Essays in Radical Empiricism*. Edited by R. B. Perry. New York: Dutton.

———. 1950. *The Principles of Psychology: Volume One*. New York: Dover.

———. 1983. *The Varieties of Religious Experience*. 1902. New York: Longman, Green; rpt. Penguin 1983.

Jameson, Fredric. 1981. *The Political Unconscious: Narrative as a Socially Symbolic Act*. Ithaca: Cornell University Press.

———. 1991. *Postmodernism, or, the Cultural Logic of Late Capitalism*. New York: Continuum.

Jaynes, Julian. 1976. *The Origin of Consciousness and the Breakdown of the Bicameral Mind*. Boston: Houghton Mifflin.

John of the Cross, St. 1953. *The Complete Works of St. John of the Cross, Vol. 1*. Westminister: Newman Press.

Jonte-Pace, Diane. 1998. "The Swami and the Rorschach: Spiritual Practice, Religious Experience, and Perception." In *The Innate Capacity*. Edited by Robert K. C. Forman. New York and Oxford: Oxford University Press.

Karl, Frederick R. 1983. *American Fictions: 1940/1980: A Comprehensive History and Critical Evaluation*. New York: Harper & Row.

Katz, Steven. 1978. "Language, Epistemology, and Mysticism." In *Mysticism and Philosophical Analysis*. Edited by S. Katz. Oxford: Oxford University Press.

Kennedy, Andrew. 1992. "Action and Theatricality in *Waiting for Godot*." In *Waiting for Godot and Endgame*. Edited by Steven Connor. London: Macmillan.

Krishnamoorthy, K. 1968. *Some Thoughts on Indian Aesthetics and Literary Criticism*. Prasaranga: University of Mysore Press.

Lacan, Jacques. 1978. *The Four Fundamental Concepts of Psycho-Analysis*. Trans. Alan Sheridan. Edited by Jacques-Alain Miller. New York: Norton.

———. 1989. "Seminar on 'The Purloined Letter.'" Trans. Jeffrey Mehlman (1973). *Contemporary Literary Criticism*. Edited by R.C. Davis and R. Schleifer. New York: Longman.

Landsberg, Alison. 1995. "*Prosthetic Memory*: Total Recall *and* Blade Runner. *Cyberspace, Cyberbodies, Cyberpunk: Cultures of Technological Embodiment*. Edited by Mike Featherstone and Roger Burrows. London: Thousand Oaks; New Delhi: Sage Publications.

Lanham, Richard. 1994. *The Electronic Word: Democracy, Technology, and the Arts*. Chicago: University of Chicago Press.

de Lauretis, Teresa. 1980. "Signs of Wonder." *The Technological Imagination: Theories and Fictions*. Edited by Teresa de Lauretis et al. Madison, Wis.: Coda Press.

LeClair, Tom. 1987. *In the Loop: Don DeLillo and the Systems Novel*. Urbana and Chicago: University of Illinois Press.

Lentricchia, Frank. 1991. "Tales of the Electronic Tribe." In *New Essays on White Noise*. Edited by Frank Lentricchia. Cambridge: Cambridge University Press.

Lem, Stanislaw. 1970. *Solaris*. Trans. Joanna Kilmartin and Steve Cox. San Diego, New York, and London: Harcourt, Brace.

Levinas, E. 1987. "Reality and Its Shadow." *Collected Philosophical Papers*. Dordrecht: Martinus Nijhoff.

Levine, I. P. 1976. "The Coherence Spectral Array (COSPAR) and Its Application to the Study of Spatial Ordering in the EEG." *Proceedings of the San Diego Biomedical Symposium* 15–24.

Lyon, David. 1999. *Postmodernity*, 2nd ed. Buckingham: Open University Press.

Lyotard, Jean-François. 1984. *The Postmodern Condition: A Report on Knowledge*. Trans. Geoff Bennington and Brian Massumi. Minneapolis: University of Minnesota Press.

Mackay, D. M. 1969. *Information, Mechanism, and Meaning*. Cambridge: MIT Press.

Magliola, Robert. 1884. *Derrida on the Mend*. West Lafayette, Ind.: Purdue University Press.

Maharishi Mahesh Yogi. 1986. *Life Supported by Natural Law*. Washington, D.C.: Age of Enlightenment Press.

———. 1972. *Phonology of Creation*, Part 2. La Antilla, Spain: Videotaped lecture, 26 December.

———. 1969. *On the Bhagavad-Gita: A New Translation and Commentary*. New York: Penguin.

Malekin, Peter, and Ralph Yarrow. 1997. *Consciousness, Literature and Theatre: Theory and Beyond*. London: Macmillan.

Malmgren, Carl D. 1991. *Worlds Apart: Narratology of Science Fiction*. Bloomington: Indiana University Press.

Mancing, Howard. 1999. "Against Dualisms: A Response to Henry Sullivan." *Cervantes: Bulletin of the Cervantes Society of America* 19, 1: 158–76.

Mangan, Bruce. 1994. "Language and Experience in the Cognitive Study of Mysticism—Commentary on Forman." *Journal of Consciousness Studies* 1, 2: 250–52.

Marshall, Brenda K. 1992. *Teaching the Postmodern: Fiction and Theory*. New York: Routledge.

Maturana, Humberto, and Fracisco J. Varela. 1980. *Autopoiesis and Cognition: The Realization of the Living*. Boston Studies in the Philosophy of Science 42. Dordrecht: D. Reidel.

McCarthy, Thomas. 1987. "Introduction." In *The Philosophical Discourse of Modernity*. Edited by J. Habermas. Trans. Frederick Lawrence. Cambridge: MIT Press.

McClamrock, Ron. 1995. *Existential Cognition: Computational Minds in the World*. Chicago: University of Chicago Press.

McGinn, Colin. 1995. "Consciousness and Space." *Journal of Consciousness Studies* 2, 3: 220–30.

———. 1997. *Ethics, Evil and Fiction*. Oxford: Oxford University Press.

———. 1991. *The Problem of Consciousness*. Oxford: Blackwell.

McHale, Brian. 1992. *Constructing Postmodernism*. London and New York: Routledge.

Miller, J. Hillis. 1982. *Fiction and Repetition: Seven English Novels*. Cambridge: Harvard University Press.

Moore, Maxine. 1977. "The Use of Technical Metaphors in Asimov's Fiction." *Isaac Asimov*. Edited by J. D. Olander and M. H. Greenberg. New York: Taplinger Press.

Moody, Todd. 1994. "Conversations with Zombies." *Journal of Consciousness Studies* 1, 2: 196–200.

Morrison, Toni. 1988. *Beloved*. New York: Plume, New American Library.

Müller, Max Friedrich, trans. 1962. *The Upanishads*, Part II. New York: Dover.

Muller, John P., and William J. Richardson, eds. 1988. *The Purloined Poe: Lacan, Derrida, and Psychoanalytic Reading*. Baltimore: Johns Hopkins University Press.

Murphy, Michael, and Donovan, Steven, ed. 1997. *The Physical and Psychological Effects of Meditation: A Review of Contemporary Research with a Comprehensive Bibliography 1931–1996*, 2nd ed. Sausalito, Calif.: Institute of Noetic Sciences.

Nagel, Thomas. 1986. *A View from Nowhere*. Oxford: Oxford University Press.

———. 1974. "What Is It like to Be a Bat?" *The Philosophical Review* LXXXIII, 4: 435–50.

Nealon, Jeffrey. 1992. "Samuel Beckett and the Postmodern: Language Games, Play and *Waiting for Godot.*" *Waiting for Godot* and *Endgame*. Edited by Steven Connor. London: Macmillan Press.

Nietzsche, F. 1974 *The Gay Science*. Trans. Walter Kaufmann. New York: Vintage Press.

———. 1968. *The Will to Power*. Trans. Walter Kaufmann and R. J. Hollingdale. New York: Vintage Press.

Norris, Christorpher. 1987. *Derrida*. Cambridge: Harvard University Press.

———. 1990. *What's Wrong with Postmodernism*. Baltimore: Johns Hopkins University Press.

Orme-Johnson, Rhoda. 1987. "A Unified Field Theory of Literature." *Modern Science and Vedic Science* 1: 323–73.

Orme-Johnson, David, and J. T. Farrow, eds. 1976. *Scientific Research on the Transcendental Meditation Program: Collected Papers, Vol. I.* Rheinweiler, Germany: MERU.

———, and C. T. Haynes. 1981. "EEG Phase Coherence, Pure Consciousness, Creativity, and TM-Sidhi Experiences." *International Journal of Neuroscience* 13: 211–17.

Pandey, K. C. 1963. *Abhinavagupta: An Historical and Philosophical Study*. Varanasi, India: The Chowkhamba Sanskrit Serries Office.

Patanjali. 1961. *The Science of Yoga*. Trans. I. K. Taimni. Wheaton, Ill.: Theosophical Publishing.

Peers, E. Allison, trans. 1961. *The Interior Castle* [Teresa of Avila]. New York: Doubleday.

Penrose, Roger. 1997. *The Large, the Small and the Human Mind: With Abner Shimony, Nancy Cartwright and Stephen Hawking*. Edited by Malcolm Longair. Cambridge: Cambridge University Press.

———. 1987. "Minds, Machines and Mathematics." *Mindwaves*. Edited by Colin Blakemore and Susan Greenfield. London: Basil Blackwell.

———. 1994a. *Shadows of the Mind*. Oxford: Oxford University Press.

———. 1994b. " 'Shadows of the Mind,' a Preview of His New Book: Interview with Jane Clark." *Journal of Consciousness Studies* 1, 1: 17–24.

Pflueger, Lloyd W. 1998. "Descriminating the Innate Capacity: Salvation Mysticism of Classical Samkhya-Yoga." *The Innate Capacity: Mysticism, Psychology, and Philosopy*. Ed. Robert K.C. Forman, New York and Oxford: Oxford University Press.

Prabhavananda, Swami. 1979. *The Spiritual Heritage of India*. Hollywood, Calif.: Vedanta Press.

Pinter, Harold. 1991. *The Homecoming*. 1965. London and Boston: Faber and Faber.

Rao, K. Ramakrishna. 1998. "Two Faces of Consciousness: A Look at Eastern and Western Perspectives." *Journal of Consciousness Studies* 5, 3: 309–27.

Radhakrishnan, S., ed. and trans. 1992. *The Principal Upanishads. Centenary Edition*. Delhi: Oxford University Press.

Radhakrishnan, S., and Charles A. Moore, eds. 1957. *A Source Book in Indian Philosophy*. Princeton, N.J.: Princeton University Press.

Ramachandran, T. P. 1979. *The Indian Philosophy of Beauty, Part Two*. Madras: University of Madras Press.

Ramachandran, V. S. 2001. "Sharpening Up 'The Science of Art': An Interview with Anthony Freeman." *Journal of Consciousness Studies*, 8, 1: 9–29.

———, and William Hirstein. 1999. "The Science of Art: A Neurological Theory of Aesthetic Experience." *Journal of Consciousness Studies* 6, 7: 15–51.

Reid, Thomas. 1969. *Essays on the Intellectual Power of Man*. Cambridge: Cambridge University Press.

Rheingold, Howard. 1993. "A Slice of Life in My Virtual Community." *Global Networks: Computers and International Communication*. Edited by L. Harasim. New York: Oxford University Press.

———. 1994. *The Virtual Community: Finding Connection in a Computerized World*. London: Secker and Warburg.

Robins, Kevin. 1995. "Cyberspace and the World We Live In." *Cyberspace, Cyberbodies, Cyberpunk: Cultures of Technological Embodiment*. Edited by Mike Featherstone and Roger Burrows. London: SAGE Publications.

Rorty, Richard. 1991. "Is Derrida a Transcendental Philosopher?" *Essays on Heidegger and Others*. Cambridge: Cambridge University Press.

Rushkoff, Douglas. 1994. *Cyberia: Life in the Trenches of Hyperspace*. London: Flamingo.

Sage, Lorna. 1992. *Woman in the House of Fiction: Post-War Woman Novelists*. New York: Routledge.

Said, Edward. 1994. *Culture and Imperialism*. London: Vintage.

———. 1979. *Orientalism*. New York: Pantheon.

de Saussure, Ferdinand. 1966. *Course in General Linguistics*. Trans. Wade Baskin. New York: McGraw-Hill.

Schechner, Richard. 1973. "Drama, Script, Theatre, Performance." *Drama Review* 17, 3: 5–36.

———, and Willa Appel, eds. 1990. *By Means of Performance*. Cambridge: Cambridge University Press.

Scholes, Robert. 1974. *Structuralism and Literature: An Introduction*. New Haven: Yale University Press.

Schouborg, Gary. 1999. "Three Approaches to Consciousness: Phenomenology, Hermeneutics, Systems-Cybernetics." *Journal of Consciousness Studies* 6, 10: 105–11.

Schwab, Gabriele. 1992. "On the Dialectic of Closing and Opening in *Endgame*." *Waiting for Godot and Endgame*. Edited by Steven Connor. London: Macmillan Press.

Seager, William. 1995. "Consciousness, Information and Panpsychism." *Journal of Consciousness Studies* 2, 3: 272–88.

Searle, John R. 1983. *Intentionality: An Essay in the Philosophy of Mind*. New York: Cambridge University Press.

———. 1986. *Minds, Brains, and Science*. Cambridge: Harvard University Press.

———. 1997. *The Mystery of Consciousness*. London: Granta Books.

———. 1992. *The Rediscovery of the Mind*. Cambridge: MIT Press.

Shankara. 1988. *Vivekacudamani*. Commentary by C. Bharati. Trans. P. Sankaranarayanan. Bombay: Bharatiya Vidya Bhavan.

Shear, Jonathan. 1998. "Experiential Clarification of the Problem of Self." *Journal of Consciousness Studies* 5, 5–6: 673–86.

———. 1996a. "The Hard Problem: Closing the Empirical Gap." *Journal of Consciousness Studies* 3, 1: 54–68.

———. 1990. *The Inner Dimension: Philosophy and the Experience of Consciousness*. New York: Peter Lang.

———. 1996b. "On the Existence of a Culture Independent Core Component of Self." *East-West Encounters in Philosophy and Religion*. Edited by Ninian Smart and B. Srinivasa Murthy. London: Sangam Books Limited, pp. 359–76.

Showalter, Elaine. 1997. *Hystories: Hysterical Epidemics and Modern Culture*. New York: Columbia University Press.

Silverman, Kaja. 1983. *The Subject of Semiotics*. New York and Oxford: Oxford University Press.

Silverstein, Marc. 1993. *Harold Pinter and the Language of Cultural Power*. Lewisburg, Pa., London, Toronto: Bucknell University Press.

Solomon, Robert C. 1988. *A History of Western Philosophy, Vol. 7, Continental Philosophy since 1750: The Rise and Fall of the Self*. Oxford: Oxford University Press.

Squires, Euan. 1994. "Quantum Theory and the Need for Consciousness." *Journal of Consciousness Studies* 1, 2: 201–4.

Stace, W. T. 1960. *Mysticism and Philosophy*. London: Macmillan.

Stevens, Wallace. 1982. *The Collected Poems*. New York: Vantage.

Sullivan, Henry W. 1999. "Don Quixote and the 'Third Term' as Solvent of Binary Dualisms: A Response to Howard Mancing." *Cervantes: Bulletin of the Cervantes Society of America*. 19, 1: 117–97.

———. 1998. "Don Quixote de la Mancha: Analyzable or Unanalyzable?" *Cervantes: Bulletin of the Cervantes Society of America* 19, 1: 4–23.

Taimni, I. K. 1986. *The Science of Yoga: The Yoga-Sutras of Patanjali*. Wheaton, Ill.: Theosophical Publishing House.

Tarlekar, G. H. 1991. *Studies in the Natyasastra*. New Delhi: Motilal Banarsidass.

Taylor, Mark C. 1999. *About Religion: Economies of Faith in Virtual Culture*. Chicago: The University of Chicago Press.

———. 1984. *Erring: A Postmodern A/theology*. Chicago: University of Chicago Press.

Throop, C. Jason. 2000. "Shifting From a Constructivist to an Experiential Approach to the Anthropology of Self and Emotion." *Journal of Consciousness Studies* 7, 3: 27–52.

Torrance, Robert M. 2001. "The Radical Tradition of Humanistic Consciousness." *Humanism and the Humanities in the 21st Century*. Edited by William S. Haney II and Peter Malekin. Bucknell, Pa.: Bucknell University Press.

Turkle, Sherry. 1995. *Life on the Screen: Identity in the Age of the Internet*. New York: Simon and Schuster, 1995.

Turner, Victor. 1998. "Are There Universals of Performance in Myth, Ritual, and Drama?" *Modern Theories of Drama: A Selection of Writings on Drama and Theatre, 1840–1990*. Edited by George W. Brandt. Oxford: Oxford University Press.

Uus, Undo. 1999. "The Libertarian Imperative." *Journal of Consciousness Studies* 6, 10: 48–64.

Varela, Francisco. 1996. "Neurophenomenology: A Methodological Remedy for the Hard Problem. *Journal of Consciousness Studies* 3, 4: 330–49.

———, Evan Thompson, and Eleanor Rosch. 1991. *The Embodied Mind: Cognitive Science and Human Experience*. Cambridge: MIT Press.

Vonnegut, Kurt. 1966. *Slaughterhouse-Five*. New York: Dell Publishing.

Wallace, Keith W. 1993. *The Physiology of Consciousness*. Fairfield, Ia.: MIU Press.

Weinstein, Arnold. 1993. *Nobody's Home: Speech, Self, and Place in American Fiction from Hawthorne to DeLillo*. New York: Oxford University Press.

Wertheim, Margaret. 1999. *The Peary Gates of Cyberspace: A History of Space From Dante to the Internet*. New York and London: W. W. Norton & Co.

Wilber, Ken. 1996a. *The Atman Project: A Transpersonal View of Human Development*. 2nd edition. Wheaton, IL/Madras, India: Quest Books.

———. 1996b. *A Brief History of Everything*. Boston and London: Shambhala.

———. 1998a. *The Eye of Spirit: An Integral Vision of a World Gone Slightly Mad*. Boston and London: Shambhala.

———. 2000a. *Integral Psychology: Consciousness, Spirit, Psychology, Therapy*. Boston and London: Shambhala.

———. 1998b. *The Marriage of Sense and Soul: Integrating Science and Religion*. Dublin: Newleaf.

———. 2000b. "Waves, Streams, States and Self: Further Considerations for an Integral Theory of Consciousness." *Journal of Consciousness Studies* 7, 11–12: 145–76.

Wolmark, Jenny. 1994. *Aliens and Others: Science Fiction, Feminism and Postmodernism*. Iowa City: University of Iowa Press.

Woolley, Benjamin. 1993. *Virtual Worlds*. London: Penguin Books.

Wordsworth, William. 1973. "Lines Composed a Few Miles Above Tintern Abbey." *The Oxford Anthology of English Literature: Romantic Poetry and Prose*. Edited by Harold Bloom and Lionel Trilling. Oxford: Oxford University Press.

Worthen, W. B. 1998. "Drama, Performativity, and Performance." *PMLA* 113. 5: 1093–1107.

Yarrow, Ralph. 2001. *Indian Theater: Theater of Origin, Theater of Freedom*. Richmond, Surrey: Cerzon Press.

Zohar, Danah, and Ian Marshall. 1994. *The Quantum Society: Mind, Physics and a New Social Vision*. London: Flamingo.

Index